D1109959

Starting Your Marriage Right

WHAT YOU NEED TO KNOW
AND DO IN THE EARLY YEARS
TO MAKE IT LAST A LIFETIME

DENNIS AND BARBARA RAINEY

A JANET THOMA BOOK

THOMAS NELSON PUBLISHERS
Nashville

Copyright © 2000 by Dennis and Barbara Rainey

All rights reserved. Written permission must be secured from the publisher to use or reproduce any part of this book, except for brief quotations in critical reviews or articles.

Published in Nashville, Tennessee, by Thomas Nelson, Inc.

Portions of this book originally appeared in *Staying Close* by Dennis Rainey.

Unless otherwise noted, Scripture quotations are from the NEW AMERICAN STAN-DARD BIBLE®, Copyright © The Lockman Foundation 1960, 1962, 1963, 1968, 1971, 1972, 1973, 1975, 1977. Used by permission.

Scripture quotations noted TLB are from *The Living Bible*, copyright © 1971. Used by permission of Tyndale House Publishers, Inc., Wheaton, Illinois 60189. All rights reserved.

IBSN 0-7852-6803-0

Printed in the United States of America
2 3 4 5 6 7 8 9 10 BVG 09 08 07 06 05 04 03 02 01 00

To Ashley and Michael Escue

To our daughter and new son, who are
off to such a great start in marriage.
We pray that Jesus Christ will be the Builder
of your marriage and family.

CONTENTS

Acknowledgments   viii

Introduction   ix

PART 1

1. "The Honeymoon's Over?"—*One Couple's Pain and Progress in the Early Years*   *1*

2. "Make Me Happy!"—*Developing Reasonable Expectations*   6

3. "How's This Supposed to Work?"—*Understanding God's Blueprints for Marriage*   11

4. "Can't You Stop By This Weekend?"— *Respectfully Leaving Your Parents*   15

5. Looking Out for the Other One—*Defeating Selfishness in Your Marriage*   20

6. "Talk to Me!"— *Open Communication Solves Many Problems*   25

7. Sex—*Just What Does God Have in Mind?*   30

8. Sex—*Her Needs, His Needs*   36

9. Soul Mating—*Building a Spiritual Foundation in Marriage*   43

10. Conflict—*Making Peace, Not War*   48

11. Prayer—*The Secret Ingredient in the Happy Marriage Recipe*   53

PART 2

12. Family Values—*Deciding What Really Matters*   59

13. BMW or Bicycle?—*Agreeing on Lifestyle Choices*   64

14. Money—*Balancing the Family Budget*   69

15. Adjust—*A Key Idea in Marriage*   74

16. Forgiveness—*The Safety Net Beneath Every Strong Marriage*   79

17. Super Glue—*The Power of Intimacy and Transparency*   84

18. The Past—*Clearing Out the Stuff You No Longer Need*   89

19. Teamwork for Husbands—*Claiming the Benefits
    of Differences in Roles in Marriage*   94

20. Teamwork for Wives—*Claiming the Benefits
    of Differences in Roles in Marriage*   99

21. Growing Faith—*Walking with Christ in Your Marriage*   104

22. Work—*Making Choices on the Mix of Career, Marriage,
    and Parenting*   108

PART 3

23. Don't Do Marriage Alone—*Becoming Accountable
    to Your Spouse and Others*   115

24. Potatoes and Pineapples—*Making Individual
    Differences a Strength in Marriage*   120

25. Fanning the Flames I—*The Five Romantic Needs of a Woman*   126

26. Fanning the Flames II—*The Five Romantic Needs of a Man*   131

27. "And the Two Shall Become Three?"— *The Decision on Children*   136

28. Vows Revisited—*Keeping the Marriage Covenant Fresh*   141

29. Decision Making—*When Flipping a Coin Just Won't Do*   145

30. The BIG Adjustment—*Getting Started As a Parent*   150

31. Married and Lonely?—*The Threat of Isolation*   155

32. "I'm All Ears"—*The Power of Listening in Expressing Love*   160

33. Dad University—*A Quick Course on Being a Godly Father*   165

34. Mom University—*Becoming a Mother of Influence*   170

PART 4

35. Great Escapes—*Getting Away to Dream, Plan, Refresh, Refuel*   177

36. The Best Day of the Week—*Choosing the Church Where You
    Worship God*   181

37. Refresher Course—*Reviewing the Basics to Keep Your Marriage on Target*   187

38. Taming Time Together—*Scheduling Busy Lives*   192

39. Facing Troubles—*Pulling Together in Tough Circumstances*   196

40. Vacations—*Making Them Delights, Not Disasters*   201

41. "Where's the Remote Control?"—*Managing the Media Monsters* 206

42. "I Only Have Eyes for You"—*Affair-Proofing Your Marriage*   211

43. Holidays—*Honoring Parents While Building Your Family's Traditions* 216

44. "I Need a Break"—*The Importance of Sabbath Rest*   221

PART 5

45. Say Something Nice—*Blessing and Encouraging Your Spouse*   229

46. Road Warrior—*Keeping Your Marriage Together When Travel Has You Apart*   233

47. Help!—*Knowing When Your Marriage Needs Outside Assistance* 238

48. Don't Forget to Laugh—*Lightening Up Your Marriage and Your Life* 243

49. Stress—*Taming Life's Pressures*   247

50. Celebrate!—*Memories Help Bind a Marriage and Family Together* 252

51. A Legacy of Light—*Building a Vision for Your Family's Future* 257

52. "What's Next?"—*Understanding Coming Seasons in Your Marriage* 262

Appendix A: The Four Spiritual Laws   267

Appendix B: Family Budget Worksheet   270

Appendix C: The HomeBuilders Couples Series®   273

Notes   274

Acknowledgments

We want to thank Bruce Nygren for his tireless efforts in piecing this book together from broadcasts and writings. Thanks for your faithfulness in the midst of difficult days. We know these days are building your faith, but not without great cost. Thank you for not losing heart in well doing. You are a good friend and comrade in the battle for a family reformation.

We also want to say three cheers for Shelley Smith. We have had the privilege of watching you grow up and grow strong. Thanks to you—and Randall as well—for making the right decisions over the past couple of years. Your contributions to this book are so numerous, there is no way we could list them. You are a talented reader, editor, and writer. Thanks for how you've sharpened and shaped these pages.

Thanks also to Betty Dillon, Dorothy English, Cherry Tolleson, and Randy Likens for help provided along the way. Thanks for tracking down transcripts, juggling schedules, running interference, putting in overtime, and cheerleading. You are a great team, and we really do appreciate you and all you do.

And to Janet Thoma, a hearty thanks for your behind-the-scenes efforts that made this book possible. We value you and the entire team at Thomas Nelson for your many contributions to this work.

Introduction

arriage for too many people is similar to an unfortunate incident that happened while we were working on this book.

On a Friday evening in July 1999, a young married couple, accompanied by the wife's sister, took off in a single-engine plane from an airport near New York City. The pilot, John F. Kennedy Jr., and his wife, Carolyn, were much in love and possessed all the qualities that so many desire—physical beauty, health, youth, success, fame, wealth, friends. Something went wrong, and after an erratic flight pattern, the plane dived into the Atlantic, killing all three passengers and suddenly ending the hopes and dreams of a beautiful couple.

No one knows exactly what happened on that flight, but the predominant theory is that JFK Jr., although a capable student pilot, was not well enough trained to properly use the sophisticated instruments on the plane. He had to fly by visual cues and quite likely became disoriented in unexpectedly hazy conditions. If he had known how to use the instruments, there's a strong likelihood that he could have piloted the plane safely to the airport at Martha's Vineyard, Massachusetts.

In a similar way, many young couples try to fly through the hazy, often stormy skies of marriage without having the right training and skills. They try to fly the marriage "without instrument training." This book has essentially one goal: to show you as best we can how to learn the skills of marriage so that you can avoid taking a plunge that for too many ends in a divorce court—a never-ending tragedy that impacts generations.

We don't pretend to know it all. Every day we learn more about marriage. But through years of Scripture study, the insights of many others, and more than twenty-eight years of takeoffs, landings, and no shortage of marital turbulence, we believe we have adequate information to keep your marriage safely airborne.

Starting Your Marriage Right contains fifty-two brief but instructive lessons on how to stay married in today's often-turbulent relational climate. Found in these "lessons" are the most important principles we could possibly pass on to you. Some couples will want to work through the chapters in chronological order, perhaps reading and discussing one chapter a week. Other couples will want to tackle first the issues that concern them. The book is designed to accommodate either approach. An ambitious couple may read several chapters a week, thereby finishing the book easily within their first year of marriage. Other more laid-back couples, who may have time only for an occasional discussion, may require several years to cover the book's content.

The most effective way to really "own" the material is to recruit and spend time with a mentor couple who have been married five or more years. We recommend that you meet with such a couple on an every-other-week basis during your first two years of marriage. You can cover a chapter or two of your choice during that time. The key objective, though, is to learn from a couple who have already been where you are and where you are headed. This could be your most important investment of time and energy to insure that your marriage will go the distance.

Regardless of how you use this book, we urge you to allow enough time to fully reflect upon and discuss the questions in the HomeBuilders section at the end of most chapters. In particular, do not skip the "To Take Action Together" segment. The instruction is designed to help you apply the principles discussed in the chapter. The suggestions often include fun activities that will further strengthen your relationship.

One technical point—to make reading the book less cumbersome, unless noted, any use of the personal pronoun *I* will mean that Dennis is speaking. All of Barbara's comments are clearly headlined or will begin with or include the phrase "I (Barbara)."

Every couple wanting to have a successful marriage must understand that since God designed marriage in the first place, He must be at the center. We believe that the information in this book is built on the solid foundation of God's Word, but no matter how great the principles and advice, each person in a marriage must be obedient to Christ through the power of the Holy Spirit, or it will be impossible to experience the joyful and fulfilling union that God longs for each couple to enjoy. Truly, anyone wanting a marriage to begin and continue right must heed these words: "Unless the LORD builds the house, they labor in vain who build it" (Ps. 127:1).

Part 1

1

"The Honeymoon's Over?"

ONE COUPLE'S PAIN AND PROGRESS IN THE EARLY YEARS

I've never met anyone who began a marriage with anything but good intentions and grand hopes. That certainly was true of a couple married in the 1990s, ready—they thought—to live out the romance of their dreams. In the following pages, Allison tells the story of the early years of her marriage to Mark (names changed). This all-too-familiar contemporary drama explains why Barbara and I chose to write this book.

My husband, Mark, and I are approaching the next year in our marriage with great delight and anticipation. In addition to the personal goals we've set for ourselves, this year we look forward to adding to our family by having our first child. After nearly four years of marriage, we're ready to leave the "young married" stage and finally feel enough like a team, strongly connected to each other and to God, to take this adventurous step! But our marriage hasn't always been on solid ground. Nearly two years ago, I was sure my marriage had ended one sunny Saturday afternoon in June.

For our two-year anniversary, my parents had given Mark and me a weekend stay at a beautiful bed-and-breakfast on the coast of North Carolina. Mark and I hoped that the time away from the financial and academic pressures of graduate school would bring an end to the constant bickering and daily shouting matches that had characterized our interactions for several months.

Unfortunately, while the getaway was a nice idea, what actually happened was a disaster. After arguing bitterly about spending money on cheaply made but expensively priced beach towels and chairs at a beach shop (we'd forgotten our towels and chairs at home), we arrived at a place the locals called Dog Beach. To my horror, I realized that the spot was aptly named. We saw lots of dogs—more than fifty—and their owners, cavorting in the water. And instead of the pristine white sand described by our innkeeper, the "beach" consisted of sandbags piled up in a one hundred-foot area to prevent erosion.

I'd had it! I was still furious with Mark for prevailing in our little "discussion" to buy the stupid beach gear. And he had brought me to *Dog Beach!* I didn't even *like* dogs!

Why bother? I thought as I turned to walk back to the car. Passing Mark on the way, I hissed at him, "This is all your fault. This weekend is *over*." Halfway to the car, I ripped the straw sun hat off my head and threw it to the ground.

"Allison!" Mark screamed after me. "Get back here and pick up the hat!"

Ignoring him, I walked away faster, head down, tears streaming from my cheeks. Later, Mark told me how my defiant refusal had made him blindingly angry.

While en route to our inn, I cried quietly. "This weekend is unsalvageable," I insisted. Out of the corner of my eye, I saw Mark's jaw clench in frustration, but he said nothing. *This marriage is over*, I thought. *We can't go on this way, feeling miserable and tearing each other to pieces.* Then bitterly I said out loud what I was thinking: "This marriage is over!"

When we arrived at the inn, Mark remained silent. We wordlessly climbed the two flights of stairs to our room. Once inside, he flopped onto the bed, staring at the ceiling. What was he thinking? Why wouldn't he talk? Weeks later he told me that he lay there wondering what he would do if I really had given up on our marriage.

At the time I wondered, *Who is this stranger I thought was my husband?* I felt he was a million miles away. Going into the tiny bathroom, I turned on the shower as hot as I could bear and sat in the tub under the stinging spray, crying.

What seemed like hours later, Mark climbed into the tub with me. He put his arms around me and rocked me, trying to quiet my sobs. "What's wrong with us?" I asked. "What can we do?" Neither of us had an answer.

Before our wedding ceremony, if someone had shown us a video of those horrible three days in our marriage—and pointed out that it would take us only two years to get there—I'm not sure Mark and I would have gone through with the wedding. While we knew, as imperfect people, we would inevitably cause each other pain, we never imagined that we would inflict deep emotional damage on each other.

As our wedding date approached, we remained blissfully ignorant of the time bombs ticking in our relationship. We thought we had our "marriage act" all together: We had both become Christians as kids, came from intact Christian families, and had done Christian ministry in college. During our engagement, we received premarital counseling from several respected Christian mentors and pastors. After three years of solid friendship and mutual attraction, God had clearly drawn Mark and me together.

The entire weekend of wedding festivities, surrounded by our families and dearest friends, confirmed a grand and glorious destiny for our marriage, concluding in and sealed by the recitation of our vows. We felt God Himself standing beside us. So why, two short years later, were we asking, *Did we make a big mistake?*

The realities and stresses of life quickly entered the picture, beginning with our wedding night. I was ill with dehydration and nausea, so making love was tremendously painful. The next morning, we got up very early and drove all day to the city where Mark had lived before our wedding. Then we drove on to spend the rest of our honeymoon apartment shopping in Washington, D.C., where we moved two months later to attend graduate school.

We recognized that we were facing remarkable challenges and changes that required rapid adjustment. But instead of pulling together as a team, Mark and I drew apart emotionally, becoming more and more isolated. Like many young married couples, we struggled financially. Though we both agreed that Mark would be the best person to handle our finances, he refused for months at a time to open the bank statement envelopes, much less balance the checkbook. Sex continued to be a miserable experience for me, and I rarely initiated or expressed interest in that aspect of our relationship. Struggling to be patient, Mark grew increasingly resentful over my reluctance. In addition to the natural challenges of graduate school, my in-laws frequently wounded me with insensitive comments and a lack of acceptance. Mark and I had a wonderful relationship with my parents; however, I frequently turned to my mom with problems when I should have turned first to God and then to my husband.

Mark contributed his problems to the garbage stew our marriage was becoming. He became defensive every time I said I wanted to "talk." Months after we finally resolved these issues, he shared how his anger over the state of our relationship—particularly our troubled sex life—consumed him. Attempting to deal with the anger, he withdrew more and more from me emotionally. Frequently, he sat passively, playing video games or reading comic books, leaving me to do all the chores by myself. "I had no idea how to lead my new family—spiritually, financially, emotionally—and I was too scared to learn," he said recently.

The end result of our selfishness was that we were locked up in our own hearts instead of sharing each other's as God intended. That horrible weekend at the bed-and-breakfast was the dramatic culmination. After two years of acting in our own individual best interests, we were left with a bone-dry marriage—empty of trust, affection, kindness, forgiveness, and grace. When I told Mark our marriage was over, I didn't mean that I was about to call a divorce lawyer. Rather, I fully expected either to kill myself in desperation or to live out the next forty years of our lives in a mockery of "what could have been." Fortunately for us (and for our future children), God chose to lift us out of that awful mess.

Through His gracious intervention, my parents asked us to spend a week with a mentoring Christian couple. Old enough to be our grandparents, wise, loving, and energetic, Ted and Jo Stone welcomed us to their mountain home and prayed and walked us through the months and years of old hurts, negative thought patterns, and selfish choices. We found the healing path our marriage needed.

Now, almost two years later, Mark and I hardly feel like the same people. And we certainly have a different marriage! With our relationship back from the dead, we still find ourselves marveling with joy at God's grace and mercy in bringing us together and through those issues, so that we could better understand His design for true intimacy in marriage. Though those selfish ways of responding inevitably resurface, we have concrete tools and means of action for dealing with them and forgiving each other.

And we keep moving forward in our marriage with the Lord's help. Mark and I tell every young married couple that if God could help *us* survive the tumultuous years of adjustment and bless us in the process, He will help *you* too. How could the Creator of marriage intend anything less in drawing the two of you together?

———

Yes, for every couple, the honeymoon ends and the hard work of building a lasting marriage begins. But as Allison concluded, God stands nearby to complete the good work He began on the day you promised to love each other forever.

Are you ready to roll up your sleeves and get on with it? First, let's look carefully at your expectations—just how do you merge fantasy and reality to make sure your marriage starts—and continues and finishes—*right*?

2

"Make Me Happy!"

DEVELOPING REASONABLE EXPECTATIONS

When two people get married, they have high expectations about their relationship. An unspoken assumption by each one is that the other will "meet me halfway."

When Barbara and I received premarital counseling from our friends and mentors Don and Sally Meredith, they warned us that we had been thoroughly indoctrinated in the world's plan for marriage. They called it the 50/50 Plan, which says, "You do your part, and I'll do mine." This concept sounds logical, but couples who use it are destined for disappointment and failure.

We spent the first year and a half of our marriage in Boulder, Colorado, where the winters are cold and electric blankets are standard equipment for survival. I can recall how both of us enjoyed sliding into those toasty-warm sheets after the electric blanket had thawed them. However, we couldn't always remember to turn off all the lights. We would snuggle in, and Barbara would say, "Sweetheart, did you remember to turn off all the lights?"

I would hop out of our comfy bed and run barefoot through the fifty-five-degree apartment, turning off light after light. It didn't happen that often, so I didn't mind—until one night when I dropped into bed totally exhausted. Just as I slipped into the third stage of anesthesia, Barbara gave me a poke and said, "Sweetheart, aren't you going to turn off the lights?"

I groaned, "Honey, why don't *you* turn off the lights tonight?"

Barbara replied, "I thought you would because my dad always turned off the lights."

Suddenly, I was wide awake. It dawned on me why I had been suffering occasional minor frostbite on my feet for several months. I shot back, "But I'm not your dad!"

Well, we stayed up for a long time discussing *expectations*—what Barbara expected me to do (because her father had always done it) and what I expected her to do (no matter *who* had always done it).

Why the 50/50 Plan Fails

The expectations Barbara and I brought to marriage set us up to buy into the 50/50 Plan for a "happy marriage." Barbara was sure that I would do my part and meet her halfway by always getting up to turn off the lights. On the night I flatly refused, I was pushing her to do her part and meet me halfway.

Our disagreement revealed the biggest weakness of the 50/50 Plan: It is impossible to determine if your mate has met you halfway. Because neither of you can agree on where halfway is, each is left to scrutinize the other's performance from a jaded, often selfish perspective.

Many times in a marriage, both partners are busy, overworked, tired, and feel taken for granted. The real question isn't, Who put in the hardest day's work? or Who faced the most pressure? The important issue is, How do you build oneness and teamwork instead of keeping score and waiting for the other person to meet you halfway?

The 50/50 Plan is destined to fail for several reasons:

• *Acceptance is based on performance.* Many people unknowingly base their acceptance of their mates on performance. Performance becomes the glue that holds the relationship together, but it isn't really glue at all. It's more like Velcro. It seems to stick, but it comes apart when a little pressure is applied. A marriage needs the Super Glue of Philippians 2:3: "Do nothing from selfishness or empty conceit, but with humility of mind let each of you regard one another as more important than himself."

• *Giving is based on merit.* With the "meet me halfway" approach, a husband would give affection to his wife only when he felt she had earned it.

If she always cooked tasty meals, balanced the checkbook, and washed his car, then he would drop her a few crumbs of praise and loving attention. She, in turn, would lavish affection and praise only when he vacuumed the carpet, always arrived home on time, and took her out to dinner every Friday night.

• *Motivation for action is based on how each partner feels.* During those first newlywed months, it's easy to act sacrificially because the pounding heart, racing blood, and romantic feelings fuel the desire to please. But what happens when those feelings diminish? If you don't feel like doing the right thing, perhaps you won't do it at all. I didn't feel like turning off the lights that night at our apartment, so I didn't.

• *Each spouse has a tendency to focus on the weaknesses of the other.* Ask a husband or wife to list the mate's strengths in one column and the weaknesses in another, and the weaknesses will usually outnumber the strengths five to one.

It's uncanny how soon after the honeymoon we can tend to focus on weaknesses rather than strengths. We log them and categorize them in the memory chips of our minds.

Ultimately, the world's plan, the 50/50 performance relationship, is destined to fail because it is contrary to God's plan.

50/50 Must Become 100/100

The 100/100 Plan requires 100 percent effort from each of you to serve your mate. The Bible describes this plan well in one of the most familiar Scriptures of all: "You shall love your neighbor as yourself" (Matt. 22:39). There's no closer neighbor than the one you wake up beside each morning! And since most of us love ourselves passionately, we are well on the way to implementing the 100/100 Plan if we take a similar approach to loving our spouses.

If marriages are to succeed and become havens of oneness rather than dungeons of isolation, Christians must do more than add a few "Christian touches" to the world's 50/50 Plan. The 100/100 Plan calls for a total change of mind and heart, a total commitment to God and each other.

Each spouse states the 100/100 Plan like this: "I will do what I can to love you without demanding an equal amount in return." In marriage you may start listening to a little voice in your head that says, *Why are you going to make the bed this morning when she wouldn't bring you a soft drink last night?* Or, *Why shouldn't I buy this outfit when he spent fifty dollars last weekend on golf?* That voice has to be silenced if you are to live out the 100/100 Plan. Yes, there will be times when one person appears to get the advantage in the relationship. But love requires sacrifice. Stick with the 100/100 Plan and you will see fruit—increasing cooperation and intimacy in your marriage.

A bit of grace always helps too. Sometimes a couple can make issues out of things that really don't matter. Maybe we had parents who did that as we grew up, and we watched them attack and pick each other apart with verbal ice picks over insignificant issues. That's not the type of person I want to be or the type of person I'd enjoy living with. Barbara and I have learned over the years to let a lot slide; we don't take issue or talk about many minor disappointments. Life is too short to daily find a molehill to build into a mountain.

Marriage is the union of two imperfect people who, in their selfishness, sinfulness, and demands of each other, will cause disappointment and hurt. You must lay aside those difficulties and hold fast to forgiveness, love, and Christ's command to love even those who don't at times appear to love you.

You will never have all of your expectations met in marriage on this fallen planet. But if you concentrate on implementing the 100/100 Plan, your life will be so full of satisfaction that you may not care.

(For more on the topic of expectations, see Chapters 5 on defeating selfishness, 7 and 8 on sex, 19 and 20 on teamwork and roles, 24 on differences, and 31 on loneliness.)

HomeBuilders Principle

Meeting each other halfway fails because
spouses often can't agree on where halfway is.

TO THINK ABOUT INDIVIDUALLY

1. The 50/50 Plan says, "You give 50 percent, I'll give 50 percent, and we'll meet in the middle." In your opinion, what is the real ratio in your marriage? How far does each of you go?

Me   1   50   100

My spouse   1   50   100

2. What expectations of your spouse did you bring to marriage? Which ones have been met? Which ones brought you disappointment?

TO DISCUSS TOGETHER

1. Discuss how you rated yourself and your spouse on the 1–100 scale. What does this exercise reveal about the role that expectations may be playing in your marriage?

2. Share your unmet expectations with each other—*gently and humbly.* Enjoy the humor of it all too. Let's face it. Both of you had some "interesting" ideas about what your spouse would do for you in marriage.

3. What steps can both of you take to bring the 100/100 Plan into full operation in your marriage? How will you measure your progress? Keep in mind that reaching the 100/100 goal is not done in a day or even in several years. It is a lifelong process.

TO TAKE ACTION TOGETHER

Exchange the unmet expectations list that each of you prepared concerning the other person. Review the expectations of your spouse that he or she says you have not met. Choose one of them that you *know* you can achieve. Keep it a secret, but start today to work toward meeting that expectation—an expectation gift to your spouse and a great way to work on fulfilling the 100/100 Plan.

3

"How's This Supposed to Work?"

UNDERSTANDING GOD'S BLUEPRINTS FOR MARRIAGE

While in southern California on a business trip, I stopped at a red light early one morning. Waiting at the intersection, I noticed a construction crew already busy renovating an old restaurant. Like ants, the carpenters and other workers were scrambling through the building, and almost every one of them possessed the same thing: blueprints. I saw blueprints carried under arms, rolled out on window ledges, and pointed at excitedly.

The light turned green and I sped away, but the scene lingered in my memory, reminding me of a simple truth: You don't build or renovate a structure without blueprints. What if the builders had two different sets of blueprints? What would the structure look like in the end? Probably pretty weird.

Unfortunately, too many couples have not compared notes on their blueprints for marriage. Like those construction workers, every husband and every wife have a set of prints, but I've seen too many relationships where his and hers don't match—their expectations and purposes differ. If you think this might be true in your marriage, how do you literally get on the same page in your relationship and build your "house" from identical plans?

The only answer I know is to put you in touch with *the* Architect, the original Designer, the One who has recorded His blueprints for marriage in Scripture. As you begin this marriage journey together, you want to grow in your love for each other, to experience life fully, and to be truly one. But what seemed so effortless when you were an engaged couple may now be an elusive dream. That's why you need to understand God's blueprints—His purposes for marriage.

What Are God's Purposes for Marriage?

You can read dozens of books about what people think, but since God created marriage, you should find out what He has to say. What were His original purposes, plans, and intentions for marriage? They include the following:

1. To mirror God's image.
2. To mutually complete each other and experience companionship.
3. To multiply a godly legacy.[1]

These three purposes give your marriage a sense of direction, internal stability, and the stamp of God's design. They lift your marriage above the everyday, run-of-the-mill relationship and place it on a high and lofty spiritual plane.

Purpose One: Mirror God's Image

After God created the earth and the animals, He said, "Let Us make man in Our image, according to Our likeness; and let them rule over the fish of the sea and over the birds of the sky and over the cattle and over all the earth, and over every creeping thing that creeps on the earth." The account continues, "And God created man in His own image, in the image of God He created him; male and female He created them" (Gen. 1:26–27).

God's first purpose for creating man and woman and joining them in marriage was to mirror His image on planet earth. Center your attention on those words, *mirror His image*. The Hebrew word for *mirror* means to reflect God, to magnify, exalt, and glorify Him. Your marriage should reflect God's image to a world that desperately needs to see who He is. Because we're created in the image of God, people who wouldn't otherwise know what God is like should be able to look at us and get a glimpse.

Purpose Two: Complete Each
Other and Experience Companionship

Scripture clearly outlines a second purpose for marriage: to mutually complete each other. That's why God said, "It is not good for the man to be alone; I will make him a helper suitable for him" (Gen. 2:18).

Adam felt isolated in the Garden, so God created woman to eliminate his aloneness. Writing to the first-century church in Corinth, Paul echoed the teachings in Genesis 2 when he asserted, "However, in the Lord, neither is woman independent of man, nor is man independent of woman" (1 Cor. 11:11). I was convinced that Barbara was "the one," because I sensed that she could complete me as well as be a wonderful companion. Now some twenty-eight years later, I really understand how much I need her. The two of us are like a PC and software. Standing alone, the computer and software are impressive, but combined as a team, the potential results are awesome! And that's exactly what God had in mind when He performed the first marriage with an original groom and bride named Adam and Eve.

You need each other. You recognize that now. But if you build your marriage according to God's blueprints, as the years go by, you will *really* appreciate the genius of how God has custom-made your mate for you.

Purpose Three: Multiply a Godly Legacy

A line of godly descendants—your children—will carry a reflection of God's character to the next generation. Your plans for children may still be in the future, but if He gives you a child, you will be in for an amazing adventure.

God's original plan called for the home to be a sort of greenhouse—a nurturing place where children grow up to learn character, values, and integrity. Too many couples today seem to be raising their children without a sense of mission and direction. They aren't imparting to them the importance of leaving a spiritual legacy of changed lives. They aren't evaluating their lives in light of the Great Commission of Matthew 28:18–20, where Christ commands us to preach the gospel to all nations.

One of your assignments is to impart a sense of destiny, a spiritual mission, to your children. Your responsibility as a couple is to make your home a place where your children learn what it means to love and obey God. Your home should be a training center to equip your children to look at the needs of people and the world through the eyes of Jesus Christ. If children do not embrace this spiritual mission as they grow up, they may live their entire lives without experiencing the privilege of God's using them in a significant way.

Your marriage is far more important than you may have ever imagined because it affects God's reputation on this planet. That's why it's essential for you to set Jesus Christ apart as the Builder of your home.

HomeBuilders Principle

> As you follow God's blueprints for marriage,
> you defeat isolation and experience intimacy.

TO THINK ABOUT INDIVIDUALLY

How well are you and your spouse fulfilling God's purposes for marriage? Go through the three purposes listed and indicate your ranking on a scale of 1 to 5 (1 = doing poorly; 5 = doing great).

God's Purposes for Marriage	How I Think We're Doing
To mirror God's image	1 2 3 4 5
To complete each other and experience companionship	1 2 3 4 5
To multiply a godly legacy	1 2 3 4 5

TO DISCUSS TOGETHER

Discuss God's purposes for marriage and the rankings each person indicated. Take a look at where you differ or both have ranked your marriage poorly. How can you strengthen your marriage in these areas during the coming year? In areas where both ranked yourselves great, congratulate each other and talk about how you can keep these areas strong.

TO TAKE ACTION TOGETHER

Go to a park or any area outdoors where you can intimately experience God's creation. As you walk, note how God's blueprints are revealed in what you see. Answer and discuss the following question: How do God's blueprints in nature help us understand why we should accept and be encouraged by His blueprints for marriage?

4

"Can't You Stop By This Weekend?"

RESPECTFULLY LEAVING YOUR PARENTS

*Y*ou may have moved out, but have you really left your parents behind?

God did not mince words when instructing a married couple to leave their parents. The Hebrew words used in Genesis 2:24, which states that "a man shall leave his father and his mother, and shall cleave to his wife," mean "to forsake dependence upon," "loose," "leave behind," "release," and "let go."

Later, Jesus addressed the issue when he said that no one was ever intended to come between a husband and a wife (Matt. 19:6). No one! No in-laws, no mother, no father was meant to divide a couple who had made a covenant with each other to leave, cleave, and become one flesh.

This pointed instruction is needed. Psychologist Dan Allender says in the book *Intimate Allies* that "the failure to shift loyalty from parents to spouse is a central issue in almost all marital conflict."[1] God knows that leaving parents will always be a difficult transition, especially in homes where the child-parent bond has been solid and warm. Unfortunately, many (if not most) couples do not cut the apron strings—they lengthen them!

What Leaving Looks Like

After our wedding ceremony, Barbara and I walked down the church aisle together, symbolically proclaiming to all those witnesses that we had left our parents. We had forsaken our dependence upon them for our livelihood and emotional support and were turning to each other as the primary relationship of our lives. The public affirmation of our covenant to each other meant, "No relationship on earth, other than my relationship with Jesus Christ and God, is more important than my relationship with my spouse."

If we do not leave our parents correctly, we will be like a couple I knew who were dependent financially on the wife's family. The situation was robbing the husband of his family leadership potential. The wife kept looking to her dad to bail them out after poor choices. Her husband wasn't able to grow up, face his responsibility to make correct choices for his family, and live with the consequences of his decisions. He was losing self-respect as a man, and it was undermining his wife's respect for him as well.

It can be equally destructive to continue to be emotionally dependent on a parent. This dependence will hinder the Super Glue-like bonding that must occur between husband and wife.

How to Leave, Yet Still Honor, Your Parents

Leaving your home does not mean you permanently withdraw and no longer have a good relationship with your parents. That's isolating yourself from your parents, not leaving. The commandment in Exodus 20:12 to honor your parents means that when you leave them, you need to go with respect, love, admiration, and affirmation for their sacrifices and efforts in raising you. But you must make a break from them and sever your dependence on them. As time passes, you must be diligent to prevent any reestablishment of dependence at critical points in your marriage.

Leaving certain kinds of parents requires special sensitivity. For example, if your mom or dad is a single parent, she or he may no longer have anyone at home to lean on and may feel terribly alone. Or perhaps you left behind a parent who endures a lifeless marriage devoid of passion. In either case, your leaving has created a big void in the home. Nevertheless, you must sever the ties.

You can honor your parents and also reap benefits by seeking their wisdom on certain issues. When you ask them to offer their insights, you

must make it clear that you are seeking information and advice, not sur-
rendering your right to make final decisions. A tip: Always try to consult
your spouse before seeking input from parents. Give yourselves some time
to become good at this. You may have depended on your parents for
twenty years but have been married only one!

When Parents Want to Reattach

Sometimes without realizing it, we may allow our parents to reestablish
the severed connections. It could occur during a Christmas visit. It might
happen during a phone call when the child mentions to the parent some
disappointment or failure experienced in the marriage relationship.

I remember how, early in our marriage, I shared a weakness about
Barbara with my mother. Now my mom is a great mother, but I was
astounded at how she rushed to my side, like a mother hen coming to aid
her wounded little chick. Her response startled me. I told Barbara about
it and apologized. I promised I would not again discuss negative things
about her with my mom.

You must not allow parents to innocently (or not so innocently) drive
a wedge between you and your spouse. Some parents may seek to manip-
ulate and control their child. For example, a father won't stop telling his
"little girl" what to do. The husband may need to step in and explain to
his wife how destructive this is to the health of the marriage. Boundaries
limiting the amount of communication between father and daughter may
need to be installed for the long or short term.

Or a mother may be trying to call the shots with her son. The wife
needs to explain carefully to her husband what she is observing. If the situation doesn't improve, there may need to be a cooling-off period where
the husband minimizes contact with his mother and directs his attention
toward his wife.

These showdowns may be intimidating for either spouse, but boundaries need clarification. You may need to call on an older mentor for
advice before you take action, but your allegiance must first and foremost
be to your spouse.

At this point, I want to encourage you husbands to be "the man" and protect your wife. Sometimes you may need to graciously but firmly step in and shield her from a manipulative parent, but I implore you to guard gently your wife's heart and your marriage from a dad or mom whose intentions may be good but counterproductive.

If as a couple you are having trouble maintaining a clean break, you may decide to spend less time at home for holiday visits. Instead of a week, perhaps the stay should be shortened to two or three days. Or skip a holiday altogether, just as a way of clarifying where your primary commitment lies.

A way to forestall some misunderstandings and help with decision making is to determine your family's values early in the marriage. For instance, one value may be establishing your own family's Christmas traditions as your children leave infancy. Having a clear idea of what you are doing and why will make it easier to explain your choices to parents.

As your parents grow older, they may need your assistance. Again, approach this issue prayerfully as a team. Take as much time as you can to make decisions, especially those with long-term ramifications. Some choices will be very difficult, but in most cases, the health of the marriage must take precedence. Although you must consider the financial situation, too, a parent may need to live at a retirement center instead of with you, if the parent's presence will adversely affect your marriage.

One final thing to keep in mind: Leaving is not a one-time event or limited to the early years of marriage. The temptation to reconnect some of the old bonding lines will continue as long as parents are alive. For example, when grandchildren come along, most parents want to share from their vast stores of experience on how to raise kids.

Both parents and their children need to remain on guard so that leaving remains just that—a healthy, God-ordained realignment of the parent-child relationship.

(For added information related to the topic of parents, see Chapters 18 on your past and 43 on holidays.)

HomeBuilders Principle

To "cleave" to your spouse, clearly "leave" your parents.

TO THINK ABOUT INDIVIDUALLY

How dependent are you and your spouse on parents? Take a sheet of paper and rank each listed item from 1 to 5 (1 = no dependence on parents; 5 = high dependence on parents).

	Me	My Spouse
Finances	1 2 3 4 5	1 2 3 4 5
Social dependence	1 2 3 4 5	1 2 3 4 5
Emotional dependence	1 2 3 4 5	1 2 3 4 5
Need for acceptance	1 2 3 4 5	1 2 3 4 5
Need for encouragement	1 2 3 4 5	1 2 3 4 5

TO DISCUSS TOGETHER

After completing your individual assessments of dependence on parents, discuss your ratings together. Do this with a gentle, understanding spirit. Talk about actions that you may need to take as a couple, based on how you and your spouse have ranked each other.

TO TAKE ACTION TOGETHER

Together, plan a parent appreciation event for each set of parents. Think of an unusual activity or action that will surprise and delight your moms and dads. Here are some ideas: make a surprise visit to take them to dinner; create a special memories scrapbook; spend a weekend day helping with fix-up or cleanup needs at their home; prepare a tribute; invite them to join you for a weekend getaway; rent a movie and bring popcorn and drinks for a family flick night.

5

Looking Out for the Other One

DEFEATING SELFISHNESS IN YOUR MARRIAGE

*A*mong my precious childhood memories are the family picnics held every summer. I played all kinds of games with my cousins, including the three-legged race, which was everyone's favorite. Moms, dads, aunts, uncles, and grandparents gathered around to watch all of the children pair off.

To make the game more interesting, partners were tied together so one faced backward and the other forward. The starter gave the signal, and what happened next is best described as chaos. Everyone would cheer as the forward-facing participants would half drag, half carry their backward-facing teammates toward the finish line. There were always plenty of grass-stained knees, piercing screams, and roars of laughter.

But occasionally we ran the race in a different way. Instead of facing opposite directions, each pair faced in the same direction. Even when facing the same direction, the three-legged race was difficult, but at least partners could work together. Locked arm in arm and stepping in unison, they made rapid progress toward the finish line. They might still stumble and fall, but they always got there faster and more efficiently.

Marriage is a lot like the three-legged race. You can run it facing in the same direction and try to stay in step with your partner, or you can run in totally different directions and stumble and fall.

Maintaining harmony in marriage has been difficult since Adam and Eve. Two people beginning their marriage together and trying to go their own selfish, separate ways can never hope to experience the oneness of marriage as God intended. The prophet Isaiah portrayed the problem accurately more than 2,500 years ago when he described basic human selfishness like this: "All of us like sheep have gone astray, each of us has turned to his own way" (Isa. 53:6).

Isaiah didn't know me, but his analysis sounds familiar. I want to go my own way, do my own thing. I'm your basic, self-centered person. We all instinctively look out for number one.

Selfishness is possibly the most dangerous threat to oneness in marriage. As I have said before, both partners enter marriage with all kinds of expectations, many of which are not met because the other partner doesn't know what is expected, is incapable of complying, or is unwilling to meet the expectation. Caught in this self-centered quagmire, the marriage ends up stuck.

In our first years of marriage, I struggled with my selfishness. After being single for twenty-five years, I was skilled at looking out for my own needs. But when I took Barbara as my wife, I assumed a new responsibility: loving Barbara as Christ loved the church. That demanded death to self, but my "self" didn't want to "die."

Just how do we avoid reaping the bitter fruit of selfishness in a marriage?

Surrender Is the Key

After we were married, it didn't take Barbara long to learn about my tendency to be lazy, which was closely linked to my enjoyment of television. I thought Saturdays were mine to thoroughly enjoy as I pleased. Following the pattern I'd learned from my dad, I would get soft drinks and chips, crawl into my chair, and settle down to watch hours of baseball, football, tennis, golf—it didn't matter what the sport. I just wanted to become a giant amoeba, a blob of molecules with flat brain waves mesmerized by hours of tube gazing. What was wrong with this picture? Barbara needed my help in doing household tasks and running errands.

Marriage offers a tremendous opportunity to do something about selfishness. Someone may say, "There is no hope; I can't get him to change," or "What's the use? She'll never be any different." Barbara and I know there is hope because we learned to apply a plan that is bigger than human self-centeredness. Through principles taught in Scripture, we have learned how to set aside our selfish interests for the good of each other as well as for the benefit of our marriage.

We have seen the Bible's plan work in our lives, and we're still seeing it work daily. Barbara hasn't changed me nor have I changed her. God has changed both of us. The answer for ending selfishness is found in Jesus and His teachings. He showed us that instead of wanting to be first, we must be willing to be last. Instead of wanting to be served, we must serve. Instead of trying to save our lives, we must lose them. We must love our neighbors (our spouses) as much as we love ourselves. In short, if we want to defeat selfishness, *we must give up, give in, and give all.*

Jesus is the original and best example of the 100/100 Plan (see page 8). C. S. Lewis powerfully described the impact that selfishness ultimately has on a human heart:

> Love anything, and your heart will certainly be wrung, possibly be broken. If you want to make sure of keeping it intact, you must give your heart to no one, not even to an animal. Wrap it carefully around with hobbies and little luxuries; avoid all entanglements; lock it up safe in the casket or coffin of your selfishness. But in that casket—safe, dark, motionless, airless—it will change. It will not be broken; it will become unbreakable, impenetrable, irredeemable. The alternative to tragedy, or at least to the risk of tragedy, is damnation. The only place outside heaven where you can be perfectly safe from all the dangers and perturbations of love is hell.[1]

Now some advice for each spouse individually:

Husband: How much time are you devoting to personal hobbies, interests, and activities that were typical before marriage but may not fit into serving your wife selflessly now?

Wife: Are you spending too much time chatting and shopping with girlfriends, neglecting tasks at home that would enhance your ability to help your husband?

If we live our lives for ourselves, thinking only of our selfish desires and interests, in the end God gives us exactly what we want: *ourselves.*

Marriage provides the opportunity to live life for someone else and to avoid the terrible conclusion, "All I've got is me. I can't depend on anyone else."

The key to solving selfishness is learning that you have to depend on someone else because you have no other choice. To experience oneness, you must give up your will for the will of another. But to do this, you must first give up your will to Christ, and then you will find it possible to give up your will for that of your mate.

Unless you can come to this giving up of the wills and learn to depend on each other, selfishness will disable or destroy your marriage as you face the difficulties that are bound to occur.

(For other material related to this topic, see Chapters 2 on expectations, 10 on solving conflict, 13 on lifestyle choices, 15 on adjustment, 19 and 20 on roles and teamwork, 32 on listening, and 45 on blessing and encouraging your spouse.)

HomeBuilders Principle

> Selfishness is defeated as you give up your will
> for the will of your mate.

TO THINK ABOUT INDIVIDUALLY

1. How are you and your spouse doing in the three-legged race called marriage? Are you running together in the same direction? Why do you feel this way?

2. How serious a threat to your marriage is selfishness? What tendencies toward selfishness or outright selfish behavior do you struggle with?

3. What will you do to become less selfish and self-centered?

TO DISCUSS TOGETHER

1. Take turns completing the following statement: "The times I feel most selfish in our relationship are . . ."

2. Concerning the selfish tendencies each has described, what steps will each of you take to become less selfish and more self-sacrificing in your marriage?

TO TAKE ACTION TOGETHER

Give each other a blank Giving Check. On a card or sheet of paper, copy the following message. Then give the blank check to your spouse, and allow her or him to write in an area where you will work on being less selfish.

_____ _____20_____
[Your name]

Pay to the
Order of_____

_____as my gift of
surrendered selfishness.

❧ GOD'S WAYS ARE BEST BANK ☛_____

Memo_____ _____

6

"Talk to Me!"

OPEN COMMUNICATION SOLVES MANY PROBLEMS

"Tap-tap . . . tap-tap-tap . . . tap-tap-tap-tap . . . tap-tap-tap . . ."

Captain Red McDaniel rapped carefully on the walls of his cell in the Hanoi Hilton, practicing the special camp code prisoners used to communicate with each other. He knew he had to be *very* careful.

His Communist captors wanted to keep all of their American "guests" isolated and vulnerable. Prisoners caught trying to communicate would be tortured, and McDaniel had already been through that.

As the interminable days went by, McDaniel came to fear isolation far more than the threats of torture by his Vietcong captors. The highlight of each day was being taken to the washroom, where he managed to whisper briefly with two other Americans brought in at the same time. They told him about the camp code, an acrostic system that involved using a certain number of taps (or other signals) to spell out letters of the alphabet. McDaniel recognized the code as his lifeline, his only link with sanity.

If a new prisoner couldn't learn the code and communicate with fellow Americans within thirty days of his arrival, he would gradually start to draw inward and deteriorate. The prisoner would slowly lose the will to live. He would stop eating, and as his stomach became bloated, he would actually start to feel "fat." Little by little, the prisoner would die alone as the strange predator, isolation, sucked his very life out of him.[1]

The Most Common Problem in Marriage

At first glance, the horrors of the Hanoi Hilton seem unrelated to a marriage relationship. But in a very real way, communication is essential to the life of a marriage, just as it was essential to the lives of the prisoners.

Good communication is a longed-for component in all kinds of relationships. In marriage, nothing is as easy as talking; nothing is as difficult as *communicating*. Using words correctly and skillfully is an important part of communication, but even more important is that both husband and wife have a willingness to communicate in ways that result in deeper honesty and openness.

The Great Cover-up

Communicating effectively begins with discovering transparency. Transparency in marriage is described in Genesis before the Fall: "The man and his wife were both naked and were not ashamed" (Gen. 2:25).

Adam and Eve were without disguise or covering, without any mask. They were uncovered physically, and they did not cover up emotionally. Before the Fall, Adam and Eve were a picture of true transparency—being real, open to each other, and unafraid of rejection.

But after the Fall, we read, "They knew that they were naked; and they sewed fig leaves together and made themselves loin coverings" (Gen. 3:7). Those famous fig-leaf aprons were only part of their cover-up. Sin introduced a lot more than modesty. It also brought deceit, lying, trickery, half-truths, manipulation, misrepresentation, distortion, hatred, jealousy, control, and many other vices, all causing us to wear masks.

Many people spend tremendous time and energy building facades to hide their insecurities. They are afraid that if someone finds out who they really are, they will be rejected. For men in particular, deep and honest communication can be very threatening. Too many wives and husbands are afraid to be honest with each other.

The Scriptures, however, emphasize being open and vulnerable. Paul modeled transparency when he wrote to the Corinthians, many of whom were not exactly his admirers: "For out of much affliction and anguish of heart I wrote you with many tears; not that you should be made sorrowful, but that you might know the love which I have especially for you" (2 Cor. 2:4). Paul was not afraid to weep or say, "I love you." Jesus wept over the death of Lazarus (John 11:35) and lamented His rejection by hard-hearted Jerusalem (Luke 13:34).

At the same time, Scripture warns about being too open and honest. Solomon wrote, "When there are many words, transgression is unavoidable, but he who restrains his lips is wise" (Prov. 10:19). The familiar saying about words is not true: "Sticks and stones can break my bones, but words can never hurt me." Words *can* hurt. They cut, rip, and wound. As Solomon also said, "There is one who speaks rashly like the thrusts of a sword, but the tongue of the wise brings healing" (Prov. 12:18). If you're a spouse who uses words rashly, then you would do well to "hold your tongue."

Many couples would improve their relationships if both partners would use words that are gentle and full of encouragement and praise. In marriage, partners need to affirm each other often.

How Do You Learn to Be More Open?

The Bible encourages deeper communication but cautions against using it recklessly. How can you tell the difference between what is appropriate and inappropriate?

Deep communication takes most of us a long time to achieve. You or your spouse may have come from a family where open communication was discouraged or even punished. It may take years to reach a deep, satisfying level of transparency, but every couple needs to be headed in the right direction.

Just as you do when you learn and sharpen most skills, with communication you start at easier levels and work your way toward proficiency. In his excellent book, *Why Am I Afraid to Tell You Who I Am?*, John Powell describes five stages or levels of communication: cliché, fact, opinion, emotion, and transparency. He says that you slowly and gently work up to transparency.

The fifth, or lowest, level is cliché conversation, "elevator talk," where you share nothing with another person: "Hello, how are you doing? Hot, isn't it? Have a nice day."

Moving up the scale a notch, level-four conversation involves reporting the facts. You share what you know but little more than that. You expose nothing of yourself and are content to report what so-and-so said or what so-and-so did.

At level three, you share your opinions—your ideas and judgments about things. You finally start to come out of your shell and reveal a little bit of who you are. But as Powell points out, you are very cautious about doing this. You watch the other person carefully, and when you sense even the slightest question or rejection, you retreat.

Emotional sharing, what you feel, starts at level two. Powell calls this "gut-level communication." Here you must be careful to avoid hurting your mate. But many marriages are in such need of sharing feelings that the risk must be taken. If you can't share feelings with your spouse, your marriage is on superficial ground. You won't grow, and neither will your partner.

Level-one communication is transparency—being completely open with the other person. Transparency means sharing the *real* you, from the heart. Level-one communication requires a deep degree of trust, commitment, and friendship.

You reserve the transparency level for your spouse and perhaps a few others who are very close to you. Becoming transparent with many people can be dangerous. For example, sharing too much of who you are with someone of the opposite sex can lead to an affair. (See Chapter 42 for more information on affair-proofing your marriage.)

When spouses reach the transparency level, they operate with oneness. One can kindly say to the other, "I think you're angry. Is something bothering you?"

And the other can answer, "I think you are right. Maybe what is making me so mad is what my boss said to me in that meeting yesterday."

Reaching this level of meaningful communication is not easy, but the rewards far outweigh the cost. We all long deeply to be heard and understood. The most natural place for this to occur is within the safe harbor of a healthy marriage. That "safe" harbor can be created and maintained only by a couple committed to each other. At its root, love is a commitment. In marriage, it's a covenant. First John 4:18 embodies the commitment that brings freedom: "Perfect love casts out fear."

(For more on communication, see Chapters 17 on intimacy and transparency, 32 on listening, and 45 on blessing and encouraging your spouse.)

HomeBuilders Principle

> A rich oneness in marriage requires an
> ever-deepening level of open communication.

TO THINK ABOUT INDIVIDUALLY

1. At what level do you communicate most, especially with your spouse?

   ___Clichés   ___Facts   ___Opinions   ___Emotions   ___Transparency

   Why do you think you are at this level?

2. At what level do you think your mate communicates—especially with you?

   ___Clichés   ___Facts   ___Opinions   ___Emotions   ___Transparency

   Why do you think your mate is at this level?

TO DISCUSS TOGETHER

Talk together about how easy or difficult it is to share feelings and be transparent with each other. (*Note:* If one mate is extremely closed, go slowly.)

TO TAKE ACTION TOGETHER

Play the Mismatched Communication game. Each partner will take turns speaking at different levels during a manufactured conversation. For example, here's a sample dialogue where the wife is communicating at the facts level, and the husband is at the emotions level.

WIFE: It's so hot—ninety degrees outside!

HUSBAND: When it's hot, I feel depressed.

WIFE: Depression is more common in women than in men.

HUSBAND: Maybe I'm like this because my mother was always angry in hot weather.

WIFE: That reminds me. Your mother's birthday is next month. What gift are you buying her this year?

HUSBAND: I think I'll buy her a portable fan. She shouldn't yell at me if I give her a nice gift like that.

You can play variations of this game. The goal is to have some fun but also to see the challenges of open, deep communication in a relationship.

7

Sex

JUST WHAT DOES GOD HAVE IN MIND?

*N*ow for a really hot topic: sex! When you and your spouse married, I'm sure you expected to have a healthy and active sexual relationship together. That's great—that's what God intended. However, sex can easily become a marital battleground, even in young marriages, because of emotional and mental baggage from past histories of sexual abuse, inappropriate sexual behavior in past relationships (or even with your spouse before marriage), or pornography. And even if these experiences or issues do not apply to you directly, our culture's messages about and portrayals of sex can unconsciously influence the way you and your spouse respond and relate to each other in bed.

That said, let me assure you once again: Sex is given to us by God and is meant to be fun and pleasurable—a bonding experience with your spouse. And this chapter and the next one are devoted to making sure it's exactly that.

What Really Matters Most: Intimacy

To build an intimate marriage, husband and wife must be committed to meeting each other's physical and emotional needs. Because most men and women have differing ideas, standards, and expectations about sex, it's no wonder that many marriages suffer in this area.

As a young married person, you might be thinking, *We already have it all! Our sex life is fantastic!* If so, that's great. Unfortunately, the daily stress of life often gets in the way of sexual intimacy, distracting the attention of a husband and wife from each other and from pleasing each other. Or you may be a couple wondering how to light that fire to begin with. Youth and a new marriage don't automatically guarantee that your sexual relationship will fall smoothly into place.

Another hindrance to intimacy may be the sexual baggage many couples haul into their marriage. The experiences of one young Christian couple illustrate the potential problems and pain.

This husband and wife both brought sexual baggage into their marriage, though in different ways. The husband had been sexually involved with his high school girlfriend. The wife had been sexually assaulted on a date. Each knew of the other spouse's past experiences, and they exchanged acceptance and forgiveness early in their relationship.

After the wedding there were new challenges, though, as the wife was unable to respond sexually to her husband, despite her desire to do so. Years of mentally and physically "protecting" herself after the sexual assault affected her perception of her husband in the bedroom. Sex was tremendously painful, and she began to display her dread of his advances. This, in turn, made her husband feel rejected. Within three months of their wedding, this couple's sexual relationship had cooled almost completely, and their emotional connection wasn't far behind. They sought counseling, received help, and continue to build the satisfying sexual relationship every strong marriage needs and deserves.

If similar baggage exists for you, don't be ashamed to seek professional help. The process may be painful, but ignoring the past may result in a "pain" that threatens the very success of your marriage.

What Does God Think About Sex?

The Designer of sex made numerous statements integral to the sexual aspect of marriage. First, sex is the process He gave us to multiply a godly heritage. He commanded us to "be fruitful and multiply, and fill the earth, and subdue it" (Gen. 1:28).

But God also designed sex for our pleasure. Scripture talks significantly more about enjoying the pleasures of sex than it does about being fruitful and multiplying. The Song of Songs, though full of spiritual meaning and application, provides an excellent description of God's intention for a husband and wife's sexual relationship. According to Solomon, the man has the freedom to enjoy his wife's body, and the woman has the freedom to enjoy his. Here's a sample of how the lover and his beloved expressed that freedom in the Song of Songs. The lover (King Solomon) said,

> How beautiful are your feet in sandals,
> O prince's daughter!
> The curves of your hips are like jewels,
> The work of the hands of an artist.
> Your navel is like a round goblet
> Which never lacks mixed wine;
> Your belly is like a heap of wheat
> Fenced about with lilies.
> Your two breasts are like two fawns,
> Twins of a gazelle . . .
> How beautiful and how delightful you are,
> My love, with all your charms! (Song 7:1–3, 6)

Men, these words give us three points on how to be great lovers for our wives.

1. *Solomon readily praised the young Shulammite woman, his beloved.* He told her how beautiful she was with vivid and picturesque language that communicated his admiration to her. I often ask the husbands at our marriage conferences, "When was the last time you wrote your wife a love letter that praised her and told her how beautiful she is?" Solomon understood how important this is in communicating love.

2. *Solomon was romantic.* His poetic words describe his beloved's entire body as a source of delight. Some husbands have an easy time being creatively romantic, but the rest of us need help in this area.

3. *Solomon's focus was physical.* A wife may be tempted to resent her husband's sex drive and physical focus, but she should understand that *much* more than a woman, a man is stimulated by sight. And God designed him this way deliberately.

A Lovely Lover

What about the bride's approach to sex? Some of her comments about her lover indicate that she focused on what she saw:

> My beloved is dazzling and ruddy,
> Outstanding among ten thousand.
> His head is like gold, pure gold;
> His locks are like clusters of dates,
> And black as a raven.
> His eyes are like doves,
> Beside streams of water,
> Bathed in milk,
> And reposed in their setting.
> His cheeks are like a bed of balsam,
> Banks of sweet-scented herbs;
> His lips are lilies,
> Dripping with liquid myrrh.
> His hands are rods of gold
> Set with beryl;
> His abdomen is carved ivory
> Inlaid with sapphires.
> His legs are pillars of alabaster
> Set on pedestals of pure gold;
> His appearance is like Lebanon,
> Choice as the cedars.
> His mouth is full of sweetness.
> And he is *wholly* desirable.
> This is my beloved, and this is my *friend*,
> O daughters of Jerusalem. (Song 5:10–16, emphasis added)

She also spoke of how she felt in her lover's arms:

> I am my beloved's,
> And his desire is for me.

> Come, my beloved, let us go out into the country,
> Let us spend the night in the villages.
> Let us rise early and go to the vineyards;
> Let us see if the vine has budded
> And its blossoms have opened,
> And whether the pomegranates have bloomed.
> Then I will give you my love. (Song 7:9–12)

Then she revealed her feelings about physical passion:

> Beneath the apple tree I awakened you; . . .
> Put me like a seal over your heart,
> Like a seal on your arm.
> For love is as strong as death,
> Jealousy is as severe as Sheol;
> Its flashes are flashes of fire,
> The very flame of the LORD.
> Many waters cannot quench love;
> Nor will rivers overflow it. (Song 8:5–7)

These passages illustrate the two main aspects of a woman's approach to love: the physical and the relational. The Shulammite woman described her lover's body as richly and colorfully as Solomon's depiction of her. But she then focused on him as a total person and their relationship.

Men often make the mistake of focusing only on the physical side of sex. Sex is much more than a physical act that ends in a few minutes. Sex actually brings two people together in body, soul, and spirit. When the soul and spirit parts of sex are missing, the woman will feel empty, undesired, and used. One woman I counseled confessed that her husband approached her only one night a month. "He never shares his life with me," she said. "He slips into bed with the lights off, we make love, and that's it." I will never forget her next comment: "Making love with him is like a bread-and-water diet." Ouch!

If a marriage is going through a turbulent period, or a spouse is struggling with an emotionally difficult issue, the problems will almost always manifest themselves in the sexual relationship. Sex acts like a gauge, measuring the depth of a relationship. For the woman I just described, the physical experience left her lonely and longing for true companionship. For sex to be truly satisfying for both partners, each has to be totally open and vulnerable to the other. Each person must feel needed, wanted, accepted, and loved sacrificially.

Sexual adjustment takes time in every marriage. Enjoy the process—that was God's intent when He created this awesome experience for intimacy in marriage.

(For additional information on sex, see the note near the end of Chapter 8, page 41.)

HomeBuilders Principle

> God intends sex in marriage to be a
> blend of relational and pleasurable oneness.

TO THINK ABOUT INDIVIDUALLY

1. With all of the inappropriate ideas about sex in our society, do you find it difficult at times to remember that God created sex? Do you have any negative attitudes about sex that are the result of Satan's lies and not God's truth?

2. List any fears you may have about sex or your sexual performance. Why do you have these fears?

TO DISCUSS TOGETHER

1. Review your answers to the questions you answered individually. Since the topic of sex may be sensitive in your relationship, neither of you should push the other to talk. Proceed gently (if at all), taking turns sharing a fear and then having your mate suggest how he or she might help overcome this fear.

2. Pray together and thank God for each other and for His marvelous gift of the sexual experience.

TO TAKE ACTION TOGETHER

Go on a date to plan the getaway event discussed at the end of the next chapter (page 42).

8

Sex

HER NEEDS, HIS NEEDS

In the previous chapter, we talked about God's view of sex in marriage—that He designed it not only for procreation but also for fostering intimacy between a husband and a wife. In this chapter, we'll cover some issues that get in the way of real sexual closeness, and what a husband and a wife can do specifically to meet the partner's physical needs more fully.

Throughout our marriage, Barbara and I have learned to know each other not just physically but emotionally, intellectually, and spiritually. After years of adjusting, sharing—and yes, occasionally arguing—we've progressed toward the total-person communication of body, soul, mind, and spirit that sex is designed both to create and to promote. And we're still working on it.

In this process, we've recognized that selfishness can be a tremendous hindrance to satisfying sex. Early in our marriage, I saw how big a problem it can be.

A good friend and his wife invited Barbara and me to go with them for a few days of relaxation in Mazatlán, Mexico. We had a wonderfully relaxing time. One evening, we enjoyed a spectacular dinner on the beach with the balmy breezes blowing gently. Then we went back to our room where the candles were lit, and through the open windows drifted strains of romantic music and the sounds of the crashing surf.

It was a perfect evening. Barbara looked spectacularly beautiful—the perfect woman. We had the perfect opportunity for love and romance, but there was one problem—an imperfect man. I tried to rush into sex, while Barbara wanted to be held tenderly and enjoy the beauty of the moment.

When she didn't respond, I got so angry that I threw a bottle of hand lotion through a window! Fortunately, the window was small, but the romantic mood shattered like the pane of glass, and the evening was ruined. We both shed tears, and I confessed my selfishness and lack of sensitivity.

Since then I have made strides in my battles with selfishness, and I make the most progress when I yield myself first to God and then to Barbara. I've learned that lessons do come at a cost—so learn them well.

How Men and Women View Sex

Nothing will melt the icicles in many marriage beds faster than the husband realizing that his wife has different perspectives and expectations about sex. The "Differences in Sexuality" chart is a general guide. (Obviously, this chart will not be 100 percent true for every person; it compares the general tendencies and differences between men and women.) These differences cause certain expectations that often lead to misunderstanding, frustration, and disappointment with sex.

DIFFERENCES IN SEXUALITY

	Men	*Women*
Attitude	Physical	Relational
	Compartmentalized	Wholistic
Stimulation	Body-centered	Person-centered
	Sight	Touch
	Fragrance	Attitudes
	Actions	Words
Needs	Respect	Security
	To be physically needed	To be emotionally needed
	Physical expression	Intimacy
Sexual	Acyclical	Cyclical
Response	Quick excitement	Slower excitement
	Difficult to distract	Easily distracted
Orgasm	Shorter, more intense	Longer, more in-depth
	More physically-oriented	More emotionally-oriented[1]

A man needs respect, admiration, to be physically needed, and not to be put down. The woman needs understanding, love, to be emotionally needed, and time to warm up to the sexual act.

The man's sexual response is acyclical, which means anytime, anywhere. The woman's response is cyclical, which means she goes through times when she is more interested in sex than others.

During sex, a man is single-minded, while a woman is easily distracted.

Understanding some of these basic differences between men and women enables you to become a student of your mate. As you learn your mate's needs, you can sacrificially act to meet those needs in a loving, caring way. What do you need to deny yourself in order to communicate love to your mate? What communicates that you care?

If You Have an Unresponsive Mate

Sexual isolation occurs when two people withdraw and no longer progressively pursue meeting each other's needs. One spouse may make what the other feels are unreasonable demands. Perhaps the wife has found responding difficult, and the husband has become angry and bitter. What once was a tender act between two young lovers has slowly deteriorated into a cool physical transaction. Ultimately, the union that God designed as the celebration of oneness erodes into sexual and emotional isolation. If you have an unresponsive mate, consider the following:

• Always be sensitive to your mate and what is going on in his or her life. He or she may be going through a particularly stressful time, which could be caused by pressures at work, an illness, the birth of a child, loss of employment, or other problems. Any of these may be contributing to your mate's disinterest in sex or lack of response.

• Ask questions. Bitterness, worry, and fear are a few causes of lack of sexual response. You may want to ask your mate: "Is there anything I have done or am doing to inhibit our enjoyment of sex together?" "Is there any problem or conflict between us that needs to be resolved?" "Is there anything in your background that is hard to talk about? Could you share it with me so I could try to help?"

• Don't be too proud to seek professional help for persistent problems. For the names of good counselors in your area, talk to your pastor.

• Find out what you can do that would really please your mate. Make a list of these things and then do them.

• Do a long-term study of your mate to learn how to create the best possible environment for him or her to respond to sex or to initiate it.

• Set aside time for frequent getaways to talk and share together. If you want romance to ignite, periodically devote large blocks of time to lighting the fire. Barbara and I try to get away for at least two consecutive nights, three or four times a year.

• If you are struggling with sexual baggage, especially issues caused by sexual abuse of either person, read *The Wounded Heart* (NavPress, 1990) or go to a Wounded Hearts seminar hosted by Dr. Dan Allender. Call 206/855-8460 for information.

A Message to Husbands from Dennis Rainey

Husbands often tell me they're "too busy for that romantic stuff—besides, that isn't reality." I always respond by saying reality shouldn't eliminate romance.

I know a man who planned a scavenger hunt for his wife. About two weeks before they were to leave on a romantic getaway, he scattered little hints around the house. Using clues he gave her, she found these hints and collected them.

On the day before they were to leave, she took all the clues and pieced together a map of New England. Then the husband told her what was happening, and she had time to pack. They took off and spent their wedding anniversary in New England—seven days of peace, quiet, and romance.

You don't have to plan scavenger hunts and trips to add adventure and romance to your marriage. Do you remember how you courted your wife before getting married? Use those same creative juices to make an area in your home an exotic love nest. For example, your bedroom needs to be a private, secure, romantic hideaway. Instead of accenting the bedroom with your golf bag and a treadmill, try scented candles, flowers in a glass vase, and a radio tuned to that soft music station.

A Message to Wives from Barbara Rainey

A good description of the kind of love your husband needs is "unconditional acceptance." In other words, accept your husband just as he is—an imperfect person.

Perhaps most important of all from a man's point of view, love means being committed to a mutually fulfilling sexual relationship. I realize there's a whole lot more to love than sex, but we're looking at how to fulfill God's command to love our husbands; therefore, we must look at love from their perspective, not just our own.

When a wife resists, is uninterested, or is only passively interested in sex, her husband may feel rejection. It will cut at his self-image, tear at him to the very center of his being, and create isolation. Each year of marriage, I realize more how crucial sex is to Dennis's self-image. Fulfilling his sexual needs and desires builds a wonderful intimacy between us, and it protects him from "wondering" about other women.

My husband's sexual needs rank higher on my priority list than exercise, menus, projects, community activities—even children. I must reserve some of my energy and creativity for him. Here are some ideas:

Decorate your bedroom as though it's a love chamber, not a storage closet overflow. And think about how you dress for your husband when it's time to entice him to bed. Have you ever asked him what he likes to see you wear on those special nights?

I believe that one reason there are so many affairs, even among Christians, is that too many wives do not value or respect their husbands' sexuality. If you don't love and accept him in this area, your other demonstrations of love will not have maximum impact.

Co-Ownership

A joint commitment to mutually satisfying sex first requires that both of you honor the spirit of co-ownership described in Scripture. The apostle Paul had this to say about sex: "Let the husband fulfill his duty to his wife, and likewise also the wife to her husband. The wife does not have authority over her own body, but the husband does; and likewise also the husband does not have authority over his own body, but the wife does" (1 Cor. 7:3–4).

Paul's advice is possibly even more practical today than it was when he wrote it. When either mate is deprived of sexual satisfaction, the temptations of our culture dramatically increase.

There are no cookie-cutter solutions for defeating isolation and achieving a fulfilling sexual relationship. Oneness can occur only as you remain teachable—willing to learn from and about the mate God has given you. Why not ask Him for fresh understanding? Then turn off the lights early tonight!

(For additional discussion of topics related to sex, see Chapters 2 on expectations, 17 on intimacy and transparency, 25 and 26 on romantic needs of women and men, and 42 on affair-proofing your marriage.)

HomeBuilders Principle

A mutually rewarding sexual relationship
demands that both husband and wife deny self.

TO THINK ABOUT INDIVIDUALLY

1. How satisfied are you with your sex life with your spouse? Use the following statements to rate various aspects of your sexual relationship on a scale of 1 (strongly disagree) to 5 (strongly agree):

_____ We view sex with positive anticipation.

_____ We have no trouble deciding when and how to have sex together.

_____ We both communicate during lovemaking (i.e., we tell each other what is most pleasing).

_____ We make love often enough.

_____ Gentleness and tenderness are sufficient parts of our lovemaking.

_____ We have enough variety in our lovemaking.

_____ We both sufficiently understand each other's sexual needs and preferences.

A score of 3 or lower on any of these statements may point to a problem area you need to discuss with your mate.

2. Complete the following statements:

When we are making love, I wish my mate would

_____

When we are making love, it discourages me if

_____

TO TAKE ACTION TOGETHER

If at all possible, schedule a long block of time (ideally a two-night stay) for special communication and sexual intimacy. Go over your responses to the statements and share your needs, fears, and questions. Treat each other with an attitude of understanding, sympathy, and forgiveness.

9

Soul Mating

BUILDING A SPIRITUAL FOUNDATION IN MARRIAGE

Early in marriage, you and your spouse need to ask, "How are we going to grow spiritually?" Since God created marriage, marriage is not merely two people in a relationship, but three—a husband, a wife, and God. Failing to address this question can almost guarantee that your marriage will not achieve the intimacy and oneness that God designed.

Three key ingredients of a dynamic Christian life are significant factors in achieving oneness as a married couple. I'll state these in the form of questions:

1. Are you and your spouse a part of the family of God?
2. Are both of you allowing Christ to control your entire lives?
3. Are both of you allowing the Holy Spirit to guide and empower your lives?

Unless you answer yes to all three questions, you will lack the power to build your home with the oneness God intends.

Marriage first and foremost is a spiritual relationship. It works best when two people are connected individually to their God, walking with Him, obeying Him as instructed in the Scripture, and praying as individuals and as a couple. If you push the spiritual dimension to the side, you are ignoring the very God who created marriage and the One who can help you make it work.

43

1. Is Your Family Part of God's Family?

When I speak of your family, I mean you and your spouse. God's ideal plan is that both partners in a marriage know Him personally, that they are first part of His family before they try to build a family of their own.

Today many people think they are in God's family because they go to church, generally live a good life, or consider themselves religious. Other people are not sure where they would spend eternity if they died today.

Regardless of which camp you fall into, I encourage you to read through the information in Appendix A on page 267. These truths will help you understand how to be sure you are included in God's family.

If you are a believer and know you are God's child, the rest of this chapter is designed to make sure that you are experiencing Him to the fullest, especially within marriage.

2. Are Both of You Giving Christ Control?

If Jesus Christ walked out of your life right now, would your life be any different next week?

If Jesus Christ has "first place in everything" with you, then next week would be devastatingly different. You would feel lost, confused, cut off from your Source of guidance, wisdom, and power. You would feel an incredible emptiness.

But if you realize that your actions, thoughts, and words would be no different with Jesus absent, you need to come to grips with the fact that Christ is not Lord of your life.

Our first Christmas as newlyweds, Barbara and I were prompted by God to do something different. Before we exchanged the few gifts under our sparsely decorated tree, we sat down separately and wrote "Title Deeds to Our Lives." Coming honestly before God, each of us listed our treasured dreams, plans, and possessions that we wanted to "sign over" to God. Then we folded our sheets and sealed them in an envelope addressed "To God Our Father." We put the letters in our safety deposit box with other important items.

Eighteen years later we retrieved that envelope and reviewed what we had deeded to the Lord. Among other things, Barbara had listed "to be settled and stable; children—at least one boy and one girl; and Dennis." I had mentioned "security; a healthy, big family—several boys; and Barbara." We realized how over the years God had continuously weaned us from perishable, unimportant things and increasingly attached us to what really counts: people and His Word. We also noted, with thanksgiving, how much more God had given us than we had given up for Him.

Where do you stand in giving God total control over your life? If you haven't ever signed over the "rights" of your lives to God, then why not consider doing that now?

3. Filled with the Spirit

When I was a little boy growing up, in our church we referred to the Holy Spirit as the Holy Ghost. For a long time I could only think of something that would be like Casper—floating through walls like a puff of smoke. But the Holy Ghost whom Jesus talked about is a person. God sent Him to do even greater works on earth through us than those done by Christ Himself. He was sent to glorify Christ as well as to be our Counselor, Advisor, Advocate, Defender, Director, and Guide. In short, if you are interested in living life as Jesus promised, and if you want a marriage where the two of you grow spiritually, then yielding to the Holy Spirit is vital.

Perhaps that's why being "filled with the Spirit" is not a suggestion; it is a clear command Paul gave in his letter to the Ephesians: "Do not get drunk with wine, for that is dissipation, but be filled with the Spirit" (Eph. 5:18). Why would Paul put being drunk with wine in opposition to being filled with the Spirit? Because he wanted to help his readers understand what being filled means. When you are drunk with wine, you are controlled by alcohol. The same is true in a positive sense when you are filled with the Spirit: You allow the Holy Spirit to control you. The results of being filled with the Spirit are holiness and joy.

We Know the Holy Spirit Works

What each of us needs in marriage is something to defeat our selfishness. On more than one occasion I can recall wanting to be angry at

Barbara and yet at the same time knowing that my life is a temple of God, and that the Holy Spirit lives in me with the same power that raised Christ from the dead. The Spirit helps me control my temper, my impatience, and my desire to say things I would later regret.

I still fail, but I have found that as I inwardly yield my will to God, the fruit of the Spirit (love, joy, peace, patience, etc.) grows within me, and these qualities move me inevitably toward a growing oneness with Barbara.

Why not stop and pray right now for God to fill you with the Holy Spirit? Here's how:

1. Confess your sins. Tell God everything, repent, and receive forgiveness and cleansing.
2. Surrender your will to God. Allow Him to be your Master.
3. By faith, ask Him to fill you with the Holy Spirit.
4. Then continue to walk with God moment by moment by reading the Scriptures, confessing your wrong attitudes or actions, and continuing to surrender and yield to Him.

Your marriage will reflect the love of God as you allow Him to fill, control, and empower you.

(*For more insight on this topic, refer to Chapters 11 on prayer, 21 on growing faith, 36 on choosing a church, and 51 on your family's legacy. See also "The Four Spiritual Laws" on page 267.*)

HomeBuilders Principle

As married partners are filled with the Spirit
and submit to each other out of reverence to Christ,
true oneness is achieved.

TO THINK ABOUT INDIVIDUALLY

1. What are your personal answers to the three crucial questions in this chapter?

Am I part of God's family? _____

Am I giving Christ control of my life? _____

Am I being filled with the Spirit on a daily basis? _____

2. In what areas of your walk with God would you like to see significant progress—prayer, Scripture study, sharing your faith, fellowship with other believers, service to others?

TO DISCUSS TOGETHER

Is the Holy Spirit directing us in our marriage? What signs of His fruit can we see?

(Use the chart to track your answers.)

	A Little	*Some*	*A Lot*
Love			
Joy			
Peace			
Patience			
Kindness			
Goodness			
Faithfulness			
Gentleness			
Self-control			

TO TAKE ACTION TOGETHER

Go for a long walk or drive, just the two of you. Take turns telling the story of your spiritual journey—when you started thinking about God, how you met Christ, the ups and downs of your walk with God, your favorite Scripture, the dreams He has given you about serving Him, and so on.

There's no "right story." Just honestly share your own.

Close in prayer, thanking God for what He has done for you as individuals and as a couple. Also discuss whether you want to sign papers giving God complete ownership of your lives.

10

Conflict

MAKING PEACE, NOT WAR

*W*hat do you argue about at your house? At our place, the answer is, "Just about everything." Conflicts in our home are as normal as breathing.

Over the years I've kept track of the things that couples fight about. Here's part of my list:

- Whether to sleep in the dark or leave a night-light on
- How many blankets to put on the bed
- Whether to leave windows open or closed
- How to "properly" blow one's nose
- Dining etiquette
- Volume of music on stereo, radio
- Where to put dirty laundry
- How to hang toilet paper
- Money—spending vs. saving

Conflict often starts with something small, even inconsequential. As someone said, people who claim that small things don't bother them never slept in a room with a mosquito. The little things, left unresolved, can rob a marriage of romance and result in bitterness, anger, and loneliness.

Does that mean that conflict is an evil to be avoided at all costs in marriage? No. Every marriage has its tensions, and the issue isn't how to avoid them, but how to cope with them. Conflict can lead to a process that develops oneness or isolation. Each couple must decide which it will be.

Soul Buddies: Anger and Conflict

When your mate hurts you, the natural tendency is to stuff it deep inside or blow it out in ways that resemble splashing gasoline on a fire. Since neither response moves your relationship in a positive direction, you need to understand what causes most anger so you can deal with it more effectively.

Anger in and of itself isn't bad. God created anger—it's a legitimate emotion. But anger that is handled improperly can quickly turn ugly. That's why Paul wrote, "Be angry, and yet do not sin; do not let the sun go down on your anger" (Eph. 4:26).

Anger in a marriage is usually sparked when you feel your rights have been violated, expectations haven't been met, or you've just plain been hurt. When you do not resolve anger but fuel it with sin (for example, selfishly refusing to tell your mate why you are giving her or him the cold shoulder), it can turn into lingering bitterness. And an angry person may blame God for the problems, which causes static in that vital relationship too.

I do not have the space in this book to fully discuss how you can learn to control anger. There are many excellent resources available. Ask your pastor or check out a local Christian bookstore. But more than anything I urge you to pray, asking God to reveal His directions for you in regard to any anger problems. And if your anger is out of control, please talk to your pastor, or seek help from someone else with experience in this issue.

Resolving Conflict Through Loving Confrontation

Over the years, I've learned to listen to Barbara because she has become proficient in the art of loving confrontation. George Herbert said, "The best mirror is an old friend." Blessed is the marriage where defensiveness is put aside, and each spouse feels the other is an "old" friend who will listen, understand, and work through whatever requires attention.

Doing this requires time, patience, and practice for every couple. A technique Barbara and I use for conflict management is called "loving confrontation." When either of us gets upset with the other person, we try not to hide or deny what is making us see red; we get the hurt in the open through direct, but loving confrontation. We let the advice of Ephesians 4:15 guide us: "But speaking the truth in love, we are to grow up in all aspects into Him, who is the head, even Christ."

If you want to practice loving confrontation, you can't believe your mate is out to get you, and you can't be out to get your mate. Be willing to hear what God may be saying through your mate. Many of Barbara's best statements to me are the ones that hurt a bit, but I need to hear them because they keep me on the right track. As I give her focused attention, I want to hear what she is trying to say, instead of plotting how I will reply and defend myself.

Perhaps the greatest roadblock to loving confrontation is the well-known "log" that seems lodged in the eyes of many husbands and wives. Jesus taught us to judge not or we will be judged. You should not criticize the speck in your mate's eye when you have a log in your own (Matt. 7:3–5). Here are some tips Barbara and I have found useful in keeping a judgmental spirit out of confrontation:

Check your motivation. Will what you say help or hurt? Will bringing this up cause healing, wholeness, and oneness, or further conflict? Prayer is the best barometer of your motivation. When you take your situation to God and He shines His light on you and the problem, you usually see your motivation for what it is.

Check your attitude. A tender spirit expressed through loving confrontation says, "I care about you. I respect you, and I want you to respect me. I want to know how you feel." Don't hop on your bulldozer and run your partner down.

Check the circumstances. The circumstances include timing, location, and setting. Perhaps the most important is timing. Barbara should not confront me as I walk in the house after a hard day's work. I should not confront her as she's helping a sick child.

Check to determine what other pressures may be present. Be sensitive to where your mate is coming from. What's the context of your mate's life right now?

Check your readiness to take it as well as dish it out. Sometimes a confrontation can boomerang. Your mate may have some stuff saved on the other side of the fence that will suddenly come right back to you.

Check the emotional temperature. Call a time-out if the conflict is escalating. Hot, emotionally charged words don't bring peace. Take a cooling-off break. Say to each other, "I'm not running away from our talk. I love you and want to work this out. But we need to set this aside awhile."

Here's a final word of advice about confrontation: When the two of you are at peace, hammer out a plan—some ground rules—on how to communicate during a disagreement. Include these ideas for your plan:

- Focus on one issue, not many issues.
- Focus on the problem, not the person.
- Focus on the actions causing the problem, not the person's character.
- Focus on specifics, not generalizations.
- Focus on using "I" statements, not "you" statements (for example, say, "*I* am upset that the car is out of gas," instead of, "*You* didn't put gas in the car again!" Also avoid the hand-grenade words that blow up many discussions—*always* and *never*, as in "You always . . ." or "You never . . .").
- Focus on observations about facts, not judgment of motives.
- Focus on mutual understanding, not on who's winning or losing.

Resolving Conflict Requires Forgiveness

No matter how well we learn to handle conflict, forgiveness ultimately acts like a soothing ointment to heal the abrasions from two people rubbing against each other in marriage. Paul stated well the formula for this: "Be kind to one another, tender-hearted, forgiving each other, just as God in Christ also has forgiven you" (Eph. 4:32). Did you catch two key words—*kind* and *tender-hearted*? If they guide your attitudes and actions in marriage, you'll reduce conflict and won't need that other key word nearly as often: *forgiveness.*

(*For information on topics relating to conflict, see Chapters 2 on expectations, 5 on selfishness, 6 on communication, 16 on forgiveness, 29 on decision making, 32 on listening, and 45 on blessing and encouraging your spouse.*)

HomeBuilders Principle
> Loving confrontation makes the most of the best
> and the least of the worst.

TO THINK ABOUT INDIVIDUALLY

1. Check yourself on your approach to handling confrontation:

a) I pray at least briefly before we deal with a problem.

____Always ____Sometimes ____Seldom

b) I pray with my spouse before beginning a confrontational discussion:

____Always ____Sometimes ____Seldom

c) When dealing with any problem, I always express loyalty, encouragement, and support to my mate.

____Always ____Sometimes ____Seldom

d) I tell my mate the truth but never try to blow him or her away.

____Always ____Sometimes ____Seldom

e) I am willing to submit to my mate and hear what he or she is trying to say.

____Always ____Sometimes ____Seldom

f) I try to make specific requests with an "I" message and avoid "you" messages.

____Always ____Sometimes ____Seldom

2. What single issue causes the most conflict in your marriage? How do you think Jesus wants you to respond to this issue? Be specific.

3. Before meeting with your mate for discussion, reread the ground rules for communication during a disagreement (see page 51).

TO DISCUSS TOGETHER

Share with each other your answers and solutions to question 2 above. Before beginning, review together the ground rules for communicating during a disagreement.

TO TAKE ACTION TOGETHER

After the hard work you two have put in on this chapter, you deserve a break. Do something together that both of you enjoy. Have some fun!

11

Prayer

THE SECRET INGREDIENT IN THE HAPPY MARRIAGE RECIPE

While I was still a newlywed, I asked my mentor Carl Wilson for his best words of advice about marriage. Carl, who had been married for many years and had four children, said, "Denny, that's easy. Pray daily together. Every night for twenty-five years we have prayed together as a couple."

Because I really wanted to succeed as a husband, I immediately applied Carl's wisdom. I went home that night and instituted a spiritual discipline that we have missed probably less than a dozen times in more than twenty-eight years of marriage. This daily habit has helped us resolve conflicts and keep the communication lines open. Most important, it has demonstrated our dependence on Jesus Christ as the Lord of our family.

I believe if couples faithfully prayed together on a daily basis, they could decrease their chances of ever divorcing by 99.9 percent. This spiritual discipline is potent in preserving and protecting the marriage covenant. God intends for marriage to be a spiritual relationship consisting of *three*—not just a man and a woman, but the two of them and their God relating spiritually and remaining committed to the other for a lifetime. Wouldn't it be natural for God, the One who initiated the relationship, to want a couple to bring their troubles, worries, and praises to Him on a regular, daily basis?

Jesus made an incredible promise related to prayer that every husband and wife need to claim daily together: "If two of you agree on earth about anything that they may ask, it shall be done for them by My Father who is in heaven. For where two or three have gathered together in My name, there I am in their midst" (Matt. 18:19–20).

With such tremendous power and hope available, why do so few Christian couples pray together? Surveys from FamilyLife Marriage Conferences show that less than 8 percent of all couples pray together regularly. And I would guess that less than 5 percent of all Christian couples have *daily* prayer together. Honestly, I don't know whether Barbara and I would still be married now if we weren't praying together daily. You may be a Bible scholar, go to marriage seminars, and never miss church, but if you don't pray with your spouse, I think you're allowing your marriage to be "at risk."

No doubt our enemy works hard to keep us from praying together because prayer can become the most intimate encounter between a husband and wife (other than sex) that builds and strengthens a marriage. When you pray with your spouse, you bare your soul in front of a person who knows your secrets, your strengths, and your weaknesses. That's a humbling moment. No wonder many people want to avoid it.

Prayer between a husband and a wife probably was not modeled for most of us when we were growing up. When we marry, what ought to be one of the most natural conversations between a man and a woman and their God is threatening and may seem unnatural. That's tragic, because I believe prayer could eradicate the divorce infection that has swept this country and infected the church. Christian marriages would have a vitality and an expectancy that would make neighbors and coworkers take note. People would experience new peace and joy at home.

Starting the Daily Prayer Habit

The daily prayer habit starts with one person in the marriage taking the initiative to begin. Husband, I encourage you—as your family's spiritual leader—to be this person. Take your wife by the hand and say, "Sweetheart, I'm not exactly sure how to do this, but I want to start praying together with you every day." If you will do this, and wife, if you will eagerly comply, you can bring your burdens to the Lord together. Then He will pour out the incredible blessings of heaven on you as you humble yourselves before Him.

I know of a man whose wife prayed for years that he would pray with her. They were faithful churchgoers but had no joint prayer life. The woman prayed dutifully, never voicing her request to her husband or nagging him about prayer. One day he took her by the hands and tenderly asked her if she would pray with him. They bowed their heads, and this private, reserved man began to pray.

I believe that bells rang and choirs sang in heaven because of this man's obedience in inviting God into the center of their intimate relationship. Again, husband, I will say that your wife will respond to your initiating in this area, but *you must begin by leading.* A woman told me, "When he [her husband] suggests we pray together, my confidence in him as a leader soars."

In turn, wife, express to your husband your desire to pray together, but then let God answer the prayer; don't nag or push your husband in this area.

Many Christians are not comfortable praying aloud, even with a spouse. If you fall in that category, don't worry about a lack of eloquence. Jesus expressed admiration for a prayer that was only seven words long and spoken by a humbled tax collector: "God, be merciful to me, the sinner!" (Luke 18:13). God wants your honesty. Tell him what's really on your heart. He knows what you want to say anyway, so your verbal ability is not what counts: "When you are praying, do not use meaningless repetition . . . for your Father knows what you need, before you ask Him" (Matt. 6:7–8).

You may want to use this simple prayer until you become more comfortable expressing these thoughts in your own words:

Dear Father,

Thank You for Your kindness and blessings to us this day. Thank You for giving us to each other in marriage. Please help us with our struggles. Thank You for forgiving our sins. Bless and care for everyone in our family. Please grant us Your peace and strength as we obey and serve You. In Jesus' name, amen.

Joint daily prayer is *the* most important spiritual discipline needed in all Christian marriages. A young married woman told me that the daily prayers with her husband held their marriage together during a period of painfully deep miscommunication and disconnection. She said, "Praying together when our marriage seemed out of control helped us hold on to what we knew was right. And now that the issues are resolved, when we pray together, my heart is sealed to his. I *feel* closer to him."

(For information on related topics, see Chapters 9 on spiritual foundation and 21 on growing faith.)

HomeBuilders Principle

Praying together daily will build intimacy
and unlock God's power in a marriage.

TO THINK ABOUT INDIVIDUALLY

1. Did your parents pray together when you were growing up? If so, how did you feel when you saw them do this? If not, what differences would there have been in the family if your parents had prayed?

2. How comfortable are you praying with your spouse? Why do you think you are comfortable or uncomfortable about such prayer?

3. What steps might you take to increase joint prayer in your marriage?

TO DISCUSS TOGETHER

Discuss your evaluations of the prayer life of your marriage. What adjustments might you want to make?

TO TAKE ACTION TOGETHER

May I ask a huge favor of you? If you are not praying daily with your spouse, would you promise to pray together at least once a day for one week? It does not need to be a spectacular spiritual event. You can pray anytime, anywhere, about anything. You can both pray or take turns. Here's the only rule: You must pray *together*—just the two of you—*out loud.*

Once you overcome some initial awkwardness, I believe you will enjoy this activity and find it encouraging to your relationship, as well as a boost in your personal walk with God.

If you are already praying together, great! The Lord be with you as you pray.

Part 2

12

Family Values

DECIDING WHAT REALLY MATTERS

There is no end of "good things" that can scramble our priorities and gobble our energy. All of us can devote much time to personal fitness, hobbies, sports, community service, church work, and so on. If our foundational values are not anchored, we will feel adrift as waves of choices wash through our lives.

That first Christmas of our marriage when Barbara and I wrote out "Title Deeds to Our Lives," in effect saying, "Lord, we are giving it all up" (see page 44), we made a significant first step in settling what ultimate values would drive our marriage. But we found out later that we needed to take another step—to state in writing the specific values that would dictate our choices and how our family would live.

Are There "Right" Values?

In our culture, one of the most despised actions a person can take is to push his values on someone else. Even some Christians have adopted this attitude, which is a tragic development because we followers of Christ have been given an explicit presentation of values in Scripture. Granted, there is room for individuals to apply differing interpretations to parts of the Bible, but the big issues of what should consume our attention and how we should behave are clear.

I think many people welcome a life with few boundaries because it allows them the freedom to do essentially what they want. But ultimately we need to ask ourselves, *What am I really living for? What are my criteria to decide on important values? What are the limits that keep me from total self-absorption? How will I know if I've been successful?*

If your foundational values are not clear, it will be difficult for you to decide these issues:

- How big a house you will live in or what kind of car you will drive
- How much money you will make—in a one- or two-career home
- How much money you will give away
- How high you will climb the corporate ladder
- How many extra hours a week you will work that will rob family time
- How involved you will be in a local church

Jesus made a number of statements that definitely guide us in answering these questions as we seek to clarify our values. Here are just two:

For what will a man be profited, if he gains the whole world, and forfeits his soul? Or what will a man give in exchange for his soul? (Matt. 16:26)

Do not be anxious then, saying, "What shall we eat?" or "What shall we drink?" or "With what shall we clothe ourselves?" For all these things the Gentiles eagerly seek; for your heavenly Father knows that you need all these things. But seek first His kingdom and His righteousness; and all these things shall be added to you. (Matt. 6:31–33)

It's obvious that we can't accept blindly the values of big job, big bucks, big house, and big car coming from our materialistic culture with only a few Christian modifications.

When Barbara and I began to list our values, we suddenly realized we were distilling the essence of our lives, who we were and what we were about. And we also could move on to answering the question, How would we measure success? Here is the order of our big-picture values:

1. Our personal relationship with God
2. Our marriage
3. Our children

All other issues, such as decisions relating to vocation and career, would have to be evaluated in light of their impact on these three supreme priorities. We agreed that no other success would matter if we failed on these three. But abiding by our values demanded tough choices and sacrifices. For example, I gave up or postponed activities I loved—fishing, hunting, and going to sporting events. Barbara set aside painting, sewing, and pursuing other creative endeavors. We gave these up so we could succeed in the values that mattered most.

The values God has for you and your marriage may differ. What's really important is that a husband and wife go before the Lord to hammer out their values with total disregard for the values of other people. If you are not sure how to begin, find an older, spiritually mature Christian couple willing to share how they shaped their family values. And if you think creating a list of family values sounds confining and will limit opportunities, you will be surprised (as we were) that this is a liberating exercise. Suddenly, you have something concrete to discuss.

The tragedy is that too many families are being swept along by the culture and are doing what their neighbors are doing or what their friends at church are doing. They're not stopping to ask, *Why are we doing what we're doing?*

Listing Values

Once you have decided the big issues, you need to take another step and be specific about the little things. Life involves a lot of little decisions that add up to large choices. Getting specific was Barbara's idea, so I'll let her tell the story.

I (Barbara) was feeling pressure from all of life's demands, so I remember sitting down one day and talking with Dennis about what we really valued as a couple. We decided we would write down separately what we valued and then compare our notes.

No surprise—we found a number of our values were different, which revealed why we were feeling some pressure and tension in our marriage. For example, one of Dennis's top values was building relationships. That was not even in my top five! I had listed work ethic as important, which wasn't on his list.

Of course, I valued relationships and Dennis valued hard work. Each of us understood better what was driving the other person. And even though some values were different, we saw how we valued some of the same things. The understanding that came from doing this exercise and talking about our values became very important in understanding each other and knowing what to expect.

Over the years, we have continued to talk about our values and to re-evaluate and redefine them. Gradually, we have come closer together. It's not that we have exactly the same values now, but we have merged in ways that wouldn't have been possible if we hadn't talked about those values.

Sticking to Values

To be honest, clarifying our values wasn't an easy process the first time the plow went through the ground. The values were muddy. Some confusion and disagreement occurred.

And after agreeing on a list of family values, it takes effort to stick to them. We schedule time to talk about this topic, at least on an annual basis. You need to keep a fresh understanding of what is really driving you individually, your marriage, and your family; changes in values are inevitable as your family matures.

We certainly have not done this perfectly. But by having values and reviewing them when we sense we are losing focus, we have maintained our odds of hitting the bull's-eye on what really counts for us.

Ultimately, the exercise of listing and reviewing our family values has helped us establish a family identity. We have been less tempted to compare ourselves with the culture or with our Christian friends—to be driven by the expectations, lifestyles, and values of others.

(For additional information related to this topic, see Chapters 13 on lifestyle choices, 14 on money, 27 on starting a family, 35 on planning retreats, and 51 on a vision for your family's future.)

HomeBuilders Principle

> Establishing your family's values will
> clarify decision making and build unity.

TO THINK ABOUT INDIVIDUALLY

On a pad, write five to ten values you believe God desires for your marriage and family. Rank them in order of importance.

TO DISCUSS TOGETHER

Compare the list and ranking of values each of you prepared. How alike or different are they? Discuss them, and merge your values into one agreed-upon list. (Again, if this value-defining process is confusing or creating conflict, seek some help from an older couple you admire.)

TO TAKE ACTION TOGETHER

Agreeing on your family values may take time. Don't let this discourage you or keep you from pressing toward the goal of having a list of values agreeable to the two of you. You may need to set a date in the future when you will talk specifically about your values list again. Pray for a unified spirit as you complete this important project.

13

BMW or Bicycle?

AGREEING ON LIFESTYLE CHOICES

The word *lifestyle* is a key part of the American vocabulary as the new millennium begins.

The prosperity our nation has enjoyed for decades means that we all assume there is a wide variety of options available in choosing how we want to live. Ultimately, though, a lifestyle represents just another set of choices driven by underlying values—the way we choose to use our financial resources and time. And if spouses do not reach agreement on this issue, conflict will be a daily indicator of their different values.

For most couples, questions related to lifestyle surface first around whose tastes will determine the appearance and furnishings of the new love nest. Barbara and I were no exception, as our differing tastes became apparent even before our wedding in 1972.

Barbara chose a silver pattern called Old Master. I asked a friend to accompany me to a department store. At the silver department I walked up to a distinguished elderly clerk and said, "I'd like to see Old Master by Towle."

"Of course, sir," said the woman. She showed me a setting of Old Master. It was pretty.

"Ahh, that's really interesting. How much is it?"

"It's $59.95," she replied.

"Did you say $59.95? That's not bad for eight place settings of silver."

The woman pushed her glasses back, looked at me a bit condescendingly, and said, "Son, that's for *one* place setting."

"You mean $59.95 for *one* place setting! Lady, do you realize how many plastic knives, forks, and spoons that will buy?" (My reaction was to 1972 prices. Today I probably would have a stroke on the spot!)

Later I called Barbara. I tried to be tactful, but frankly, I was trying to discover if she was losing her mind. She assured me that the silver was a bargain. So, basic, functional fiancé followed along dutifully and we registered for Old Master by Towle.

This searching for common ground in a new marriage can be humorous, but just how should you go about deciding the values in your marriage and family related to lifestyle? Will your tastes be more of the shiny BMW variety, or will you drive what my friend Bob Horner calls a "Rolls-canardly"? Rolls down the hill, can hardly get back up!

What Really Is Important?

For Christians, the spiritual should be more important than the physical. If partners do not make a point of defining what's important to them, the culture, peers, advertising, and a host of other influences will rush in to accomplish the task. Three powerful influences work together that drive many newly married couples over the financial cliff.

First, we live in a culture that worships material things. Every day we are bombarded by advertising and other messengers that shout, "You are what you own!" The media also tell us that what we have is definitely not enough, and we should aspire to bigger and better things.

Second, we compare what we have with what our parents have or with what others have been able to accumulate. Even among the Christian community the pressure to make comparisons arises.

Third, we are selfish. We want nice things. Winston Churchill once remarked, "I am easily satisfied with the very best." With abundant, instant credit a young couple may satisfy their latest cravings. And many in this generation have grown up having just about anything they wanted.

I encourage you to evaluate and discuss the value you place on material possessions, your tendency to compare, and your ability to deny what your eyes see and want. Hold each other accountable for purchases by establishing a budget and being in agreement about what you will buy.

This generation needs a clear understanding of Jesus' teachings about money and possessions. He commanded us not to worry about physical needs or material things but to seek first "His kingdom and His righteousness" (Matt. 6:33). He told His disciples to travel light and encouraged them to be ready to give away their coats if people asked for them. Jesus did not have a home and was definitely not into collecting stuff. He is our model.

As a couple, you need a godly mentor couple who can model budget management and impart to you God's heart about money, possessions, and materialism.

Your Choices Will Empower or Hamper Future Options

As you and your spouse discuss the specifics of lifestyle, please remember one critical truth: Decisions made early in marriage about how to invest resources will have a dramatic ongoing impact on your family. I wish I could reach through these pages, put my arms around you, look you in the eyes, and ask, "Are you listening? This is really important. I'm going to warn you about a trap that is destroying many families today."

A typical scenario is for one or both persons coming into the marriage to bring along a sizable debt. For many this deficit is a result of college loans. For others it may represent money obtained on credit to buy a car, computer equipment, vacations, or a long list of other stuff.

The debt may not seem a big deal when both husband and wife are working. In fact, the dual-income situation may encourage adding more debt, perhaps a mortgage for a nice house.

Everything may be going smoothly until the couple decides to add a little third person to enjoy the nice house and other things. But their ability to consider having a child, much less the possibility for Mom to stay home to provide care, is limited or nonexistent because of debt and the cost of their lifestyle.

Before getting in this predicament, the wise couple will do what Jesus suggested (insert the word *lifestyle* in place of the word *tower*): "Which one of you, when he wants to build a tower, does not first sit down and calculate the cost, to see if he has enough to complete it? Otherwise, when he has laid a foundation, and is not able to finish, all who observe it begin to

ridicule him, saying, 'This man began to build and was not able to finish'"
(Luke 14:28–30).

Counting the cost, as well as setting financial boundaries and staying
within them, results in financial freedom. Choices about lifestyle often
have significant spiritual ramifications too. The couple burdened with
debt and lifestyle expenses that threaten to break their budget may be
unable to give liberally to their church and other kingdom efforts. An
opportunity for one or both to help with a short-term mission project, for
example, may be denied because they can't afford it.

My intent here is not to imply that enjoying elegant things, living in a
large home, and taking a nice vacation are wrong. My point is that each
couple needs to examine their situation and decide whether their chosen
lifestyle fits in with the important values of life and allows them to honor,
obey, and serve God as He calls them to do.

A Strategy for Lifestyle Choices

The best way I know for a couple to forge an agreement on lifestyle is
to go through the process of determining family values. Once the two of
you have a clearer idea of what is really important in your marriage and
family, decisions on lifestyle matters will be more obvious.

In the next chapter we look more specifically at issues related to money.
As we all learn, often the hard way, lifestyle and money are tightly
linked—both servants of our true, deeply held values.

(*For other information related to this topic, see Chapters 12 on family values
and 14 on money.*)

HomeBuilders Principle

The lifestyle you choose today will restrict or expand
your choices—including service to God—for years to come.

TO THINK ABOUT INDIVIDUALLY

1. What impact have these three influences had on you?

a) A materialistic culture

b) Comparison of what you have with what others have

c) Selfishness

What actions do you need to take to protect you from making poor choices on lifestyle issues?

2. What material possessions and activities are most important to you—those you would hate most to give up?

3. Is there anything about your lifestyle that may be in conflict with God's values or may place a heavy strain on your family budget?

4. Can you think of a mentor couple who could teach you God's perspective on money and possessions?

TO DISCUSS TOGETHER

1. Share your answers to the questions you answered individually. What may God be saying to both of you about your lifestyle?

2. What actions should you take as a couple in this area of your marriage?

TO TAKE ACTION TOGETHER

Together, take a tour of your home. Are there any possessions that you may not need? Should you consider selling some stuff to reduce your debt or consider giving some of it to people less fortunate than you? A less cluttered, less expensive lifestyle could reduce the cash drain as well as reduce tension in your marriage.

14

Money

BALANCING THE FAMILY BUDGET

A memorable moment happens to almost all newlyweds at the end of their first month of marriage: Husband or wife assembles a pile of bills and receipts on the kitchen table, looks at the checkbook balance, and then breaks into a cold sweat! If the differing expectations and value systems present in every home have not collided before now, they are about to.

There's no question that the way to handle money causes stress in most marriages. The expert on money matters, Larry Burkett, once said on our *FamilyLife Today* radio broadcast, "Of the couples who end up getting a divorce, every survey shows between 85 to 90 percent of them say the number one problem they were having was finances."[1]

Most of us believe that the only real money problem is "not enough." A friend of mine said, "I know I can't take it with me. But could I at least keep some through the weekend?" Deep down we all know that a money shortage usually is not the real issue. We need the knowledge and discipline to use wisely the money we already have.

As I read Scriptures about money, and as I have experienced money challenges in our marriage for more than twenty-eight years, I believe that God uses money to test us. He tests our faithfulness to His Word—whether we are going to trust Him to supply our needs as we give, share, and become wise stewards of the financial resources He has placed under our care. Many times, money issues have sent Barbara and me back to dependence on God.

The most important point we all need to remember about money is that it is just another part of life, not the essence or goal of our existence. If we keep our attention on God and His objectives, we will walk in obedience and help build His kingdom, and our needs will be richly supplied (1 Tim. 6:17–18).

In this chapter I offer "hard-knock university" knowledge on finances. I am no guru on money management; bookstore shelves bulge with many good books on this topic, a number of them by Christian financial experts such as Ron Blue and Larry Burkett. But having been around the block a few times, I have some pointers I believe will be of benefit to any couple.

Money Sense

I love Ron Blue's summary of the proper attitude toward money:

1. God owns it all.
2. Money is never an end in itself, but is merely a resource used to accomplish other goals and obligations.
3. Spend less than you earn, do it for a long time, and you will be financially successful.[2]

Having already alluded to his first two points, I want to get practical and review the thrust of Ron's third point—the basics.

Talk about money. On our radio broadcast, Larry Burkett said about couples, "I have said a million times and I believe it, if you are not communicating about money, it is because you are not communicating about anything."[3] How true this is. It may be difficult at first to talk about this sensitive topic; but if you don't, you will talk about it eventually, and it probably won't be a pleasant conversation. Bite the bullet early! Talk about your finances, your goals, and the money-related strengths and weaknesses that will help or sabotage you.

Minimize debt. Openly discuss your level of debt. Unfortunately, it's not unusual for a couple to start marriage in significant debt, perhaps $20,000 or more due to unpaid college loans or other premarital purchases. Put a plan in place to reduce such debt and to prevent adding more because the really large investment—a home—usually waits just around the corner.

Study to learn the basics, for example, a budget. Despite the modern aids such as sophisticated computer software to track money, an alarming number of people don't know how to balance a checkbook. If you have never been taught the basics of preparing a budget, managing your check-book, and paying bills on time, swallow your pride and learn. There are many people and resources waiting to help you. (A simple budget work-sheet is included on page 270. You may also want to invest in some inex-pensive money management computer software like Quicken Basic.)

Decide who will do what with finances. Just because the husband is the spiritual head of the home does not mean he has the gift of book-keeping. Honestly decide between you who is best suited to do what with your money. In our home, I learned too late that Barbara was a far better financial record keeper than I could ever be. I was doing it to "protect" my wife. I should have let her do it to protect both of us!

Give and save. You should never give to get from God—that's not how He operates. But God blesses you for being obedient, and He wants you to give liberally to care for the needs of others. He also urges you to be a faithful steward (Luke 16:10–13). A critical part of stewardship is to set aside a portion of earnings for the future—the needs of your house or someone else's needs. Obviously, I'm not talking about selfish hoarding but prudent preparation for future known and unknown expenses that await every family.

Make dual-income choices. Spend a lot of time in prayer and discus-sion over this topic, because the ramifications of unwise decisions may influence a family for decades.

Don't develop a plastic addiction. Very, very few people handle credit cards well. Odds are good that you are not one of the minority. Easy plas-tic credit is a lure to tempt you to think you can escape from reality through the fantasy of getting whatever you want *right now.* Don't fall for it. If you need a credit card for travel or emergencies, keep it locked up at home and agree with your spouse that it can be used only by mutual consent.

Consider carefully loans or gifts from parents. When our daughter Ashley married Michael, I started thinking about the amount of money they were going to chunk out for rent. We had a little bit of wedding funding left over, so I thought maybe we should help them put together a down payment on a home.

But then I remembered that a young couple should stay focused on each other during their first year together (Deut. 24:5). Buying a house is a huge distraction and can definitely take the focus off the relationship.

At some point Barbara and I may decide to help our children after marriage. But again I will heed our financial mentor, Larry Burkett, who said, "There is nothing wrong with the parent helping. Just be sure you are helping, not hurting. It might be better to take the same amount of money and buy them a car so that they owned a car for cash. Then tell them, 'Now, I want you to take the same amount of money you would have been paying on the car and save it up for the down payment on your home.'"[3]

Consider accountability. If you are struggling with money, seek help. You may need a staff member at your church or an older couple to hold you accountable to your monthly and long-term financial decisions. There is no shame in this; doing what's right for you and your family is always right.

Use resources developed by experts. Every newly married couple should go through a Christian book or Bible study that teaches God's perspective of finances. Ron Blue worked with the FamilyLife team to create a HomeBuilder study called *Master Money in Your Marriage.* I can't overstate the importance of going through a Bible study like this together. I also recommend Crown Ministries for their hands-on financial training.[4]

Jesus spoke probably the most compelling words related to money and possessions in the Sermon on the Mount: "Do not lay up for yourselves treasures upon earth, where moth and rust destroy, and where thieves break in and steal. But lay up for yourselves treasures in heaven, where neither moth nor rust destroys, and where thieves do not break in or steal; for where your treasure is, there will your heart be also" (Matt. 6:19–21). That financial planning sounds good to me.

(For more study on related topics, see Chapters 12 on family values, 13 on lifestyle, 22 on career and marriage, and 29 on decision making.)

HomeBuilders Principle

The way you handle money
can prosper or bankrupt your marriage.

TO THINK ABOUT INDIVIDUALLY

1. How does the way you spend your money (or would spend it if you had more) reveal your attitudes toward the importance of money in your life?

2. What are your strengths and weaknesses in managing money?

3. What strengths in managing money do you see in your spouse? How might the two of you better use each other's strengths in money management?

TO DISCUSS TOGETHER

Share and discuss answers to the questions in the previous exercise. Approach this topic with prayer and care—it's a hot one for most couples. But congratulate each other for pressing on; many husbands and wives seldom have a good, honest discussion about money.

TO TAKE ACTION TOGETHER

If you don't have one, work on a family budget (see the sample form on page 270). If you have a budget, does it need attention and review?

15

Adjust

A KEY IDEA IN MARRIAGE

*I*n at least one aspect, marriage is like football.

In a close game, the winning team is usually the one that made the most significant adjustments in strategy along the way. That's what effective coaches do at halftime—give their players the key adjustments that will gain them the advantage in the final quarters.

A winning marriage requires the same mind-set. A husband and wife need to recognize that surprises requiring proactive adjustments await them in their relationship.

Barbara and I were no exception. Perhaps the biggest adjustment we faced early in marriage resulted from differing backgrounds. Barbara grew up in a country club setting near Chicago and later in a suburb of Houston. I grew up in Ozark, Missouri, a tiny town in the hills of southwest Missouri. Barbara came into our marriage a refined young lady. I was a genuine hillbilly and was not refined. In some ways, we seemed to have come from two different countries, and on some issues, different galaxies.

Some issues triggering the need for adjustments in marriage are major: being raised in a dual- or single-parent family; being an only child or growing up with several siblings; coming from an economically challenged family or a well-to-do family; growing up with parents who did or did not embrace religious faith. The list goes on and on: opposite personalities, differing racial or cultural backgrounds.

Minimally, a couple will have to adjust to differing traditions, values, habits, and rules learned in unique backgrounds. As time passes, other adjustments to sexual performance, financial pressures, and job demands may be required. And let's not forget a big adjustment in a small package—spelled B-A-B-Y! That's right: the first child.

Often the minor differences cause the most frustration and require the most creative flexibility. Someone has said, "We are worn down less by the mountain we climb than by the grain of sand in our shoe."

One of those tiny grains of sand can be the toilet seat. The husband may come from a family of all boys where the toilet seat's default position was *up*. If this guy marries a girl from a family of all girls, where the seat remained in the horizontal dimension, you know the potential for conflict and the need for adjustment.

In our home, for years a grain of sand was the way I "helped" Barbara by putting my socks in the clothes hamper wrong side out so that "the dirty side got washed." She has finally trained me to do it the "right" way.

Every married individual must adjust to qualities in a spouse that were not noticed or were ignored during the dreamy days of dating.

Settle the Big Issues First

How many people have encountered a painful frustration in marriage and asked themselves, *Why did I do this? Did I marry the wrong person?*

If these questions arise, confront them immediately. If you don't resolve these doubts promptly, they will hang indefinitely like a distant cloud on the horizon of your relationship.

Anyone struggling with this question should go back to the biblical admonition in Genesis 2:24–25 where spouses are commanded to leave, cleave, become one flesh, and be completely transparent with each other. If you are bothered by such doubts, face them by getting away alone for a weekend to seek out the Lord and pray for His peace on this matter.

Let me assure you that you are married to the right person. How do I know this? Because God hates divorce and wants your marriage to last. You may have gone against some biblical admonitions in getting to where you are in your marriage, but the Scripture is clear: You are not to try to undo a "mistake" and, in the process, make a second mistake.

The Game Plan for Making Adjustments

The solution to handling issues of adjustment lies in regarding your relationship as more important than your individual values and desires. If you hold on tightly to what *you* want, you'll never get to the point of understanding that the well-being of the overall relationship is what ultimately matters.

Here are some points to remember as you make adjustments in your relationship:

1. Recognize that adjustments are inevitable. Every married couple has to deal with the grains of sand in their shoes. It's 100 percent normal. If you realize up front that you will have to make changes in your behavior and learn to tolerate frustrating traits in your spouse, your attitude will be more in line with what James wrote: "Consider it all joy, my brethren, when you encounter various trials" (James 1:2). He said to consider it all joy *when* you encounter trials, not *if* you encounter them.

2. Understand that adjustments have a divine purpose. God uses these issues to combine two unique people into something new called "us." I also believe that God uses adjustments to teach us how to love another dramatically different, imperfect human being. At prime moments, God will use your marriage to show you how to love the unlovely.

3. Ask God for wisdom on how to live with this person who's different from you. Instead of trying to change your spouse and correct all of the bad habits, how can you accept the situation or adjust yourself? Barbara realized this early in our marriage. She recalls, "I had to realize that God had to change Dennis. I couldn't." Marriage may be an institution, but it isn't a reformatory.

4. Be more concerned about your own rough spots than those of your spouse. Jesus said we should take the log out of our own eye before trying to take the speck out of someone else's eye. If I'm not willing to make changes, how can I expect Barbara to change?

5. Make a commitment to hang in there, to work through the inevitable adjustments. The apostle Paul provided guidelines for handling adjustments when they come your way: "Do nothing from selfishness or empty conceit, but with humility of mind let each of you regard one another as more important than himself" (Phil. 2:3). That's a description of a grace-based marriage—giving your partner room to be different and flexing on his or her behalf.

Your Spouse Is Your Friend, Not Your Enemy

Sometimes at our FamilyLife Marriage Conferences, the speaker asks couples to face each other and say aloud, "You are not my enemy." Later in the conference husbands and wives go a step farther when they say to each other, "You are my friend."

Do you consider your wife or husband a friend? If not, is it possible that the two of you have not adjusted to each other's differences and are letting the nitpicky issues in life rub away the good feelings in your relationship?

Making adjustments is usually not easy, but the rewards are worth the effort. What changes could you make that will communicate clearly that your spouse is a dear friend, not an enemy?

Using a Preferences Meter to Facilitate Adjustments

My cohost on the radio program *FamilyLife Today,* Bob Lepine, has used a very practical tool to ease adjustments in his marriage. According to Bob, he and his wife, Mary Ann, express their individual preferences on a given topic by degrees. For example, when trying to decide where to eat out, both persons state their wishes on several restaurants. If neither one wants to champion a particular eating place, it's eliminated.

Then Bob may say, "I've got a mild preference for Chinese food." Mary Ann may respond, "Well, I have a pretty strong preference for Mexican food." Bob probably replies, "Well, your strong preference beats my mild preference. Let's eat Mexican."

Of course, the next time it may switch—by then Bob may be dying for some Chinese, and Mary Ann acquiesces.

The person with the weaker preference is usually the one who winds up flexing and letting the other person have his or her strong preference. But the person not getting his wish—this time—experiences the joy of seeing the other person get pleasure out of the strong preference.

(For added insight on the topic of adjustment, see Chapters 2 on expectations, 24 on differences, and 30 on the first child.)

HomeBuilders Principle

Your marriage is more important
than your individual preferences or values.

TO THINK ABOUT INDIVIDUALLY

1. What adjustments have I made in our marriage? (Be specific; give examples.)
2. What adjustments has my spouse made? (Again, give examples.)
3. In what areas are we still making adjustments? Why?

TO DISCUSS TOGETHER

Talk about adjustments to each other you have made. List some areas where adjustments may still be going on. How can you help each other make these adjustments?

TO TAKE ACTION TOGETHER

Over a cup of coffee or a soft drink, each of you write on separate slips of paper three adjustments that you know your spouse would appreciate *you* making. Hold up the back of your slips like a hand of cards, and each of you draw one from the other person's "deck." For the next week, this is your "adjustment gift" to each other (examples: put away the toothpaste; don't overuse the remote control on the TV; turn off lights; don't say negative things about an in-law; etc.).

16

Forgiveness

THE SAFETY NET BENEATH EVERY STRONG MARRIAGE

Without the cleansing power of forgiveness, at best marriage will be very hard duty. At worst it will be disaster. No matter how hard two people try to love and please each other, they will fail. With failure comes hurt. And the only ultimate relief for hurt is the soothing salve of forgiveness.

The key to maintaining an open, intimate, and happy marriage is to ask for and grant forgiveness quickly. And the ability to do that is tied to each individual's relationship with God.

About the process of forgiveness, Jesus said, "For if you forgive men for their transgressions, your heavenly Father will also forgive you. But if you do not forgive men, then your Father will not forgive your transgressions" (Matt. 6:14–15). The instruction is clear: God insists that we are to be "forgivers," and marriage—probably more than any other relationship—presents frequent opportunities to practice forgiveness.

To forgive means "to give up resentment or the desire to punish."[1] By an act of your will, you let the other person off the hook. And as a Christian you do not do this under duress, scratching and screaming in protest. Rather, you do it with a gentle spirit and love, as Paul urged: "Be kind to one another, tenderhearted, forgiving each other, just as God in Christ also has forgiven you" (Eph. 4:32).

The real test of your ability to forgive comes on the battlefield when you and your spouse are ticked off and angry with each other. That is when you need the power of the Holy Spirit and must ask, "God, You need to help me here. I need to move to forgiveness because You have commanded me to do so. I need You to empower me, to enable me to give up the right of punishing my spouse and to forgive."

It took practice early in our marriage, but Barbara and I learned how to keep our relationship healthy most of the time by not burning excessive emotional energy on resentment. We grant forgiveness and ask for it freely—even when we don't feel like it.

Why Is Asking for Forgiveness Difficult?

Admitting you're wrong and asking for forgiveness is humbling. Both sexes have trouble with this situation, but I think men struggle more. The celebrated male ego makes it hard for husbands to say, "I was wrong. I'm sorry. Will you forgive me?"

In the first years of our marriage, I occasionally struggled to admit I was wrong. When I did, I often said, "If I was wrong when I did this, I'm sorry." I admitted there was a remote possibility I could have been wrong, but I withheld all-out confession. After all, it seemed to me that there were really few times when I was totally wrong. Asking for forgiveness when you're 100 percent wrong is one thing, but what about the times when you're 60 percent right and only 40 percent wrong? During the first years of our marriage, the 60/40 situations seemed to come up regularly, and I struggled admitting I was at fault. I was deploying what might be called the If Maneuver—using that tiny word *if* to give myself an out, to avoid admitting I was 100 percent responsible.

At one of our FamilyLife Marriage Conferences, a husband and father of several boys boasted to me, "You know, I've been married twenty-four years, and I've never once apologized to my wife for anything I've done wrong."

"Oh, really?" I said in a tone that urged him to tell me more.

"Yeah," he said with obvious pride. "Every time we get into a squabble or any kind of disagreement, I just tell her, 'I'm sorry you're mad at me.' I don't admit anything. I just tell her it's too bad she had to get so mad."

Then with a smug grin, he admitted, "And all these years she's never realized that I have never once apologized."

I had the strongest urge to give the guy a piece of my mind. What a pitifully selfish attitude to bring into a love relationship!

Instead I tactfully attempted to explain that he was missing a blessing. He didn't listen. He went away quite sure he was a very clever fellow. He didn't realize that he was hurting not only his wife, but also himself and his children. Just think of what he was modeling for his sons.

Granting Forgiveness Is Also Tough

As difficult as it is to ask for forgiveness, it can be hard to grant forgiveness when you have been wronged.

I often advise married couples to take out a joint membership in the Seventy Times Seven Club. This club began when Peter asked Jesus how many times we must forgive one another. Peter wondered if seven times would be enough. Christ answered, "No—seventy times seven" (Matt. 18:21–22). In other words, forgive an infinite number of times, not just when you feel like it.

You can tell whether you have forgiven your spouse by asking yourself one question: *Have I given up my desire to punish my mate?* When you lay aside that desire and no longer seek revenge, you free your spouse and *yourself* from the bonds of your anger.

Forgiveness cannot be conditional. Once you forgive, that's it. Feelings may still be raw, and it is not hypocritical to not feel like forgiving your spouse. If someone has hurt you, you can choose to forgive immediately but still be processing feelings of disappointment or rejection. Forgiveness is a choice, an act of the will—not an emotion. It may take a while for your feelings to catch up with your will. But your will needs to respond to the scriptural mandate to forgive your spouse.

If you're not careful, though, you may unintentionally dilute the power of forgiveness. How many times have you heard someone say, "I'm sorry; will you forgive me?" And the other person quickly says without apparent reflection, "Sure, I forgive you!" The two people move on, but then the offender may offend again, and the scenario repeats, perhaps many times.

True, cleansing forgiveness will be difficult if there is no authentic repentance on the offender's part. I believe there is a tough love that must break this cycle by saying, "You know, if you are really serious about being forgiven, your actions need to show some believable repentance."

A mate can administer this "love with teeth," but outside help may be needed, particularly in the early years of marriage. Most churches offer counseling to couples experiencing marital stresses. Or you may ask an older couple to serve as marriage mentors. If problems persist and forgiveness is absent, tell someone—seek help.

What About Major Wrongs?

There are some hurts, such as adulterous affairs or a spouse's addiction to pornography, that are extremely difficult to forgive and get over. There may be some pain and distrust in the heart of a person who has been so deeply offended. But we are still commanded by God to move beyond the circumstances and forgive.

That does not let the other person off the hook for completing necessary restitution and demonstrating repentance. Some boundaries may need to be erected in the relationship to prevent the sinful behavior from happening again. An intervention by a pastor, counselor, or mature friend may be required to make the sting of pain from the sin felt so sharply that the offending spouse will finally realize that the behavior has to change. No one should be allowed to continue perpetrating serious harm on a mate.

Ultimately, though, forgiveness must rule. Anyone who says, "I cannot forgive you," really means, "I *choose* not to forgive you." If forgiveness seems impossible at that point, if prayer and reading the Scriptures do not seem to work, go to a mature Christian. Seek out a wise counselor—an elder at your church, a wise Bible teacher, a same-sex friend to confide in—and say, "Can you help me get beyond this?"

As Christians, we do not have the option of becoming embittered with our spouses. The result of obeying God and forgiving is not bondage, but freedom. Ruth Bell Graham said it well: "A good marriage is the union of two forgivers."

(*For further insight on forgiveness, see Chapters 5 on selfishness, 10 on conflict, 21 on growing faith, 45 on blessing and encouraging your spouse, and 47 on knowing when your marriage needs outside help.*)

HomeBuilders Principle

A good marriage is impossible
without the healing power of forgiveness.

TO THINK ABOUT INDIVIDUALLY

1. In your relationship with your spouse, what issues have arisen that seem the most difficult to forgive? Why do you think that is so?

2. Get alone for fifteen to twenty minutes and ask yourself these questions:

- Is there any bitterness in my heart toward my spouse?
- Am I punishing my spouse for something he/she has done that has hurt or disappointed me? If yes, list those hurts/disappointments.
- In prayer and as an act of your will, give up "your rights" to punish your spouse.
- Write across your list of hurts your statement of forgiveness.
- If appropriate, go to your spouse and tell him/her of your forgiveness.

TO DISCUSS TOGETHER

Together review your personal responses to the questions in the previous exercise. If some issues need forgiveness—asking or granting—do so now in the spirit of Ephesians 4:32.

TO TAKE ACTION TOGETHER

Since forgiveness is a liberating process, if you and your spouse have given each other a clean slate, the two of you need to liberate each other to celebrate! Do something together that you enjoy—perhaps a picnic, a walk in the park, a concert—to remind each other as you go of the goodness of a God who gives us wonderful tools for life, such as *forgiveness.*

17

Super Glue

THE POWER OF INTIMACY AND TRANSPARENCY

*E*veryone needs a relationship with another person who accepts him unconditionally. The irony is that it doesn't take long after the honeymoon to discover that the closer one moves toward one's mate, the greater the risk of rejection. This delicate pull-push dance is called intimacy.

The pain and frustration of this human dilemma compare to the predicament of two porcupines caught without shelter in subzero weather. Shivering in the frigid air, the prickly pair moves closer to share body heat. But then the sharp spines poke painfully, and they move apart, victims again of the bitter cold.

Marriage is like that. We can't stand the cold (isolation) and desperately need to learn how to overcome the sharp barbs that are part of moving together. Such a close marriage requires a husband and wife crafting intimacy, trust, transparency, and understanding. The couple chisel out a common direction, purpose, and plan for their lives. A "oneness marriage" is more than a mere mingling of two human beings who share interests and communicate well. It's a tender and total merger of body, soul, and spirit.

This incredible experience requires tenacious, unending effort. Just how can two "porcupines" find intimacy?

Transparency and Intimacy Basics

Because many people live fast-paced lifestyles, move frequently from place to place, and often come from broken or dysfunctional families, emotional closeness is difficult to achieve. But no marriage will reach a level of mutual satisfaction for both husband and wife without the essentials of personal honesty, openness, and deep emotional sharing.

When transparency is missing, the deep desires for emotional and physical intimacy will not be met. And without both transparency and intimacy, trust will not develop. These separate qualities are like three cords that, when woven together, form a marriage rope of incredible strength and durability. But if one is removed, the others weaken, and the relationship suffers.

The ability to develop deeper transparency and intimacy is not a gift or secret available only to a chosen or lucky few. Typically in a marriage, one person is more cognitive or fact-oriented, while the other is more emotional or feelings-oriented. A significant first step in building transparency and intimacy is knowing each person's basic orientation. Each person then needs to give the other the freedom to be different. Being different is *good* before we get married, but many times it becomes unacceptable just months into the marriage. *Different is good!* Period.

Developing transparency is difficult for several reasons. Perhaps in childhood, an individual received little encouragement to freely express opinions and feelings. Maybe a poor self-image makes a person especially guarded and fearful of rejection. Many men struggle with sharing feelings because in American culture, little boys are often told that to shed tears or express emotions (except anger) is not manly and a sign of weakness. Maybe warped religious ideas are a factor, for example: "A Christian is not supposed to struggle, so there can be no negative feelings." Whatever the barriers, they need to be exposed and understood. Becoming more transparent involves risk, but that's the only way deeper intimacy and trust will flourish.

Transparency begins with a firm commitment to create a safe environment for total openness. Inside Barbara's wedding band is the inscription "1 John 4:18." That verse says, "There is no fear in love; but perfect love casts out fear, because fear involves punishment, and the one who fears is not perfected in love." From the beginning, we knew our love required us to be open without fear.

Early in our marriage that verse took on significant meaning as Barbara *felt* my commitment. As she felt secure, my love began to "cast out fear," and she began to open up to me even more. She was like a rosebud that needed the right environment to bloom. Over the years she has opened up and become a magnificent, beautiful rose.

Becoming more transparent requires vulnerability, and only through vulnerability will deeper intimacy and trust grow. It begins as you entrust yourself to God. He loves you and gave you your mate to start with, so take a deep breath and begin sharing yourself with your mate.

Emotional transparency includes expanding your ability to share the following aspects of yourself:

- Thoughts. What do you really think? In a marriage there should be little holding back of what each person thinks and feels deeply.
- Feelings. How have experiences affected you? Are you sad, angry, depressed, happy, hurt, or discouraged?
- Needs. Are you willing to say what you really need: "I'm missing being close to you; could we make love tonight?"

You may need tutoring on basic expression, especially when you want to communicate on a deeper plane. Here's a review of a three-step plan:

1. Determine *what* you want to say. Prepare your thoughts ahead of time; outline in your mind in specific terms what you want to express.
2. Determine *how* you want to say it. What emotions do you want to portray that will convey your message—sad, excited, passionate?
3. Determine *when* you want to say it. Timing may not be everything, but it's important. Pursuing more transparent conversations has a proper time and place. Study your mate and learn the time and environment that are best for sharing—and understand your own needs and moods as well.

A Transparency Breakthrough

For most couples the struggle to become transparent is long and arduous, so take heart if the process seems to drag. A couple married thirty-one years came to a FamilyLife Marriage Conference after relatives had insisted that they attend. The husband was almost totally closed as a communicator, and because I knew of their problems, I monitored the pair carefully throughout the weekend. At the end, I drew them aside and asked, "What did you get out of the conference?"

The husband stood facing me while his wife sat on the stage, chin in hand, staring at the floor. I could tell he was struggling to express himself, but he finally said, "Well, I guess the most significant thing is that we've been married thirty-one years, and I haven't told my wife I love her until this weekend."

He reached down to tenderly squeeze his wife's arm and went on to admit, "This is the first weekend in twenty-four years we've been away from the children."

I looked over at his wife, who had begun sobbing quietly. Although they had made progress toward oneness, it obviously had been a painful time. Her tears were mixed—the pain of isolation blended with the joy of a breakthrough in transparency and oneness they had never known before. She had been a very lonely wife, but they had taken one small, yet significant, step toward a better marriage.

Please don't wait thirty-one years (or thirty-one minutes, for that matter!) to make that kind of progress. Yes, the path to true intimacy is steep and long. Like marriage itself, transparency and intimacy are a journey—one that leads you to a destination of an unshakable closeness and trust in the one you love more than any other. The risk is worth it!

(For more insight on this topic, see Chapters 6 on communication, 7 and 8 on sex, 18 on the past, 23 on accountability, 24 on differences, 31 on isolation, 32 on listening, and 45 on kind words.)

HomeBuilders Principle

Transparency, the path to true intimacy, begins
with a joint commitment to create an atmosphere
where it is safe to be totally open.

TO THINK ABOUT INDIVIDUALLY

1. Here's an exercise to help determine the level of transparency in your marriage. Take this little test for both you and your spouse.

Transparency Index

I am:

Totally closed   1   2   3   4   5   6   7   8   9   10   Totally open

My spouse is:

Totally closed   1   2   3   4   5   6   7   8   9   10   Totally open

2. If you are the open, transparent type, analyze how you relate to your mate, particularly if he or she is more closed and less transparent. Do you overwhelm your mate, or do you try to draw him or her out gently and lovingly?

3. If you are the more closed and less transparent partner of your marriage, what are you doing to try to open up? Do you make an honest effort to respond to questions that your mate may ask to get communication going?

TO DISCUSS TOGETHER

A good place to start in reviewing each of your answers to the questions in the previous exercise (and in moving toward transparency) is to tell each other how doing the Transparency Index made you *feel*. It may be difficult, but explain your current feelings in the middle of *this* discussion. This is often the tough part—telling how you feel right *now*. Don't quit until you have made progress in being more open.

TO TAKE ACTION TOGETHER

Perhaps the greatest hindrance to growing transparency is a lack of focused time together. It's hard to achieve intimacy when both of you are speeding along at 110 miles per hour on different tracks. Give your marriage and each other a precious gift—make an appointment each week to set aside two hours of uninterrupted time alone without significant distractions such as TV, a movie, or a child. Just the two of you take the opportunity to catch up and connect.

18

The Past

efore you married, did you and your beloved take any time to clean out the attic?

I'm not referring to a housecleaning of childhood artifacts such as Little League trophies, Ken and Barbie wardrobes, Lego boxes, or Baby-Sitters Club books. What about the memories we all know are best described as garbage? Any two independent human beings arrive at the wedding altar with significant histories—good and bad memories and habits stored in their personal "attics."

When Barbara and I married, neither of us realized what was in the attic. We had shared a bit by opening a few boxes and peering into an old trunk or two holding long-forgotten relics. But we had no idea how some of this junk would reappear at the most awkward times.

If anything, because of our culture's lax morality and the number of broken homes today, couples marrying now have attics more stuffed than when Barbara and I wed. But if the past isn't discussed, the shame, guilt, and fear may appear years later to play a role in tarnishing your marriage covenant.

Just what are you to do with your past? If God has forgiven your past sins, is it necessary or even right to look at them again? And how much of your history should you share with your spouse?

Is Digging Up the Past a Good Idea?

Paul wrote, "Therefore if any man is in Christ, he is a new creature; the old things passed away; behold, new things have come" (2 Cor. 5:17). If "old things passed away," should you not forgive, forget, and move on?

It is true that those of us who have accepted salvation through Jesus have received a new nature. We have been given grace and are forgiven. But past sins have left us with scar tissue that affects how we respond to one another in a relationship.

Marriage is tough. Even with Jesus Christ helping you build it, marriage will at times test your commitment to the core. There are enough surprises in marriage without putting on a blindfold by saying, "We're not going to talk about those issues that have shaped our lives in the past." You must get into those issues and create a level of understanding and compassion to truly *know* each other. Then deep trust for each other will be in place when life's inevitable trials come along later.

A marriage relationship has to be built on a love-based lifetime commitment: "Perfect love casts out fear" (1 John 4:18). You can't risk hiding something important from your spouse, some pain in your life from a past guilt or shame that is now accusing you by saying, "Don't share that! She'll reject you!" If you are experiencing this, your relationship is controlled by fear, not love.

When love encounters past mistakes in the loved one, it says, "I embrace you. I receive you. I accept you. I cherish you. And, yes, I forgive you."

All of us need to know that we are forgiven and loved because the truth is that we are fallen and have something to hide. Christianity offers us grace, forgiveness, cleansing, and wholeness in plentiful supply.

The Stuff in the Attic

All of us have made bad choices and wrong turns. Some of them earned us a spanking, while others may have cost us our innocence, our virginity, or even our basic human dignity. The bad decision may have involved alcohol, drugs, pornography, or illicit sex that resulted in a sexually transmitted disease.

Some junk in the attic may have been put there by someone who harmed us, maybe a parent who gave abuse instead of love. Or maybe our parents had an unhappy marriage, and we learned from them all the wrong ways of relating.

No matter what the error or who is responsible, your sin—if not forgiven and cleansed away by the blood of Christ—can hang around in the form of shame and guilt. And even knowing that your sins are forgiven does not prevent the accuser, Satan, from reminding you of past garbage in your life.

Ultimately, you must both receive and claim God's forgiveness. Claiming it can sometimes be tough when your feelings are shouting that *God could never forgive me for what I did.* If this is a struggle for you, you must put your mind on the facts about forgiveness, such as the truth found in these verses:

> As far as the east is from the west,
> So far has He removed our transgressions from us. (Ps. 103:12)

> If we confess our sins, He is faithful and righteous to forgive us our sins and to cleanse us from all unrighteousness. (1 John 1:9)

Memorize similar verses, and when doubts or negative feelings arise, repeat the Scriptures. As a precious child of God, claim your inheritance of forgiveness.

There are times, however, when you may need others to help you fully experience forgiveness. Obviously, the most important person in helping you finally claim forgiveness in an area affecting your marriage will be your spouse. When the one who knows you best understands and forgives, you more likely will be able to forgive yourself.

Packages from the attic may continue to show up many years after the wedding. This does not mean necessarily that the person finally sharing has been deceitful. Transparency and trust may have to reach a significant depth before sharing is safe.

How to Share Your Past with Your Mate

Any discussion of sensitive material from the past must occur between two people who understand and have experienced God's grace and forgiveness (see Eph. 4:32). *If at any time you are unsure about the wisdom of sharing something from your past or how exactly to go about it, seek assistance from a pastor or professional Christian counselor who has been recommended by your church.*

If you are confident that you should proceed and a forgiving climate exists between you and your spouse, here are tips on how to divulge or confess information from your past:

1. Explain why you are sharing this information now and haven't before. Make clear that your desire is to deepen trust in your relationship. You want a clean ledger between you.

2. Give the big picture, not the details. Don't provide specifics of how you sinned, for example, the exact circumstances of a sexual encounter. And if you are the one receiving the information, do not ask probing questions to feed your morbid curiosity. Vivid images will haunt you more than general statements.

3. Ask for and grant forgiveness. Don't ever treat forgiveness flippantly, but on the other hand, ask for and grant forgiveness eagerly. Used correctly, forgiveness is a powerful tool for healing in your marriage.

4. Don't expect an immediate resolution. Keep a leash on your expectations. Your spouse may or may not respond positively to your disclosure. Understandably, your mate may need time to process this new information.

Difficult Issues

Some issues arising from the past (sexual abuse, abortion, and rape, for example) are both excruciatingly painful and complex. Although sharing on these matters may cause jolting tremors in the marriage, they need to be brought to light sooner rather than later. The truth has a way of becoming known, and if it has been concealed, its impact will be more devastating.

The great hope is that when we deal with the past in the right way, then we really can move on. Scripture encourages us to do so. "Forgetting what lies behind and reaching forward to what lies ahead," Paul wrote (Phil. 3:13).

In our marriage, after having discussions with Barbara about items from our attics, the ability of two imperfect sinners to express God's love, compassion, and forgiveness and put the past away is a beautiful and awesome thing! It's what a Christian marriage is all about.

(For additional insight on topics related to handling the past, see Chapters 4 on parents, 6 on communication, 16 on forgiveness, 17 on intimacy and transparency, 21 on growing faith, 32 on listening, and 47 on knowing when you need outside help.)

HomeBuilders Principle

Don't let personal junk from the past
clutter your marriage now or in the future.

TO THINK ABOUT INDIVIDUALLY

1. Can you think of any events, relationships, or personal actions from your past that may be causing current difficulties in your marriage?

2. If you are carrying any guilt or shame about your past, ask God now for forgiveness.

3. What information from your past do you think you need to share with your spouse? Pray about what to say, how to say it, and when.

TO DISCUSS TOGETHER

If both of you want to discuss past issues raised during your personal reflection, go ahead and do so after praying together. If one or both of you do not want to talk about past issues now, that's fine. There should be no pressure to do this. Both of you need to be comfortable about such a discussion. Pray for the right time.

TO TAKE ACTION TOGETHER

The past is not only about "bad" memories. Take turns sharing fun memories from the past—some things your spouse may not know about. It might be an activity that both of you would enjoy doing together now, such as roller-skating, jumping in raked leaf piles, or getting a snow cone. Be creative. Go have some fun!

19

Teamwork for Husbands

CLAIMING THE BENEFITS OF DIFFERENCES
IN ROLES IN MARRIAGE

BY DENNIS RAINEY

Note: Chapters 19 and 20 are designed to be studied at the same time—19 by the husband and 20 by the wife.

I wish someone had sat me down in my early days of marriage and sternly exhorted me in the how-to's of becoming the servant-leader of Barbara and our family. I was naive about what my role was and how I should go about meeting Barbara's needs. It's no wonder. Barbara and I grew up in an era when our culture was radically redefining the responsibilities of husband and wife.

These cultural pressures have taken their toll. James Dobson has pointed out that you can't redefine the role of women, who make up half the population, without drastically affecting men—the other half. Many men are confused and insecure about their leadership role in the family.

Fortunately, there is an answer. The Scriptures clearly give us the model for being a man, a husband, and a father. When correctly interpreted and applied, these concepts not only will result in freedom for the husband and wife, but also will help you work better as a team in building a satisfying marriage.

God's Plan for the Family

According to the scriptural model, God's organizational structure for the family begins, not with the husband, but with Christ. The apostle Paul spelled this out when he wrote, "Christ is the head of every man, and the man is the head of a woman, and God is the head of Christ" (1 Cor. 11:3). In another well-known passage, Paul wrote, "For the husband is the head of the wife, as Christ also is the head of the church, He Himself being the Savior of the body" (Eph. 5:23).

In the church the meaning of the word *head* has been hotly debated. Some completely deny the man's leadership and opt for total equality between husband and wife. At the other extreme are those who strongly emphasize a man's authority over the woman and her need to submit blindly to him without question.

It is true that God has given the husband a position of authority and headship, but instead of emphasizing how his wife should submit, the husband should *concern himself with how he should lead.* Being "the head" does not mean that the man lords it over the woman and demands her total obedience to his every wish and command. God has never regarded women as second-class citizens. His Word clearly states, "There is neither Jew nor Greek, there is neither slave nor free man, there is neither male nor female; for you are all one in Christ Jesus" (Gal. 3:28).

When Paul penned those words to the church at Galatia, they came as good news for women, who often endured second-class treatment in ancient cultures.[1] Jesus had welcomed women among His followers, and according to the teaching of the New Testament, women are to be respected, revered, and treated as equals with men.

Because there are so many ideas floating around about the roles of men and women in marriage, I urge you to put some time and effort into studying Scripture and reading good books on the topic. Two titles I recommend heartily are *Rocking the Roles* by my friend and pastor, Robert Lewis (with William Hendricks), and *The Christian Husband* by Bob Lepine, my cohost on the radio broadcast *FamilyLife Today.*

The biblical view is that though their roles differ, the husband and the wife are to be interdependent—that is, they need each other. God made men to need women and women to need men. Paul explained, "In the Lord, neither is woman independent of man, nor is man independent of woman" (1 Cor. 11:11).

Dr. Scott Stanley has written, "In great marriages, couples walk like a team and talk like a team. Mutual deference, respect, and love character-ize them. Sure, in certain areas, you'll see one or the other take the lead. But at the root, these relationships are not competitive; they are more about mutual love and support."[2]

What Is a Real Leader?

As a husband seeks to fulfill his God-given title of "head of his family," he faces three key responsibilities that outline his job description: to lead, to love, and to serve.

Are you a leader? A man who is a "natural-born" leader has no trouble answering yes. But what about the man who is not naturally gifted as a leader, or who is married to an assertive, take-charge woman?

Paul's words about the man being the head of the woman are intended for every man. God has placed the husband in a position of responsibility, and the challenge of leadership comes along with it, whether or not the husband feels capable.

God gives men different personalities, so leadership styles will differ. The important thing is that every man, regardless of his abilities or the personality of his wife, must take the responsibility to lead, to ask God for strength and wisdom to do it well, and to act obediently as the godly servant-leader in his home.

When a husband loves and serves his wife properly, his leadership and her submission to him seem reasonable. She should willingly follow his lead because he obviously values her and creates an environment that encourages her to express her God-given gifts and be effective as a woman.

A Good Leader Is a Good Lover

Flowing out of the responsibility to lead is the responsibility *to love your wife unconditionally*. Ephesians 5:25 reads, "Husbands, love your wives, just as Christ also loved the church and gave Himself up for her." This kind of love seeks the best for the object of that love. I suggest that you become a student of your wife and learn her strengths, her weaknesses, her gifts, her fears, her dreams—everything about her. Then love her just as Christ loved the church and gave Himself up for her.

I think you'll find that a great lover knows how to deny himself and to give up his desires in loving his wife. When was the last time you gave up something you value for your wife, such as your golf game, day off, or your hunting or fishing trip?

A Loving Leader Is a Servant

Rounding out your responsibilities as a loving leader is caring enough for your wife to be willing to serve her. There is no question that words communicate love, but so do actions. You need both.

Christ, the Head of the church, took on the very nature of a servant when He was made in human likeness (Phil. 2:7). Jesus didn't just talk about serving; He demonstrated it when He washed His disciples' feet (John 13:1–17). I've washed Barbara's feet, and I'd recommend washing your wife's feet as a clear statement to her that you want to serve her and meet her needs.

There is no better way to serve your wife than to understand her needs and try to meet them. If she works outside the home, do you help with meals and household chores? Does she have time to exercise and visit with her girlfriends? What is one of her favorite "night out" activities?

There's one last piece of advice that I wish a mature man had given me early in my development as a husband: Find an older husband you respect and ask him to mentor you in becoming a servant-leader. If I had my first years of marriage to do over again, I'd "go to school" with a seasoned veteran husband.

(Related information on this topic can be found in Chapters 2 on expectations, 3 on God's blueprints for marriage, 20 on teamwork for wives, 24 on personality differences, 29 on decision making, and 33 on being a dad.)

HomeBuilders Principle

The husband is accountable to God
for leading, loving, and serving his wife and family.

TO THINK ABOUT INDIVIDUALLY

1. Use the following statements to rate yourself as a husband. Mark each statement from 1 (strongly disagree) to 5 (strongly agree).

_____ My leadership style makes submission easy for my wife.

_____ My leadership style is a reflection of high integrity.

_____ My leadership style is characterized by a servant attitude.

_____ My leadership style causes our home to be well-managed.

_____ I convey acceptance to my wife.

_____ I show love for my wife with sacrificial acts.

_____ I demonstrate love even when I don't "feel" it.

_____ I am willing to listen to my wife frequently and patiently.

_____ My wife knows that I am aware of her needs.

_____ My wife knows she is a big part of my life.

If you scored less than a 4 in any of these areas, analyze why and what you can do to change.

2. List your wife's five greatest needs. What are you doing to meet those needs? How could you improve?

TO DISCUSS TOGETHER

Get together with your wife and discuss your responses in the previous exercise. If leadership and submission are sensitive areas for you, do this when there are no major tensions or distractions. Go slowly and listen carefully to what your wife says, especially about her needs and your leadership style.

TO TAKE ACTION TOGETHER

Identify one thing you can do today that will demonstrate your desire to lovingly *serve* your wife.

20

Teamwork for Wives

CLAIMING THE BENEFITS OF DIFFERENCES
IN ROLES IN MARRIAGE

BY BARBARA RAINEY

Note: Chapters 19 and 20 are designed to be studied at the same time—19 by the husband and 20 by the wife.

erhaps more than at any other time in history, women need a clear understanding of their responsibilities as teammates with their husbands in marriage. Particularly, the significant social changes brought about by the women's movement have created grassroots confusion. But beyond our contemporary experience, God's design for husbands and wives still stands.

Scripture delineates reasons for our existence as human beings common to both men and women, but women have been created for an additional higher purpose—completing men where they are lacking. Genesis tells us that God realized it wasn't good for man to be alone, and that He decided to make a "helper suitable for him" (Gen. 2:18). The Hebrew meaning of the word *helper* in this passage is found hereafter in the Bible to refer *only* to God as He helps us; applying the same word to a wife's role signifies that we women have been given tremendous power for good in our husbands' lives as God's divinely called agents.

God has designed wives to help their husbands become all that God intends for them to be. I love the story told about Pete Flaherty, former mayor of Pittsburgh, and his wife, Nancy. They were standing on the sidewalk, surveying a city construction project, when one of the laborers at the site called out to them. "Nancy, remember me?" he asked. "We used to date in high school."

Later, Pete teased her, "Aren't you glad you married me? Just think, if you had married him, you would be the wife of a construction worker."

Nancy looked at him and said, "No, if I'd married him, *he* would be the mayor of Pittsburgh."

As I fulfill my God-given purpose as helpmate to my husband, I see three specific commands in Scripture that comprise the basis of my responsibility to him: submitting to his leadership, showing him respect, and loving him. Meeting these responsibilities builds oneness between the two of us. If I don't, tension, troubles, and isolation occur.

The *S* Word

Just mention the word *submission*, and many women immediately become angry and even hostile. Admittedly, the dictionary defines *submission* in a negative way, using ugly synonyms like *subservience*, *subdued*, *surrender*, and *abasement*. Who wants to be submissive like that? I certainly don't. Misinterpreting the true definition of submission can lead to abuses of the biblical concept, particularly by husbands who don't understand the biblical context of submission or a man's role in marriage.

Some husbands and wives believe submission indicates that women somehow are inferior to men. Christian women frequently struggle with this marital model because of the competing messages we hear from the church and from the world outside. Women may feel that if they submit, they'll lose their identity and become nonpersons. Others fear (some with good reason) that submission leads to being taken for granted and used.

Submission does not equal slavery. Husbands need their wives' input. Our friend and pastor, Robert Lewis, wrote: Man "needs a 'helper,' and without his wife's special attention, he is prone to imbalance and blind spots."[1]

Submission Is Voluntary

We've looked at the world's definitions of submission, but what does God have to say? According to Scripture, a wife should submit voluntarily to her husband's sensitive and loving leadership. Building oneness in marriage can work only when *both* partners choose to fulfill their responsibilities with no pressure or coercion. To become the servant-leader God has commanded him to be, Dennis needs my gracious respect and submission. And when Dennis loves me the way he is commanded to, I can more easily submit myself to that leadership.

I do this with an attitude of entrusting myself to God. In one of his letters, Peter told us that even though Jesus suffered terrible pain and insults, He did not retaliate "but kept entrusting Himself to Him who judges righteously" (1 Peter 2:23). When you entrust your life to the Father, it's much easier to be the wife of an imperfect man, particularly when you may have disagreements.

A Warning

Some readers may live with abuse or in excessively unhealthy and destructive conditions. At times, it may be inappropriate or even life-threatening for you to apply unquestioningly the principles of submission. For example, if you are being physically or verbally abused, you need wisdom on how to be wise, strong, and safe. You may have to say to your husband, "I love you, but enough is enough." If you are in that situation, please discerningly seek out someone wise who has been trained to help with your specific issue. (For constructive and practical help on this subject, see *Love Must Be Tough* by James Dobson [Nashville: Word, 1996].)

Giving Respect

In finishing his description of male and female responsibilities, Paul made an interesting summary statement that includes the second responsibility for wives. He commanded a man to love his wife as himself and added that the wife must "respect her husband" (Eph. 5:33).

Respecting your husband means honoring him, valuing his opinion, and admiring his strength, intellect, wisdom, and character.

Expressing Love

Third in God's responsibilities for wives is "to love their husbands" (Titus 2:4). Your husband needs unconditional acceptance. In other words, embrace your husband just as he is—an imperfect person.

Perhaps a woman's most important expression of love—from a man's point of view—is her commitment to a mutually fulfilling sexual relationship. Surveys consistently show that sex is one of a man's most important needs—if not *the* most important. When a wife demonstrates resistance, only mild interest, or active disinterest, her husband will feel rejected; rejection will cut at his self-image, tear at him to the very center of his being, and create isolation.

Is God Big Enough for You?

For wives who don't agree with their husbands on an important issue, I have three questions:

1. Have you clearly, and as unemotionally as possible, communicated (perhaps in writing) the facts to your husband? Has each of you taken the time to hear the other on the issue?

2. Do you trust God in your circumstances, or do you allow circumstances to overwhelm you?

3. Is God big enough to take care of your husband without your help?

That's often the hard part—wanting to be *too much* of a helpmate, especially when you're sure he's wrong and you're right. But you ought to ask yourself, *Is God big enough to take care of my husband without my help in this situation? Will I follow Jesus' example and entrust myself to the Father?*

With our Lord, everything is possible—even conquering the toughest challenges of being a loving team player in marriage.

HomeBuilders Principle

A wife fulfills her responsibilities as a helpmate
by submitting to, respecting, and loving her husband.

TO THINK ABOUT INDIVIDUALLY

1. Use the following statements to rate yourself as a wife. Mark each statement on a scale of 1 (strongly disagree) to 5 (strongly agree).

____ My attitude toward submission and respect reflects respect for my husband.

____ My attitude toward being a helpmate reflects trust in God.

____ My attitude toward my husband is love and a desire for oneness.

____ I understand my husband's responsibilities.

____ I devote adequate time to my husband.

____ I concentrate enough on his needs.

____ I am a positive encouragement to him.

____ I accept him regardless of his performance.

____ I express much love in our sexual life.

____ I sacrifice myself for him.

If you scored less than a 4 in any of these areas, analyze why and what you can do to change.

2. List your husband's five greatest needs. What are you doing to meet those needs? How could you improve?

TO DISCUSS TOGETHER

Get together with your husband and discuss responses in the previous exercise. If his leadership and your submission are sensitive topics for you, do this when there are no major tensions or distractions. Go slowly and listen carefully to what your husband says, especially about his needs and his perception of your attitude.

TO TAKE ACTION TOGETHER

Identify one choice you can make, a decision you can support, or an outward action you can do *today* that will demonstrate your desire to submit lovingly to your husband.

21

Growing Faith

WALKING WITH CHRIST IN YOUR MARRIAGE

*J*would be guilty of marital advice malpractice if I failed to address the effects of a couple's neglect of their individual and joint relationship with Jesus Christ. All of us are wounded, imperfect, broken sinners who do not have the ability to love another wounded, imperfect, broken sinner the way we need to in the relational furnace called marriage. The shortest route to a godly marriage and family is to first invest the ongoing effort and time each day in becoming a more passionate, committed, and skilled disciple of Christ.

You may be saying to yourself, "Well, that's easy for him to say, but I'm just not that religious or spiritual." If that's how you feel, then I need to remind you that most of those who followed Jesus when He was on earth were not spiritual professionals but very ordinary people. They had in common a desire to follow the greatest Person who ever lived because He knew how to live life to the fullest.

Jesus spoke about two different foundations for a life. His statements are equally applicable to a couple building a home together:

Therefore everyone who hears these words of Mine, and acts upon them, may be compared to a wise man, who built his house upon the rock. And the rain descended, and the floods came, and the winds blew, and burst against that house; and yet it did not fall, for it had been founded upon the rock. And everyone who hears these words of Mine, and does not act upon them, will be like a foolish man, who built his house upon the sand. And the rain descended, and the floods came, and the winds blew, and burst against that house; and it fell and great was its fall. (Matt. 7:24–27)

Jesus was talking about the need to build your spiritual house on a solid foundation, and the way to support your life through increasing obedience to God and His Word. When you build your house on that Rock, you can withstand the cultural storms and the "currents" of your selfishness and shortcomings.

Many couples never stop to consider that storms, floods, wind, and the like will assault their marriage. They aren't prepared spiritually, so these elements overtake them. Perhaps they don't understand God and His love for them. They think that if they give Him total control of their lives, He will punish them or send them to work in a developing nation. Hampered by this basic misunderstanding of who God is and what He desires for His children, people don't take the Scriptures seriously. They live their lives based on their own understanding, not according to the light of God's Word. It's no wonder so many marriages fail.

How do we help each other set Jesus Christ apart as Lord and Master in command of our lives? We must know Jesus Christ personally and diligently follow in His steps, growing toward Christian maturity. Paul wrote, ". . . we are no longer to be children, tossed here and there by waves, and carried about by every wind of doctrine, by the trickery of men, by craftiness in deceitful scheming; but speaking the truth in love, we are to grow up in all aspects into Him, who is the head, even Christ" (Eph. 4:14–15).

Is there an insider's secret on how to make the most of time and build a marriage on the solid-rock foundation of Jesus Christ? Many people in our "do your own thing" world may not care for the answer, but followers of Jesus for centuries have recognized its critical importance: *discipline.* Certain spiritual activities contribute to the training of a growing disciple. I am not proposing a lifeless list of legalistic tasks that will turn the Christian life into a graceless, joyless religion based on works. No, these are basic exercises that will change a flabby, weak faith into a strong one.

Prayer. Every good relationship survives or dies on its communication. Prayer is the way we communicate with God. You need to pray as individuals and as a couple. Perhaps the two of you can pray briefly before you go to sleep at night.

Bible study. In the Word we learn so much about God, His principles, and what He wants from us—and we see Jesus, our Leader, in action and can learn better how to follow Him. Make use of time available during a commute or exercise session by carrying a pocket-sized Bible or listening to Bible audiotapes.

Worship. We are commanded to worship God, individually and collectively. If we are not worshiping God, we probably are worshiping something else. Find a vibrant Christ-worshiping, Bible-believing church. (See Chapter 36 for help in choosing a church.)

Giving. We are stewards of resources on loan to us from God. We need to be diligent in sharing with others so their needs are met and they in turn give thanks and glory to God. Regular tithing (giving 10 percent of your income) to your local church and other Christian ministries is a great beginning point for every couple.

Fellowship. The body of Christ is our family; we need others and they need us to accomplish the work of the kingdom as a loving team. How about joining or offering to lead a small group Bible study at your church?

Service. It is a privilege to serve others in the name of Christ, particularly those who are needy or alone. In every community of any size there are churches and agencies that need volunteers to feed the hungry and help the poor. Seek one out.

Witness. Jesus entrusted to His followers the task of reconciling the lost to God. That involves all aspects of the process, from cultivating friendships with neighbors and others who are not believers, to planting seeds by sharing testimony and the Word, to actually reaping the harvest by asking those made ready by the Holy Spirit to receive Christ. Do you work with someone who needs you to live out the gospel by showing genuine love?

Other spiritual disciplines bear much godly fruit, including fasting— going without food or other daily necessities as a sign of total dependence on God for strength.

I encourage you to sink your spiritual roots deep by giving yourself to these vital disciplines of a disciple's life.

(For more discussion of spiritual maturity, see Chapters 51 on legacy and 52 on the coming seasons of your marriage.)

HomeBuilders Principle

Obedient, growing followers of Christ
make great marriage partners.

TO THINK ABOUT INDIVIDUALLY

1. Are you building a solid foundation for your life on Christ? What steps might you take to go even deeper in your love and devotion to Him?

2. Some spiritual disciplines were listed in this chapter. Using the following scale (1 = poor and 5 = great), how would you rate your commitment to each of these disciplines?

Prayer	1	2	3	4	5
Bible study	1	2	3	4	5
Worship	1	2	3	4	5
Giving	1	2	3	4	5
Fellowship	1	2	3	4	5
Service	1	2	3	4	5
Witness	1	2	3	4	5

3. What changes might you make in being more faithful in exercising these disciplines?

TO DISCUSS TOGETHER

Share and discuss your answers to the questions in the previous exercise. How might you help each other live a more spiritually disciplined life?

TO TAKE ACTION TOGETHER

Most of us benefit from having someone who knows us well to hold us accountable in areas where we want to improve. Each of you choose at least one spiritual discipline that you know needs improvement. Decide how you can hold each other accountable for the next month. Remember, these disciplines are not meant to be a burden but a tool to increase your joy in knowing and obeying God.

22

Work

MAKING CHOICES ON THE MIX OF CAREER, MARRIAGE, AND PARENTING

Work—and its impact on the home—is a hot issue in marriage, especially a new marriage, where both spouses may work. In this chapter we'll discuss work and career from both the husband's and the wife's perspective.

A Challenge to Men from Dennis Rainey

Let's get personal: What would happen if you switched the energy you give to your job with the energy you give to your home and family?

I realize that may be an unfair question because by necessity many men must work long hours. But too many husbands and fathers give almost all their energy to the job and leave little for the family. I have a friend who keeps an index card on his desk that reads: LEAVE SOME FOR HOME. He realized that without that reminder shouting at him daily, he'd go home on "empty" most of the time.

Good management in a business means being close to the people you manage; this takes time and physical proximity. The same is true for your "managerial duties" as a husband and father.

Time and proximity are not the only issues, however. Many families think they require two incomes to keep all the bills paid. In some cases, this may be true, but we all need to consider how we're spending our money. Do our bills arise from *needs* or *wants*? We might be able to get by on less, especially during those early, formative years of our children's lives. Statistics show that three out of four mothers of school-age children work outside the home, and by the time American children are twelve years old, nearly 35 percent of them are regularly left on their own.[1]

I know of one man who insisted that his wife work outside the home for much of their marriage. When his wife was finally able to stay home, their children were grown up, out of the house, and emotionally disconnected from their parents. After seeing the difference in his wife as a result—her increased energy and creativity given to him and their home—this man admitted, "This is so much better. I wish we'd done this while the children were still here."

The responsible husband should take a long, hard look at why his wife works and how it affects her and the rest of the family. Is she exhausted? Is a child feeling lonely and ignored? Is there time to talk and play and live together?

One final observation about men, especially younger ones: Be particularly careful that you are not encouraging your wife to work so that you can enjoy hobbies, adult toys, or activities you grew accustomed to while single. Don't plant a seed of bitterness in your wife by forcing her to work primarily to support your obsession with sports or leisure.

A Challenge to Women from Barbara Rainey

The caricature of the male executive in the three-piece pinstriped suit working long hours to make it to the top has been around for decades, but the female counterpart is a more recent development. Today many women share with men the struggle to find the right balance between work and family.

I am not opposed to women working outside the home. But I want to discuss the issue of mothers—especially those with young children—devoting time and energy to another full-time occupation.

A majority of mothers now work outside the home either part-time or full-time. Reasons include survival needs, lifestyle needs, and personal fulfillment needs. Some women work because they fear a possible divorce would leave them unable to provide for themselves. Let's look at what is really taking place in our culture.

Working mothers are not a new phenomenon. What is new is the shift in career focus: from full-time mother with a job on the side to a full-time career while attempting to mother in whatever time is left over.

I don't believe Scripture supports this notion. A familiar passage in the New Testament summarizes what young wives and mothers are to do: "To love their husbands, to love their children, to be sensible, pure, workers at home, kind, being subject to their own husbands, that the word of God may not be dishonored" (Titus 2:4–5).

Notice the priority of commitments given women in this passage: husband first and children second. Based upon this instruction, I think every woman needs to ask herself, *Is a job the best use of my time? Will I have more influence for the future through my employment or through my children?*

I'd also like to challenge you to look honestly at your finances with your husband and determine whether the extra money you bring in meets *needs* or *wants*. Some families could get by on the husband's income if they cut back on expenses.

If in fact you must work or feel you cannot quit anytime soon, here are some guidelines and suggestions:

1. A mother should have a job only if her husband is in total agreement. A lack of oneness at this point can be critical. The two-career marriage may solve financial difficulties, but it creates others.

2. A mother should consider how much of her capabilities, time, energy, and creativity she gives to work. James Dobson notes that there is only so much energy within the human body for expenditure during each twenty-four hours, and when it is invested in one place, it is not available for use in another.[2]

If a woman must work, I think a job with a flexible time frame that can be pursued at home is the best option. With computer technology and changes in the workplace, many opportunities are available.

3. A mother should consider her child's needs. Noted child development expert Burton White wrote, "I firmly believe that most children will get off to a better start in life when they spend the majority of their waking hours being cared for by their parents."[3]

Evaluate whether to work outside the home as part of your life focus. To what will you give your life—your children or your paid vocation?

Mothering is more than a full-time job; it's a twenty-four-hour career. I don't believe mothers can serve their families and outside occupations without one or both suffering. Please pray and think carefully about your choices. They will have an impact in the lives of future generations.

If Both Must Work

Regardless of the reasons, if both husband and wife work full-time outside the home, these suggestions make the situation as positive as possible for the marriage and family:

- Accept the idea that you have made choices, and acknowledge that you can't have it all. Much pain and frustration come from unmet expectations. If both of you work, your time for other activities will be limited. Don't beat yourself up because you can't cook a five-course meal every night, coach soccer, teach Sunday school, change the oil in your car, and make your own clothes. Concentrate on the most important things—time with God, your spouse, and your children.

- Simplify your life. Always look for ways to make daily activities less complicated.

- Be focused; don't waste time. A time-use study reported that Americans spent 38 percent of their free time watching television.⁴ If both of you have jobs, resist the temptation to say, "I'm tired—I think I'll just relax and watch some TV." Your time is too scarce and valuable to waste doing that. Early in our marriage we took the television out of our dining room—a great decision!

- Be a team. If you both work, you both are tired and have more to do than possibly can get done. Don't make things worse and lose time by fussing over who is doing or not doing his share. Commit to help each other as much as possible at home. Doing this will ease the load, and you'll have more time together to talk and stay connected.

- Communicate. More than ever, with your two busy lives often heading in opposite directions, you must stay connected. Hold family meetings weekly, and the first appointment listed should be a date for the two of you alone every week.

Values are the bottom line on the role of work in your lives. Your agreement on what really matters in your family will make work/career decisions clearer, although not always easy.

(For additional information on this topic, see Chapters 12 on family values, 13 on lifestyle, 14 on money, 27 and 30 on children, 33 and 34 on being a dad and mom, 38 on scheduling, 44 on rest, 46 on work-related travel, 49 on stress, and 51 on legacy.)

HomeBuilders Principle

> Work and career must not become
> the most important things in life
> for either husband or wife.

TO THINK ABOUT INDIVIDUALLY

1. As you think about all of your life and your most treasured values, do you think your job or career is receiving the right amount of time, energy, and resources? Why do you feel this way?

2. Do you need to make adjustments in the priorities for your spiritual life, work, marriage, family, and other matters?

TO DISCUSS TOGETHER

Compare individual answers to questions 1 and 2 in the previous exercise, and discuss any changes both of you may need to make.

TO TAKE ACTION TOGETHER

Over a cup of coffee or a soft drink, discuss how peer pressure, advertising, and/or expectations of parents may influence your thinking about the kind of job and career either or both of you feel you must have to be "successful." Are there new options you need to consider?

Part 3

23

Don't Do Marriage Alone

BECOMING ACCOUNTABLE TO YOUR SPOUSE AND OTHERS

*A*llow me to be frank. Most of us live more responsibly when we know another person who cares about us—a parent, a coach, a boss, a friend, a spouse—will mentor us, check up on us, monitor us, in other words, hold us accountable.

If you want your relationship to deepen and go the distance, I strongly encourage you to welcome loving accountability from your spouse and others. For many newly married couples, developing accountability relationships may be one of the most important steps they take.

Accountability with Your Spouse

The wise preacher declared, "Two are better than one because . . . if either of them falls, the one will lift up his companion. But woe to the one who falls when there is not another to lift him up" (Eccl. 4:9–10). That Scripture shouts the value of mutual support or accountability in marriage.

Here are some areas where Barbara and I have learned to practice accountability in our marriage:

1. Spiritual health. As I mentioned earlier, every marriage—every *life*—must involve daily communication with and dependence on God in order to remain on track. Most of us are prone to laziness or distraction when it comes to taking care of our spiritual needs. A loving spouse, who has our permission to encourage us in our devotion to Christ, can help by asking open-ended questions: "What has God been teaching you lately?"

and "What are you praying about these days?" Honest discussion around questions like these can result in growth and a hunger to know more about God. A husband and wife praying together on a daily basis will have an accountability mechanism already in place.

2. Emotional and sexual fidelity. This is a potentially sensitive but critical area in any new marriage. The way in which the issues of temptations and moral struggles are handled will chart the course for every married couple.

Neither spouse can risk opening the door to inappropriate intimacy with someone of the opposite sex. In a Bible study group I once led, Barbara sensed that one of the men was acting a bit too friendly toward her. At first she thought she might be imagining it, but after more of the weekly sessions, she knew the man had an interest in her.

Although she was embarrassed and not sure how I might respond, she confided her suspicions and discomfort to me. When I responded with understanding and kindness, I saw relief spread across her face. This unsettling secret quickly lost its negative power as we discussed her feelings openly.

Looking back on that incident, we saw that it was a test for both of us regarding accountability. Fortunately, both of us did the right thing—she shared and I did not get angry—and the incident strengthened our commitment. It also helped us see the value of open communication and mutual accountability.

3. Schedules. We try to help each other make good decisions by monitoring each other's workload and schedules. Making good decisions means saying yes to some things and no to others. And saying no can be easier when you can honestly add, "*We* have decided that I don't have time to do this."

4. Money and values. Nothing created the need for accountability more than the checkbook. Early on it was a fork in the road as to what each of us felt was important. I recall some early accountability tests. Would I listen to her? Would I really consider her advice? Would she trust me with a final decision? These were all natural opportunities to practice godly, caring accountability to each other.

5. Parenting practice. When Barbara and I had our first child, we began the lifelong process of being accountable to each other for our performance as parents. Early on we interacted and sharpened each other on our parenting styles. We all tend to draw on the parenting techniques modeled for us by our parents. When Barbara and I noticed the good or bad tendencies, we could either encourage or help each other improve.

Secrets are primary tools in dividing couples. Accountability between husband and wife is a superb way to keep them from messing with your marriage.

Accountability with Others

Isolation is another strategic ploy of the enemy. He wants you separated from others so that you think you are the only couple in the whole world who ever had a particular problem. That's why you need to start early to find other couples who are kindred spirits and grow together by sharing the struggles and triumphs in your lives and marriages.

At least one other couple needs to know *how you really are doing in your marriage*. This point is so important that I will say it again: *You need at least one or two other couples who know how you are doing in your marriage.*

You may choose to participate in a small group devoted to building godly marriage and family. The group offers the opportunity to grow spiritually, and it provides an environment of support and accountability for couples. Lifelong friendships can be cemented in such Bible studies.

We've found that most churches are full of couples who earnestly desire a genuine relationship with other couples. In this hurried culture of fast food and shallow relationships, we need to feel connected. Ideally, your church already has a small group you can join. If not, ask a pastor whether a group could be started, or start a group yourselves. Many excellent materials are available that make leading a group a manageable and enjoyable task.

You may consider using the HomeBuilders Couples Series produced by our organization—FamilyLife. Many couples have started a group in their neighborhood. People who have no religious affiliation or background feel comfortable in these groups because they are formed around the felt needs of marriage.

If you are interested in starting a HomeBuilders group, follow this simple action plan:

Step One: Go online at <www.familylife.com> and review a copy of the HomeBuilders study you want to lead. Call FamilyLife at 1-800-FLTODAY for more information. (See Appendix C for a list of available titles.)

Step Two: Prayerfully make a list of people you'd like to join your group (four to seven couples) and then invite them. You may need to ask more than the number of couples you hope will come. Don't think only of those in your church; ask those in your neighborhood or associates at work who would benefit from your time together.

Step Three: Set your first meeting date, get the participants' materials, and begin.

God Put Their Marriage Back Together

One woman wrote to tell us how a HomeBuilders group had been "very instrumental in rebuilding a relationship that I thought was forever torn apart." The letter went on to explain the family was ripped open at the seams by divorce. Trying to escape all the pain and memories, the woman moved to a new city and started attending a church where she eventually gave her heart to Christ. Still struggling with hurt and anger, she agreed to attend a HomeBuilders discussion. She wrote, "It [the series] knocked my socks off! I was still so very angry over the way my marriage had ended and with my life in general, but something was beginning to happen inside of me."

Through the HomeBuilders study, the woman read the Bible and understood it in a way she had never experienced before. She wrote her ex-husband to tell him what she was learning, and he immediately called her. They talked for the first time about what God wanted to do in their lives.

The next week he flew out and attended one of the HomeBuilders sessions. That weekend they put their lives in the hands of Jesus Christ, and when he asked her to remarry him, she said, "Yes!"

What a tremendous testimony to the power of God working through a group committed to doing marriage and family His way! If you are not experiencing such fellowship and accountability, please consider joining or starting a group soon. I believe it's one of the top two or three things you can do that will ensure your marriage lasts for a lifetime.

(For more information on related topics see Chapters 9 on building a spiritual foundation in marriage, 21 on growing faith, 36 on choosing a church, and 49 on managing stress.)

HomeBuilders Principle

Accountability, with a spouse and in a small group,
is one of God's tools for building
a strong and lasting marriage.

TO THINK ABOUT INDIVIDUALLY

1. Who are the people in your life you have given permission to hold you accountable for issues of purity, integrity, and character? If you don't have such people, why do you think this is the case? How might you change this situation?

2. Concerning your marriage, in what areas do you know your mate holds you accountable? Are there other areas that need to be added?

3. In what areas do you hold your mate accountable? Are there other areas that need to be added?

TO DISCUSS TOGETHER

Share your answers to questions 2 and 3 in the previous exercise. Discuss how being accountable already helps your marriage—and how increasing accountability might make it even better.

TO TAKE ACTION TOGETHER

Do the two of you participate in a small group like one of those discussed in this chapter? If not, contact your pastor or a key leader at your church and request to join such a group. You may desire to start and lead your own group. It doesn't matter how it happens—"just do it!" Participation in a small group is too good a benefit to miss.

24

Potatoes and Pineapples

MAKING INDIVIDUAL DIFFERENCES
A STRENGTH IN MARRIAGE

I am constantly amazed by how easy it is to overlook one of the more obvious facts about men and women: They're *different!*

Feminists and others in the recent past have worked to blur the distinctions between the sexes. But this effort is ultimately doomed because God created us male and female—different.

When this Ozark country boy married the refined city girl, our differences came out in dozens of ways. For instance, Barbara believed that grass and flowers were meant to be tamed and made to grow beautifully inside a freshly painted white picket fence. I had a philosophy I learned from my dad, who discipled me in the fine art of avoiding yard work. He would let the yard die a slow death in July, so he didn't have to mow it the rest of the summer. In turn, I believed that if God had intended for leaves to be collected, He would have had them fall in plastic bags to begin with.

Barbara and I have worked through many of our differences. Some were funny, but others were not. And it's no coincidence that our present home sits back on a heavily forested hillside that overlooks a beautiful lake. We enjoy the sunsets, but you won't find much of a lawn. I'm trying to change, though. One summer, the children and I surprised Barbara by hauling tons of rocks to outline a trail and some flower beds.

All of us know that men and women are separated by more than basic, biological nuances. But just how different are we? After considerable research, an author named Cris Evatt developed a general summary of male and female personality traits. Of course, these are generalizations that may only apply in degrees to any particular person, and some items on the list probably relate more to social conditioning than real personality differences. But you will enjoy reviewing and discussing the list with your spouse.

Differences Between Men and Women

Men	Women
More self-focused	More other-focused
Needs less intimacy	Needs more intimacy
Fears engulfment	Fears abandonment
Feels less resentful	Feels more resentful
Needs less approval	Needs more approval
More independent	Less independent
Often detached	Often emotional
An attention-getter	An attention-giver
Highly competitive	Less competitive
Strong drive for power/money	Less important drive for power/money
Respect very important	Respect less important
Often obsessed with sports	Sports less important
Talks mostly about "things"	Talks mostly about "people"
Less talkative in private	Less talkative in public
Takes things literally	Looks for hidden meanings
Language more direct	Language more indirect
Less responsive listener	More responsive listener
Decisions made quicker	Takes more time to decide
Gossips less	Gossips more
Engages in put-downs	Engages in backbiting
Focuses more on solutions	Likes to discuss problems
Less apologetic	More apologetic
Tells more jokes/stories	Tells fewer jokes/stories
Less willing to seek help	Seeks help readily
Boasts about performance	Boasts less frequently
Nags less often	Nags more often

Often intimidates others	Seldom intimidates others
Issues orders	Makes suggestions
Often seeks conflict	Tends to avoid conflict
Likes to be adored	Likes to adore others
Fearful of commitment	Eager for commitment
Sexually jealous of mate	Emotionally jealous of mate
Accepts others more	Tries to change others more
Thrives on receiving	Thrives on giving
More polygamous	More monogamous
More sadistic	More masochistic
More sex-oriented	More love-oriented
Has fewer close friends	Has many close friends
Likes group activities	Prefers intimate encounters
Worries less about others	Worries more about others
More sensitive to stress	Less sensitive to stress
Less trusting	Often too trusting
More aggressive	Less aggressive
Initiates war	Does not make war
Posture leans back more	Posture leans forward more
Cooler/seductive sexiness	Warmer/animated sexiness
Has more testosterone	Has more estrogen
Less into dieting	More into dieting
Less concerned about health	More concerned about health
Worries less about appearance	Worries more about appearance
Takes more physical risks	Takes fewer physical risks
Shops out of necessity	Often shops for enjoyment[1]

Whew! A list like that makes it clear why combining two people with different qualities and approaches to life into a marriage is a challenging task. And to complicate things more, sometimes a quality that attracted you to your mate—"He's *so funny!*"—can frustrate you after marriage: "Why can't he be serious once in a while?" That's why you should often remind each other, "You are God's perfect gift for me." You need to trust Him and His plan.

Let's review how it's His intention that the mate He's chosen for you—differences and all—is His way of making you complete.

Receive Your Mate

Before a truly united, oneness-type marriage can take wings, the two individuals have to accept or receive each other. To understand this, we need to go back to the drama that unfolded in the Garden of Eden.

God makes Adam, but then says, "It is not good for the man to be alone; I will make him a helper suitable for him" (Gen. 2:18). Our paraphrase of this passage says, "I have chosen, according to My infinite wisdom, to make Adam incomplete, and now I will do something about that. In fact, I'm going to complete him by handcrafting a person who is a perfect fit for him in all ways!"

Adam may wonder what God means. After all, he has the perfect Boss, a perfect job, even perfect retirement benefits. But he needs something—more precisely—*someone* else. Adam needs a helper, specifically made for him. In the original text, the Hebrew word for helper means "wholeness."

As the drama continues, God causes a deep sleep to fall upon Adam. He takes one of his ribs and fashions it into the woman. After making Eve, God presents her to Adam. He doesn't send her, tell Adam to pick her up, or have Adam find her under a Christmas tree all wrapped up. Instead, God personally brings her to the man (Gen. 2:22). The Lord God was the original Father of the bride, intimately involved in the first wedding in history.

But how will Adam receive Eve? He had been busy naming the animals but had not found a helper suitable for himself. And he had never seen an "Eve" before. In many Bible translations, Adam's response seems rather ho-hum:

> This is now bone of my bones,
> And flesh of my flesh;
> She shall be called Woman,
> Because she was taken out of Man. (Gen. 2:23)

The Living Bible paraphrase comes closest to capturing the real spirit of

Adam's response: "This is it!" Another way to interpret the Hebrew here is, "Wow! Where have you been all my life?" In other words, Adam is excited; he is *beside* himself!

Obviously, Eve looked better to Adam than all the animals he had just named. But there is something more here we don't want to miss, a cornerstone principle for marriage. *Adam had faith in God's integrity.* He knew God could be trusted. Eve had done nothing to earn Adam's response. He accepted her because God had made her for him.

To reject your mate is to reflect negatively on the character of God. It's as if you say, "God, You slipped up. You didn't know what You were doing when You provided this person for me."

Cleave to Your Mate

After each receives the mate God has provided, the next step for the husband and wife is to join forces. The Bible's word for this is *cleave,* which literally means to stick together like glue in a permanent bond.

As the melodrama of God's presentation of Eve to Adam comes to a close, the script says, "For this cause a man shall leave his father and his mother, and shall cleave to his wife; and they will become one flesh" (Gen. 2:24).

Cleaving is not just about sex, although the beautiful act of sexual intercourse certainly illustrates the physical aspect of becoming "one flesh." Cleaving is much more. Another good word for it is *commitment,* a total lifelong decision to stick together physically, emotionally, and spiritually.

Without question, it's a challenge for both spouses to accept all the differences in each other when they marry. But this is God's plan; in spite of the things in your mate that repel, He wants you to receive and cleave. And the result is a partnership of exponential strength and awesome potential.

(For more information related to differences, see Chapters 15 on adjustment and 19 and 20 on roles and teamwork in marriage.)

HomeBuilders Principle

> When God's plan is accepted and trusted,
> differences are welcomed
> as a source of strength in marriage.

TO THINK ABOUT INDIVIDUALLY

1. Is there anything about your mate that you don't accept? Why?
2. Are there areas in which you don't feel accepted by your mate? Why?

TO DISCUSS TOGETHER

Together, look over the "Differences Between Men and Women" list on pages 121–122. Working as a team, place check marks by items you believe are true of each other. Thinking of your marriage, what basic differences between you have caused the most enjoyment in the relationship? What differences have caused the most frustration? How are you doing in resolving them?

TO TAKE ACTION TOGETHER

Choose a task or activity that the two of you can do together that will reveal how combining your different personalities and other traits results in a dynamite team. Consider these examples: leading a home Bible study—one person makes all administrative arrangements while the other leads the discussion; planting a flower garden; giving the dog a bath; balancing the checkbook and paying the monthly bills; writing a letter to a parent; finding information on the Internet. Be creative!

25

Fanning the Flames I

THE FIVE ROMANTIC NEEDS OF A WOMAN

Note: In this chapter, after an introduction to the topic of romance, we discuss the five romantic needs of a woman. In the next chapter, we cover the romantic needs of a man.

en and women think of romance differently. When asked to describe the purpose of romance, a woman will use words such as *friendship, relationship, endearment,* and *tenderness.* Given the same question, a man will answer with one of the shortest words in the English language—*sex.* For him, physical oneness and affirmation of his manhood equal romance.

Can two people with such different perspectives have their expectations met? Absolutely! But creating adventurous romance requires planning and enthusiastic effort. The relationship has to be a top priority. One reason so many marriage beds are frozen over or boring is that couples just don't have time for romance and sex. Too many husbands and wives try to work sex in between the evening news and the top ten list on the *Late Show with David Letterman.*

Let's face it. Many of our activities and other important things get the best of our resources and energy. Jobs get our best. Children get our best. Hobbies, civic duty, and church work get the rest of our best. But are we saving any of our best for romance in marriage?

At the Rainey house, Barbara and I work hard to save some energy for each other. Our children have learned over the years that Mom and Dad often like to have quiet evenings alone. When the children were younger, we occasionally turned the kitchen into a famous big-time restaurant called the Rainey Rainbow Room and let each child order a meal from a special menu. Barbara and I served as chef and waiter, and the kids had a great time learning a little bit about how to eat out.

Later in the evening, they knew they were to go to their rooms and stay there, not coming out for anything except bathroom runs. At 8:00 P.M., Barbara and I turned our bedroom into our own romantic cafe, complete with a small table, candles, and flowers (when I remembered to pick them up). There we would eat, talk, and relax. As we communicated, we were reminded of what attracted us to each other, and romance had an opportunity to ignite. We didn't have to worry about a baby-sitter and didn't have to leave the house to get away alone.

To make evenings like this work, you must schedule them and then take the time to follow through. If I have learned anything in marriage, it is that romance, our relationship, and sex take time. And they deserve our best.

The Five Romantic Needs of a Woman

I have spent the better part of twenty-five years of marriage learning and adjusting this summary of a woman's romantic needs. The list was developed through much observation and conversation with Barbara and counseling other couples. I also have learned a great amount from the best book ever written on romance, passion, and sex—the Song of Songs. Obviously, a woman has more than five romantic needs, but I consider these to be the top five:

Need #1: To Be Spiritually Ministered to by Her Man

Are you surprised that something to do with candy and flowers isn't number one? A woman wants a man eager to be her protector, someone who cares not just about her security and physical needs but also (and even more importantly) about her spirituality, the well-being of her very soul. She needs a "soul protector."

A husband can be a spiritual protector and advocate for his wife by praying with and for her daily, putting his arms around her, and saying, "I want to ask God to bless you. I want to take any needs you have in your life right now to the Lord. And I'm going to pray for you throughout this day." A wise husband takes the lead in sharing Scripture and eagerly initiating conversation on spiritual issues.

A husband can contribute to his wife's spiritual well-being by encouraging her to pursue her spiritual growth. For example, he might watch their child while she attends an evening Bible study.

I suggest that every young husband who wants to better understand his wife and his job description should read my friend and colleague Bob Lepine's book *The Christian Husband.*

Need #2: To Feel Safe and Secure with Her Husband

A woman needs to feel her husband's covenantal commitment to stay married and to love her and accept her. Then she feels safe to give him the gift of who she is in the marriage relationship. The Shulammite woman, who was the object of Solomon's passion, said, "I am my beloved's and my beloved is mine" (Song 6:3). She obviously had a strong sense of contentment and security.

A wife needs to know that romantic intimacy is just between her and her husband, that he will not share any personal details with his friends. She should not feel pressured or fearful, experiencing the love that casts out all fear (1 John 4:18).

Need #3: To Share Intimate Conversation

According to researchers, the typical couple spends only four minutes a day in meaningful conversation with each other. Many husbands don't realize that for our wives to consider us romantic, we first of all have to be a great friend and a conversationalist.

Grunts and one-word answers to questions will not satisfy her need for intimate conversation. Too many women don't feel that their husbands really need them, and bare-bones conversation confirms their sense of low personal value. Many men who were accomplished at romantic, deep conversation during courtship seem to lose this talent later. Make a commitment to learn to make intimate conversation a priority with your wife. You need to talk and fill her in on the details of your life—not just facts, but *feelings.*

When a husband sincerely shows his desire for conversation and a deepening relationship—emotional intimacy—he will find that his wife is much more interested in sexual intimacy. Her dreams, hopes, desires, and disappointments then are not divorced from the marriage bed but are a part of it.

Need #4: To Receive a Tender Touch and Hear Gentle Words

Before marriage, two people in love can hardly keep their hands off each other because they find the touch of their beloved thrilling. What happens after the wedding? Some couples married for a while would find a firm handshake a wildly intimate encounter. This should not be the case in a marriage. There is great power in tender touch, even if it's just a long, full-body hug or a lingering kiss. Or the touch may be a gentle caress of her face that has no motive to make sexual demands but communicates, "I love you, Sweetheart, and I care for you tenderly."

Gentle words have similar power. I have made a partial list of some things that I think any husband could use in complimenting and praising his wife: charm; femininity; faithfulness to God, you, your children; hard work; beauty; personality; her love, including her receptivity and responsiveness to you as a man; her advice and counsel; character; desirability; friendship and—that's just a start. What wife won't respond to a husband who praises her regularly with gentle words for all these qualities?

Need #5: To Be Pursued and Set Apart by Her Man

A wife wants a husband who will swoop her off her feet, carry her away to the castle, and say, "Let's spend time together." Focused attention is like precious gold in a relationship.

One time Barbara and I had a little unresolved argument over a weekend. A couple of days later we went on our customary weekly date. We finally had the time and environment to fully discuss and resolve our differences. What it took was several hours away from phones, papers and bills, and the needs of our children. Your wife craves this focused attention from you.

The Song of Songs has taught me much, but maybe the most important truth I found there is that a relationship needs time for romance, for two people to connect, to understand each other, to enjoy each other's company, and to build mutual trust.

(*Additional material on related topics can be found in Chapters 6 on communication, 7 and 8 on sex, 11 on prayer, 17 on intimacy and transparency, 35 on getaway escapes, 42 on affair-proofing, and 45 on blessing and encouraging your spouse.*)

HomeBuilders Principle

A husband who wants more romance
must practice the three *T*'s—talk, time, and tenderness.

TO TAKE ACTION TOGETHER

Since this chapter was all about the need to have more romance in marriage, here are some ideas for a husband on how to spark the blaze of love with his wife:

- Create a romantic setting with candles and sparkling grape juice, rent a romantic movie, and watch it together.
- Draw a bubble bath for your wife after she's had a hard day.
- Talk with your wife about your future plans for your life together.
- Court her again by recreating something fun you did when you first dated each other.
- Surprise her with a cup of hot chocolate, coffee, or tea.
- Do a project around the house that has been on the "back burner."
- Take her for a walk at dusk.[1]

26

Fanning the Flames II

THE FIVE ROMANTIC NEEDS OF A MAN

Husbands don't always understand the subtleties of creating a romantic love nest. I heard about a stockbroker who had a ticker tape machine installed in his bedroom and kept it running twenty-four hours a day. Another guy tore down his Harley-Davidson motorcycle in the master bedroom.

Wives can be guilty of deromanticizing the bedroom too. Mounds of laundry that need to be washed or folded and ironed are sure romance dampeners. I know one man whose wife had so many African violets in their bedroom that he was afraid he would be swept away some night in a plant avalanche.

Romance in a marriage is best when both husband and wife are thinking of each other romantically. In this chapter we'll concentrate on helping the wife understand her husband's romantic needs. Remember, a woman spells romance R-E-L-A-T-I-O-N-S-H-I-P. A man spells it S-E-X!

The Five Romantic Needs of a Man

The Shulammite woman described in the Song of Songs was definitely interested in romance and was wholly unashamed of her sexual attractiveness. One time she merely gave Solomon a look while twisting a single bead of her necklace. She did this in such a way that the king said, "You have made my heart beat faster." Since he probably wasn't jogging at the time, we know he was sexually excited. She intentionally lit a flame within him, using her powers as a woman to fuel the romance in their relationship. There's much to be learned from this story when outlining the top five romantic needs of a man.

Need #1: A Wife Who Communicates Respect for Him as a Man

One of the greatest needs of any man is respect. In Ephesians 5:33, Paul addressed wives, "And let the wife see to it that she respect her husband." Just as a husband is to love his wife, so a wife is to honor, esteem, and value her husband.

A man needs to know that his wife respects how God made him sexually as a man. A wife may have no idea how insecure her husband may be in this area of their relationship. He may not be able to acknowledge it. Because you are his wife, God has selected you to uniquely provide the loyalty and affirmation of his sexuality.

A wife may misunderstand these issues, and by her responses, she causes her husband to feel his sex drive is dirty, frowned on by God, even borderline sinful. In our sexually confused culture, some wives may feel that their husbands should be less sexual. But the Bible constantly urges men, as part of their sexuality, to initiate, to stand firm, to be strong, to be courageous.

A wife needs to understand that the sex act for a man is a risky venture because he must perform by physically consummating the relationship. (By this I'm *not* saying that the woman doesn't also face risks in the sexual relationship.)

When a wife responds eagerly to her husband's masculinity, she affirms him. Consistently pushing him away or demeaning his sexuality can so disappoint and crush him that he may look elsewhere to have his needs met.

Need #2: A Wife Who Wants and Entices Him Sexually

This need is closely connected to Romantic Need #1. A man needs to feel that out of the whole male part of the human race, she desires him—not Tom Cruise, Brad Pitt, or Kevin Costner—and him alone. This is the other side of the coin—a woman expressing her sexual hunger enthusiastically as she enters into this aspect of the relationship.

A wife can demonstrate this easily by what she wears to bed. If you ask any husband to name his wife's favorite nightgown, I'll guarantee that he knows. But a more telling question is, Does every wife know which of her nightgowns is her husband's favorite? And if she knows, why wouldn't she want to wear that one more often?

In the Song of Songs, the Shulammite woman wasn't afraid; she wasn't ashamed; she didn't feel guilty; she was open and responsive to him. She used her sexual power in her man's life to draw him back to herself. At one point she literally drove Solomon crazy when she approached him and said, "Come on. Let's go to the country and spend the day together." It wasn't a fruit-picking venture! They were going on a romantic picnic in the vineyard to make love. And *she* invited him to her special picnic!

If at that moment a device had been attached to Solomon that measured his feelings, it would have stuck on the reading, "WOW! This woman *wants* me." Do you think he was willing to adjust his schedule to fit in a little foray to the vineyard? Absolutely!

A wise woman understands what her attitude can mean to her husband. Obviously, you can't go to the vineyard nightly. But taking regular responsibility for romance will let him know that *he is your man* and *you are his woman!*

Need #3: A Wife Who Communicates
She Enjoys Sexual Love with Him

Yes, a pattern is emerging related to a man's romantic needs! *Romance* and *sex* are nearly synonymous for a man. That's the point. A man likes to hear his wife talk positively and excitedly about her sexual intimacy with him. The Shulammite woman verbally communicated her anticipation, excitement, and physical enjoyment of Solomon. She made it clear that Solomon was more than a companion and friend; he was her lover.

I think I can speak with some authority on behalf of 50 percent of the human race when I say a man is truly thrilled to know that his wife is aroused, excited, and enjoying this act of being one. He wants to know how he's done in the past, how he's doing as you are making love, and afterward how he did! You can't overcompliment your husband on his prowess as a lover.

Need #4: A Wife Who Is Adventuresome, Fun, and Impulsive Sexually

Every wife needs to find ways to add flavor, something out of the ordinary, to the romantic relationship. Hire a baby-sitter. Go for a ride, a trip, a hike. I know it's not easy to unplug your mind from the day-to-day demands of job, house, food, laundry, maybe children—a hundred things. Save time, creativity, and energy to have some fun, to do something that sparks your adventurous, daring side. Step on out and express yourself in an appropriate way that will send your husband's meter off the chart as well as have him agreeing with Solomon that "You have made my heart beat faster." (I recommend that every wife read *Intimate Issues* by Linda Dillow and Lorraine Pintus. It contains godly advice for every woman.)

Need #5: A Wife Who Lets Him Know He Has Satisfied Her

Yes, this one is about sex too! But a man's needs don't revolve only around his own sexual pleasure. He wants to be a fully competent giver of pleasure and to know he has succeeded. His male identity needs the reassurance that his wife has been fully satisfied and feels terrific.

Obviously, having truly enjoyable sexual relations means that both parties are totally involved and consumed with giving and receiving pleasure. A husband likes to see the grin on his wife's face that says, "You *are* the man!" When he sees that smile, he knows his risk in initiating, in stoking the fire, was well worth it.

I encourage you to make it a goal as a wife to become a student of your husband and his needs. Make a secret list of what brings true affirmation and encouragement to him in this area of your marriage relationship. And then regularly encourage him.

(Additional material on related topics can be found in Chapters 6 on communication, 7 and 8 on sex, 11 on prayer, 17 on intimacy and transparency, 35 on getaway escapes, 42 on affair-proofing, and 45 on blessing and encouraging your spouse.)

HomeBuilders Principle

A wife who wants more romance
must accept and encourage her husband's sexuality.

TO TAKE ACTION TOGETHER

Since this chapter was all about the need to have more romance in marriage, here are some ideas for a wife on how to spark the blaze of love with her husband:

- Write an "I love you, _____," message to your husband in a creative way, such as in the snow or sand.
- Call him at work and tell him you can't wait until tonight when you can be together.
- Get a sitter for the kids, fix a candlelight dinner, and meet your husband at the door in lingerie.
- Order pizza, turn the television to a game he wants to watch, and view it with him. If there's no game on, rent a video of his favorite adventure or war movie.
- Write a seductive message on a card that he will find after he arrives at work. It will give him something to think about and anticipate all day.
- For Valentine's Day, fix a bubble bath and serve him dinner in the bathtub.
- Surprise him by getting in bed naked without him knowing about it.[1]

27

"And the Two Shall Become Three?"

THE DECISION ON CHILDREN

ehold, children are a gift of the LORD; the fruit of the womb is a reward," Solomon wrote (Ps. 127:3).

Is that your attitude about children? Okay, let me guess. Maybe you have a few questions about having children. Possibly some fear and feelings of inadequacy. Perhaps you don't even like children. And just maybe, you aren't ready to give up all the freedoms the two of you enjoy right now. Am I right?

I must confess that before I married, Psalm 127:3 was not a verse included in my personal memory plan. I don't recall even *liking* children when I was single. I didn't take care of a little tyke or think about the number of children I'd like to have. I had no interest. God had to do some serious heart surgery on me when it came to children.

But after Barbara and I married, we started having children—one after another. God blessed us with a full house (six!), and as He did, He enlarged our hearts. Then we understood another truth that Solomon wrote about children, "Blessed is the man whose quiver is full of them" (Ps. 127:5). I can honestly say that having children is one of the best things that ever happened to me. Once you become involved in the process of loving these precious young souls and connecting your heart to theirs, you realize that becoming a parent is a great reward.

It's a Scary World Out There!

When should you start your family?

Let's take a look at your situation. You and your spouse are learning to enjoy each other. Your marriage has had ups and downs, but it's growing. Life is already full of challenges. And you're not so sure you're ready to strap on this thing called a child. Plus, plenty of reasons abound for waiting to start your family. Maybe you're thinking:

It's a scary world out there! Without question, the world into which you will bring a child is a frightening place. School shootings, diminishing morality (even among Christian youth), and a plethora of media choices, such as the Internet, are very real dangers. Raising a family and being good parents have never been more valuable—or more challenging—in our nation's history.

My parents' marriage didn't work out. Our divorce culture has left more than one scar on this generation's heart; the fear of a failed marriage is one of these wounds. Many couples wait to have children because they aren't certain their marriage will go the distance. As adult children from broken homes, they don't want to bring a child into a family to experience what they did.

I feel so inadequate to be a mom/dad. You don't know how parenting works. You spent sixteen years or more in school but received little or no preparation for raising the next generation. Where do you start? How do you do it?

Where Do You Begin?

Your fears can be overwhelming; paralysis can set in; years can pass. You need to begin now discussing this decision. I offer this important piece of advice: *Look* at children through the eyes of God, *feel* about children with the heart of God, and *think* about children with the mind of God. To do this, you need to get into the Scripture to find out what God says about children.

1. God commands us to have children. In the very beginning, God explained His desires related to children when He commanded Adam and Eve to "be fruitful and multiply, and fill the earth, and subdue it; and rule over the fish of the sea and over the birds of the sky, and over every living thing that moves on the earth" (Gen. 1:28).

Children aren't "optional equipment" for a married couple. For those who can have children, the command is clear: "Be fruitful." Many couples who want children are unable to get pregnant; infertility can create a profound sense of loss in a marriage relationship. I urge you, though, if God does not allow you to bear your own children, consider adoption. Welcoming otherwise unwanted children into your lives is certainly a noble response to Jesus' comment that when we help one in need, we help Him (Matt. 25:40).

2. God says children are a blessing. "The fruit of the womb is a *reward*. *Blessed* is the man whose quiver is full of them." Yet even within the Christian community, you'd think children were a curse. Barbara and I have heard many jokes and hurtful comments about having a large family. Very few Christians have communicated to us the great blessing God bestowed when He gave us six.

At this point, I'll avoid a lengthy discussion about the size of your family, but let me encourage you to get your marching orders from God, not the world or the misguided notions of some in the Christian community. "Two and no more!" seems to be the culture's—and far too many Christians'—cry. God says it's a blessing to have a full quiver. Some quivers, I fear, are never fully filled. And quivers come in different sizes. Don't assume you have the small size. If children are a blessing, why not ask Him for a large quiver? If God loves us and knows what's best for us, why wouldn't we *want* His blessing?

I'm not advocating that all families should be large, or that a small family is wrong. But I believe Christians are becoming unduly worried about overpopulating the world. The world needs Christians to produce godly offspring. If Christians don't replicate a godly heritage and legacy to carry biblical values and Scripture's truth to the next generation, others will—including Muslims, Hindus, Buddhists, humanists, and atheists.

Parents should nurture children in a Christian home. God's original plan called for the home to be a greenhouse—a nurture center where children grow up to learn character, values, and integrity. Psalm 78 instructs parents to teach their children to know God and to carry that knowledge to the next generation, and through these lines of godly descendants, Satan's kingdom will be defeated.

Children are divinely appointed "generational messengers" who carry the truth about God and His kingdom to future generations. What a privilege we have in receiving these gifts and passing on the message of Christ's love and forgiveness.

God highly values children. Jesus was speaking about someone who would lead children astray when He sternly warned, "It would be better for him if a millstone were hung around his neck and he were thrown into the sea, than that he should cause one of these little ones to stumble" (Luke 17:2).

3. Children are redemptive. They call us to die to self and to yield to Christ as Master and Lord. Barbara and I have learned that the more children you have, the less selfish you can be. We have determined that we can't simultaneously raise six children (and do it well) and be selfish. We've tried! God uses our children to teach us about His love, His forgiveness, and His grace.

A Noble Calling

I'd like to address you as though you were my own children—not with a sermon in my hand, but from the very center of my heart. Having children is one of the highest and holiest callings God has ever given us. There's no sweeter refrain than being called "Daddy" or "Mommy." There's no more memorable rhythm than that of a running toddler right before he jumps into bed with you on a Saturday morning. And there's no nobler mission in all of life than wholeheartedly embracing the privilege of shaping the soul of a boy or girl.

Parenthood is like a season that begins and has no ending. It's an adventure beyond anything Hollywood could ever conceive, and it's more fun than ten thousand trips to Disneyworld. Yes, raising a child is one of life's most profound gambles. Children aren't robots. And, yes, they'll break your heart, but they'll also fill it.

I doubt that at the end of your life, you could name a single thing that surpasses or even approaches the grand calling of being a parent. It is indeed a glorious mission.

(For additional study of this topic, see Chapters 12 on family values, 30 on the first child, 33 on being a father, 34 on being a mother, 50 on building family memories, and 51 on your legacy.)

HomeBuilders Principle

Children are gifts from the Lord
that bring enormous joy.

TO THINK ABOUT INDIVIDUALLY

1. What is your attitude toward children? Why do you think you feel the way you do?

2. Why do you want or not want to have children? Have you ever considered whether your attitudes about having a family line up with God's attitudes toward children? Why or why not?

3. How many children do you think you want, and why?

TO DISCUSS TOGETHER

• Discuss your answers to the questions in the previous exercise. If you disagree on some issues, agree to pray individually and together that God will bring unity on this vital topic.

• If you were to encounter difficulty in conceiving, would you consider adopting a child of another race or from a different country? If this interests you, consider calling Bethany Christian Services at 1-800-BETHANY and inquire about adoption.

TO TAKE ACTION TOGETHER

• Begin praying about your family together. Ask God to enlarge your heart for children, to bless your marriage with children, to give you wisdom in raising them, and to make you of one heart and mind as you support each other as parents.

• If you are unable to have children, think of some ways you can help influence children for Christ. Is there a program such as Big Buddies or the YMCA through which you can volunteer some time to develop a one-on-one relationship with a child? Can you teach a children's class in your church?

28

Vows Revisited

KEEPING THE MARRIAGE COVENANT FRESH

In the summer of 1997, I was sitting at my computer writing an article, praying, and asking myself, *How can we rebuild the family in America?*

I felt the weight of this question not just because I'm involved with FamilyLife and have devoted much of my adult life to researching, writing, and speaking on how to build strong marriages and families. More important, I wanted new insight because our oldest daughter's marriage was only days away. Was there something I could say or do that would help Ashley and Michael begin a marriage that would go the distance?

God brought to my mind the concept of covenant, which literally means "to cut." In the Old Testament they split an animal in half and laid the two sides on the ground. The two people making a covenant then walked through those bloody pieces and pledged, "May God do also to me if I break my covenant with you!"

I knew that hacking a steer in half during my daughter's wedding wouldn't cut it, but I thought, *How can we incorporate covenant?* I had an inspiration. We took Ashley and Michael's vows to a calligrapher who inscribed them on a sheet of pure cotton paper.

During their wedding ceremony, after stating their vows verbally, the couple turned and signed their marriage covenant. There was space at the bottom of the covenant for others to sign, and the pastor asked if anyone in the audience wanted to witness the marriage covenant. By doing so, people would pledge to pray for Michael and Ashley and promise to hold them accountable for keeping their covenant. A line formed quickly.

In the life of our family at least, that marked the return of the marriage covenant.

Why Is the Marriage Covenant Important?

Our God is a Covenant Maker and Keeper. The Bible is filled with the covenant idea because God chose covenant as His way of relating to people. The covenant is the most sacred of all pledges and promises.

The first marriage covenant was achieved when God united Adam and Eve in the first wedding. Later Jesus expressed the importance of the marriage covenant when He said, "Have you not read, that He who created them from the beginning made them male and female, and said, 'For this cause a man shall leave his father and mother, and shall cleave to his wife; and the two shall become one flesh?'" Then Jesus added, "Consequently they are no more two but one flesh. What therefore God has joined together, let no man separate" (Matt. 19:4–6).

The covenant Jesus described was a solemn oath made by the two partners to each other and also to God. In contemporary marriage ceremonies, words and symbols hint at covenant through the stating of vows and the exchanging of rings. But the marriage license is more like a contract than a covenant.

A contract has an end date. A covenant is permanent. A contract usually specifies a part of a person's property or services. A covenant involves a person's total being, which in marriage means a commitment that extends beyond performance, health issues, and financial prosperity.

I will never forget some of the best premarriage counseling that Barbara and I received. A good friend, Don Meredith, looked me in the eyes and said, "Dennis, will you still be committed to Barbara if she someday commits adultery?"

And then Don looked Barbara in the eyes and said, "Will you remain committed to Dennis if he becomes an adulterer?" That may have seemed a stunning question to ask a couple who were still dating and only considering marriage, but the sober question matches the serious nature of the marriage covenant—a promise to never sever the marital bond.

Living Out the Marriage Covenant

Since most of us were married in a ceremony that did not emphasize the marriage covenant, here are five ideas that will make a covenantal commitment a reality in your marriage:

1. Pray together every day as a couple. As I described earlier (Chapter 11), when Barbara and I were first married, I asked a man I highly respected for his best counsel on marriage. He told me that Barbara and I should pray together every day. My friend Carl said, "I've prayed every day with my Sara Jo for more than twenty-five years. Nothing has built our marriage more than our prayer time together."

We took his advice. Barbara and I usually pray together before going to sleep, but there have been nights when neither one of us felt like praying. The Lord has gently reminded me, *You need to pray with her.* And even though on occasion I've not even wanted to talk to her, I have finally rolled over and said, "Let's pray." Our obedience to this spiritual discipline has reminded us of who really is the Source of strength in our marriage.

2. Never use the D word. Marriage is tough, and at times every one of us probably has thought about giving up. The key word is *thought.* No matter how hopeless the situation seems or how lousy you feel, I urge you not to *say* the D word—divorce—in your home.

In Proverbs 18:21 we read, "Death and life are in the power of the tongue." Words have power. If you first think about divorce and then talk about it, before long what was once unthinkable becomes an option.

If you or your spouse in times of anger has threatened divorce, there is a wonderful restorative cure called grace. Forgive each other for talking about ending your marriage.

3. Sign a marriage covenant. Whether you are newlyweds or you have been married awhile, why not consider having a covenant-signing ceremony? You could do this with other couples at your church or in your home with the witnesses being family members or close friends. After the covenant signing, hang the document in a prominent spot. (See page 144 for information on obtaining a wedding covenant.)

4. Do what you promised. It won't ultimately make any difference if you sign a piece of paper but later break your covenant. The famous

British pastor Charles Spurgeon said, "It was by perseverance that the snail reached the ark." Don't let temptations and heartaches keep you from finishing strong in your marriage and family. I love the definition of *commitment* evoked by Winston Churchill, who said, "The nose of a bull-dog is slanted backwards, so that he can continue to breathe without letting go." Don't let go! Fulfill your vows.

5. Urge others to keep their covenant. In the Christian community we need to band together to fight divorce. We serve a God who has gone on record on this topic: "I hate divorce" (Mal. 2:16). We need to combat divorce in the most positive way—by honoring our covenants and encouraging others to do the same. Together we can become known in our culture as the keepers and protectors of the marriage covenant.

Now, Ashley and Michael's covenant hangs above the fireplace in their home, a constant reminder of their promise of fidelity to each other and of the promise of God to guard and sustain their marriage. It also reminds the rest of us to pray for them. And now another party is benefiting from that covenant, a sweet baby named Samuel, our first grandson.

Renewed devotion to the marriage covenant could help countless couples stick to their vows. Will you be a part of this movement by signing your own marriage covenant?[1]

(For additional information on this subject, see Chapters 3 on God's blueprints for marriage, 11 on prayer, 37 on the critical tools needed in a lifelong marriage, 51 on legacy, and 52 on the coming seasons of marriage.)

HomeBuilders Principle

The wise couple builds their relationship
on the solid foundation of a marriage covenant.

TO TAKE ACTION TOGETHER

Would you like to make a covenant a part of your marriage? I encourage you to take this meaningful step. If you want creative ideas on this event for you or your church, or would like to order a printed covenant suitable for signing and framing, please contact FamilyLife at 1-800-FLTODAY or on the Web at <www.familylife.com>.

29

Decision Making

WHEN FLIPPING A COIN JUST WON'T DO

*E*arly in our marriage, Barbara and I resolved that we would always make decisions together, and if at all possible, we would be in agreement with each other.

The only exception to these rules would occur when we reached an impasse after much discussion and prayer. Then I would have the responsibility as the head of our home to decide the matter.

Some husbands may think erroneously that it works best to pull rank with their headship and force their wives to submit to their decisions. This foolish attitude violates Scripture, and it is demeaning to a wife. God's blueprints for marriage teach that each spouse is made complete by the other. Paul's statement applies here: "In the Lord, neither is woman independent of man, nor is man independent of woman" (1 Cor. 11:11). We need each other. Why would anyone knowingly choose to ignore the other in decision making?

Some among the Christian community hold the notion that there is no head of the home (a roleless marriage), and that a husband and a wife should share in all decisions equally. In this chapter you will see that sometimes you won't agree, even after days of discussion, prayer, and carefully listening to each other. In a roleless marriage, who decides—especially on a major decision?

The structure of responsibility and authority established by God in the home addresses this dilemma. God's structure doesn't limit life for us but enables us to experience life to the fullest, the way He designed it. As you will someday experience with your children, structure, boundaries, and rules provide the protection and security that bring freedom, not bondage.

Barbara and I make a lot of decisions on a daily basis. We have learned to consult each other on those decisions that we know both of us need to talk about before making a final determination. Rarely have I gone against her counsel, but on occasions I have had to make a tough call that she disagreed with. Barbara will present the remainder of this chapter's information on this topic.

Decision Making in the Rainey Marriage

As Dennis said, when we have to make a decision, we usually do it by unanimous agreement. Even if we begin talking about a decision from opposite perspectives, we typically work through the process of sharing our thoughts, come to an agreement, and make the decision as one. It is rare that we continue to disagree, but it has happened.

When our oldest daughter, Ashley, was four and a half, we faced our first schooling decision. Ashley's birthday is in late August, meaning she would be the youngest child in her class.

I had enrolled her in an excellent preschool program to prepare her for kindergarten. The director of the school and Ashley's teacher said she had done beautifully and would do just as well in kindergarten. I agreed.

I came home and reported all these facts to Dennis. I laid it all out carefully and convincingly, but to my surprise, he didn't agree. I couldn't believe that he wasn't buying my persuasive logic! He said, "I think we should hold her out for a year."

I pursued with my arguments: "She makes friends easily. The teachers think she should be in school next year. Why can't you agree with me?"

Dennis expressed that Ashley would have a profound advantage if she was the oldest, rather than the youngest, in the class. He also felt that this advantage would really pay off during the teenage years when she would be making important moral choices.

I backed off and waited a couple of weeks, prayed about it, and tried again. I presented all my facts, trying to beef up every point to make my position more convincing, but Dennis didn't budge.

We went on like this for several weeks, and I realized I wasn't making any progress. I was becoming more entrenched in my position, and he was immovable in his. We had reached an impasse.

I decided I had to do something, so I prayed and said, "Okay, Lord, You know that I'm right and he's wrong! And I pray that You will change his mind. But, Lord, if I'm wrong and he's right, I want You to change my attitude. I'm willing to do whatever You want me to do, but You know I think he's wrong."

My attitude and perspective changed. In the days that followed, God gave me peace. And as my stance softened, I saw Ashley more objectively as a little girl who needed another year to be a child without the pressures of school.

As it turned out, starting Ashley in kindergarten as a young six-year-old was the right move. We discovered several years later that she was dyslexic, and the extra year at home gave her a much better chance to deal with learning to read.

I'm glad the Lord broke our impasse by reminding me that I needed to have the right attitude. I needed to trust God with Dennis's decision and submit my will to his.

It works both ways, though. Many times Dennis has changed his mind and followed my advice and instincts in the decision-making process. When we first began thinking about sending our children to college, we discussed how we would come up with the money. I felt led consistently to advise him not to make a particular type of investment. It wasn't because of my knowledge of financial matters; it was purely an intuitive feeling. Dennis heeded my input in every case that I can remember. In most of them it was wise that he did.

Decision making for the Christian couple should not be reduced to an issue of who is right and who is wrong. In those rare situations when we disagree, I am glad that Dennis and I have a biblically based structure that enables us to decide and move forward. It has meant that he must assume his responsibility as head of the home, but in assuming that position, he has learned that the role of a leader is that of a servant. As he serves me by listening to my perspective and really taking into consideration my advice, he has made my submission to him easier. I didn't say it was easy—just easier.

What if your husband and you have already begun to reverse roles and you make the decisions? Maybe he's not as gifted nor as aggressive in his personality. What should you do?

First, as a couple, you need to revisit God's blueprints for how a husband and wife are to live with each other. The position of the head of the family should not revolve around one's personality or giftedness. Too often a husband can become passive when his wife takes over. It isn't right, but in those situations he may find the road of least resistance appealing.

Talk about this as a couple. Discuss how decisions should be made in your home and how both can share in them. Then when the next decision comes along that you are tempted to decide for him, don't. Toss it in his lap. Engage him around the issue. Ask for his help and perspective. Make this a matter of prayer as a couple. Ask God to help you complement each other in the area of decision making.

A profound promise appears in Scripture repeatedly: "For nothing will be impossible with God" (Luke 1:37). Think about that for a minute. Nothing is too hard for God! Your ability to make decisions together may seem impossible now, but nothing is impossible for God. Nothing.

(For additional information, see Chapters 3 on God's blueprints for marriage, 6 on communication, 10 on conflict, 12 on family values, 15 on adjustment, 19 and 20 on teamwork and roles, 24 on personality differences, and 32 on listening.)

HomeBuilders Principle

Two heads are better than one.

TO THINK ABOUT INDIVIDUALLY

1. Using a scale (1 = poor, 5 = great), how would you rate the quality of joint decision making in your marriage?

1   2   3   4   5

Why did you assign this rating?

2. What issues present the greatest challenges to making good joint decisions?

3. What can you do to make decision making better in your marriage?

TO DISCUSS TOGETHER

Review and share your individual answers to the questions in the previous exercise. What decisions do you need to make to improve your decision making?

TO TAKE ACTION TOGETHER

Together, choose an issue in your marriage or family where a decision needs to be made. Using information in this chapter as well as insights gained in your discussion, work through the process of making this decision—*together*. If you reach an impasse, pray about next steps. Should you seek outside counsel? Postpone the decision while committing it to prayer? Is it time for the husband to make the decision on his own?

30

The BIG Adjustment

GETTING STARTED AS A PARENT

*J*ust a few days before our second anniversary, Barbara went into labor with our first child. After twenty-four hours of watching the agony, I nearly passed out. I had to leave. I took a walk, and when I returned, I was just in time to put on my scrubs.

Then Ashley was born. The doctor pulled that baby out, held her up, and introduced all of us to one another. It was a magnificent moment, a time when we totally lost ourselves in the wonder and miracle of birth. But at that point, the doctor could have said, "Hey! Do you want her?"

I could have wheeled Barbara to a corner of the delivery room and said, "What do you think, Sweetheart? She has a lot of yucky-looking purplish white stuff all over her. And her face—it's all pointy and scrunched up!" Of course, we didn't do that! We received that baby and laid that warm bundle on Barbara's stomach, and we looked at her and shed tears. We received our daughter as God's gift.

This is how it begins for every parent, receiving a child as a gift from God. But now that your baby has been born, what's next? The ultimate goal of parenting is to release your child someday to become dependent upon God and interdependent with others. You will hear and read much about parenting in the future, but please heed this wise suggestion from Stephen Covey in his book *Seven Habits of Highly Effective People*: "We must begin with the end in mind."

Although he wasn't specifically referring to raising children, there's no greater place to apply that than in raising kids. Covey also quotes E.M.

Gray, who wrote, "The successful person has the habit of doing the things failures do not like to do. They do not like to do them either necessarily. But their disliking is subordinated to the strength of their purpose."[1] The strength of our purpose is to raise our kids to love and fear God. And that keeps me going some days when I don't feel like parenting.

Five Things Parents Need

As we began our parenting career, Barbara and I were nearly overwhelmed by children—we had six in ten years. And we were definitely not parenting on purpose. Based on all our experiences, here are five things we believe parents need.

1. Parents need to understand the times. Paul wrote, "Therefore, be careful how you walk, not as unwise men, but as wise, making the most of your time, because the days are evil" (Eph. 5:15–16). You represent the first generation of future parents in our nation's history who are starting out with so many questions, yet with so few relationships that provide answers. The ways we think, act, and feel about our families and children have changed enormously. In past societies, the culture reinforced values. Today, because absolutes are up for grabs, parents scramble to help their children maintain the right values.

As you raise your children in this culture, you need a community of faith, a church that will help you succeed as parents. You need to be able to ask questions of other like-minded parents somewhat ahead of you in the family cycle. And you need resources and training in being a mom and dad. (For a complete listing of resources for parents, visit our Web site at <www.familylife.com>.)

2. Parents need a sacred commitment to each other. An eleven-year-old boy's essay on what he liked best about his home said this:

My mother keeps a cookie jar in the kitchen, and we can help ourselves, except we can't if it's too close to mealtime. Only my dad can anytime. When he comes home from the office, he helps himself, no matter if it is just before we eat. He always slaps my mother on the behind and brags about how great she is and how good she can cook. Then she turns around and they hug. The way they do it, you'd think they just got married or some-thing. It makes me feel good. This is what I like best about my home.[2]

Your kids need to see your vows lived out, in every circumstance, in times of peace and conflict. I will never forget when I was about age six, my mom and dad had a quarrel. I remember thinking, *Are my parents going to get a divorce?* Divorce was not even discussed back then. But if I had such anxious feelings in the mid-'50s, what does the average first grader today feel?

Your marriage must be built to outlast your kids. If you come from a bro-ken family, and you're unsure what you can offer children, let me assure you that your children need to see your devotion and commitment to your spouse even more than they need your devotion and commitment to them. Resolve conflicts with your spouse; forgive each other; remain faithful. These quali-ties of love build a powerful, profound sense of security in children.

3. Parents need to know what they believe. As your child grows, his little radar unit will lock in on you and your spouse. Parents are the text-books a child reads. Your belief system may not seem tremendously impor-tant when your baby is in diapers, but not long thereafter, your deeply held values about life will influence your interactions with your child. Your beliefs will affect how you discipline, what kinds of TV shows and movies you allow your child to watch, and who your child may date.

As parents you don't need a list of 101 values; choose a half dozen or so that represent your unshakable convictions about how you will raise your child. Here are a few of ours:

- We will first and foremost train our children in the Scriptures to love, obey, and experience God and His mission for their lives.
- We will train our children to relate to others with respect; when they fail, they will ask one another for forgiveness.
- Love and discipline go hand in hand. Broken rules, disobedience, or neglect results in discipline.
- We will fiercely protect and preserve our family, and we will be loyal to one another.
- We will attempt to impart God's heart for the world and train them to be part of the Great Commission.

Together hammer out your core beliefs.

4. Parents need to maintain God's perspective on children. Someday, you might feel like the woman who heard her doorbell ring. Standing on her front step was a man who said, "I am asking for donations for the new children's home we are building. Could you contribute?"

The tired, beleaguered mother responded, "I will tell you what I will do for your children's home; I will give you two children!"

Although we don't begin as parents with this attitude, it represents how we feel about children at times. God's perspective on children (mentioned in Chapter 27) has three aspects: (1) Children are a gift from God, (2) raising your children is a privilege and responsibility He has given to no one else, and (3) they need to be raised for the glory of God.

5. Parents need to possess a purpose and a goal for children. A man approached three construction laborers working with mortar and bricks. He went to the first man and said, "What are you doing?" The man replied, "I am laying bricks." He went to the second man and asked him the same question, and he answered, "I am building a wall." When asked the question, the third man said, "I am building a cathedral."

It's easy to see only the daily "bricks," forgetting you are raising children for the glory of God in the next generation.

Most parents have a life plan for their children, but often it doesn't go far enough. Parents may know the educational goals they want their children to achieve, the activities they want to encourage, and the type of person they want each child to marry. But on the spiritual side, their plan usually doesn't go much farther than making sure their children live a good life, go to church and, they hope, receive Christ.

Don't settle for a vision of your child's destiny that is less than what God has in mind. God wants to help us raise our children. And we wouldn't want it any other way because "unless the LORD builds the house, they labor in vain who build it" (Ps. 127:1). God will help us build our homes. And He is the best home builder of all.

(For more information on this topic, see Chapters 12 on family values, 27 on children, 33 on fathers, 34 on mothers, and 51 on legacy.)

HomeBuilders Principle

When raising a child, parents need to begin with the end in mind.

TO THINK ABOUT INDIVIDUALLY

1. On a sheet of paper, write down six values or character qualities you want your child to possess on the day he graduates from high school.

2. What do you think will be the most difficult challenges to overcome in making sure your child accepts your important values and qualities? How might you face each challenge?

TO DISCUSS TOGETHER

Share and discuss your answers to the questions in the previous exercise.

TO TAKE ACTION TOGETHER

Before your child is three months old, during the baby's nap or on a night out when someone is caring for your child, come up with your agreed-upon master list of values for your child. Frame and hang them in a prominent spot in your home.

31

Married and Lonely?

THE THREAT OF ISOLATION

$\mathcal{I}$f there's one thing worse than a miserable, lonely single person, it's a miserable, lonely *married* person. The irony is that no husband or wife marries with the intention of being isolated from a mate. Most people believe that marriage is the *cure* for loneliness, but I want to warn you: You began battling the dreaded foe of isolation as soon as you drove off on your honeymoon.

Isolation has reached epidemic proportions in the most intimate of human relationships. In addition to more than a million legal divorces each year,[1] isolation saps the strength from millions of marriages that still appear intact.

A psychology professor writing in *Psychology Today* observed:

I know of no more potent killer than isolation . . . no more destructive influence on physical and mental health than the isolation of you from me and us from them. Isolation has been shown to be the central agent in the development of depression, paranoia, schizophrenia, rape, suicide, and mass murder . . . The devil's strategy for our times is to trivialize human existence and to isolate us from one another while creating the delusion that the reasons are time pressures, work demands, or economic anxieties."[2]

I believe that isolation is Satan's chief strategy for destroying marriage. Barbara and I feel its dividing tug in our relationship when we have disagreements and misunderstandings. Our busyness repeatedly invites its presence into our marriage.

Like a terminal virus, isolation invades your marriage silently, slowly, and painlessly at first. By the time you become aware of its insidious effects, it can be too late. Your marriage can be disabled by boredom and apathy, and even die from emotional malnutrition and neglect.

What Is Isolation?

The dictionary will tell you that *isolation* is "the condition of being alone, separated, solitary, set apart," but I like what our daughter Ashley said once when she slipped into my study to ask me what I was writing about.

"Isolation," I explained. "Do you know what that means?"

"Oh," our ten-year-old replied, "that's when somebody excludes you."

Ashley's answer is a profound observation on human relationships. When isolation infects a marriage, a husband and a wife exclude each other. When you're excluded, you have a feeling of distance, a lack of closeness, and little real intimacy. You can share a bed, eat at the same dinner table, watch the same TV, share the same checking account, and parent the same children—and still be alone. You may have sex, but you don't have love. You may talk, but you don't communicate. You live together, but you don't share life.

Because of the alarming number of couples in good marriages who are unaware of this problem, I must state forcefully a sobering truth: *Every marriage will naturally move toward a state of isolation.* Unless you lovingly, energetically nurture and maintain intimacy in your marriage, you will drift apart from your mate.

The soul was not created to live solo. We yearn for intimacy, and marriage is where we hope we'll find it. The tragedy is that few couples achieve it.

Telltale Signs of Isolation

Barbara and I have seen this death of hope occur in the marriage of some friends. In many ways their story is typical of many others.

This couple enjoyed dating and were married in their early twenties. After a brief honeymoon, they packed up their belongings and moved to a new city. On the two-day drive to their new home, they began to notice their differences. She felt alone and apprehensive about their new life together; he felt puzzled that their conversation had dried up so quickly. Isolation had already begun.

She took a demanding job, and he was promoted in his. Busyness and fatigue set in as they moved into the stream of everyday life. Instead of having companionship, they felt alone. She felt undiscovered, unknown. He felt uncared for.

Initially, the birth of their first child seemed to bring them back together. Later, when she returned to her job, she adjusted her hours to maximize her time with the baby. Life became focused on the child. Their marriage wore down under the draining influence of isolation.

She would bring up a problem. He would quickly deny it or say, "When this phase in our lives passes, things will get better."

Because their frequent spats became increasingly painful, each retreated and learned to feel safe that way. Both realized that life was smoother when they wore their masks, and they played the marriage game as if there wasn't anything wrong.

Although they seldom missed church, and no one who knew them would have guessed it, isolation had firmly entrenched itself in their marriage. Had this couple not attended a FamilyLife Marriage Conference, their marriage might have continued its spiral farther into isolation and, ultimately, divorce. But at the conference they recognized they had a problem. They realized they needed to take steps toward oneness as a couple by biblically resolving conflict, listening to each other, and making God the Builder of their home.

As it happened with this young couple, isolation starts when husband and wife slowly drift apart in ways they may not recognize at first. Signs include the following:

- Feeling that your spouse isn't hearing you and doesn't understand.
- Having attitudes of, "Who cares?" "Why try?" "Tomorrow we'll talk about it—let's just get some sleep."
- Feeling unable to please or meet the expectations of your spouse.
- Sensing that he's detached from you.
- Feeling that she's going her own way.

- Refusing to cope with reality: "That's *your* problem, not mine."
- Feeling that keeping the peace by avoiding the conflict is better than experiencing the pain of dealing with reality.

Couples will present a happy facade, keeping house and playing at marriage while real needs go unmet. While unmet needs indicate isolation's presence in a marriage, the irony is that slipping into a state of isolation seems to offer protection and self-preservation. Silence feels like a security blanket but is perilously deceptive.

Many marriages continue for years in a state of armed truce. Competition replaces cooperation, and ugly reality dashes the dreams of hope as conflict unravels the fabric of love and concern. Broken hearts stain pillows with bitter tears.

The Choice Is Yours

Every day, each partner makes choices that result in oneness or in isolation. May I recommend three important choices you need to make?

Choice #1: Resolve to pursue oneness with each other, and repent of any isolation that already exists in your marriage. Remember, you don't have to be married a long time to be isolated.

Choice #2: Resolve never to go to bed angry with each other. Find a way to resolve your differences and move toward oneness. Realize that often it's easier to hold a grudge than to forgive. Resentment and oneness cannot coexist.

Choice #3: Resolve to take time to share intimately with each other. Allow your spouse into your life. Ask questions of your spouse, and listen patiently. Learn the art of healthy, transparent communication.

What if you're already in deep trouble? Swallow your pride. Get help. Call a mentoring couple, your pastor, or a counselor. Don't allow isolation to take up residence in your home by ignoring it.

Make the right choices, and you'll know love, warmth, acceptance, and the freedom of true intimacy and genuine oneness as husband and wife. Make the wrong choices, and you'll know the quiet desperation of living together but never really touching each other deeply.

We were not meant to be alone in the most intimate human relationship God created. Choose today to move toward warmth in each other and away from the chill of isolation.

(*For other material on this topic, see Chapters 6 on communication, 10 on resolving conflict, 11 on prayer as a couple, 17 on intimacy and transparency, 23 on accountability to spouse and others, 25 and 26 on romance, 35 on romantic getaways, and 47 on knowing when your marriage needs outside help.*)

HomeBuilders Principle

Intimacy destroys isolation.

TO THINK ABOUT INDIVIDUALLY

1. Have you ever thought of isolation as a threat to your marriage? How else might you have described the state of your relationship?

2. Are there any areas in your relationship with your mate where you feel isolated, distant, or unknown? Why?

TO DISCUSS TOGETHER

1. Pick a time when you and your mate can talk openly without distractions. Discuss your answers to the questions in the previous exercise. Be sensitive to what each person has to say.

2. Ask each other, "What are the greatest threats we face in our marriage that could lead to isolation?"

TO TAKE ACTION TOGETHER

The threat of isolation is sobering, but the promise of God to unite you in a lasting marriage of deepening intimacy is exciting. *Celebrate* your oneness. Spend special moments together telling each other of your love and restoking your passion for the beautiful relationship He made by giving you each other.

32

"I'm All Ears"

THE POWER OF LISTENING IN EXPRESSING LOVE

very cell phone user has experienced this: While you are speaking to a spouse, a business contact, or a friend, the connection breaks. Only you don't know it immediately. You continue to talk until you sense something is wrong and ask, "Are you still there?" The silence or a static screech provides the answer—the person on the other end is gone. And then you wonder, *Just how much of what I said wasn't heard?*

How often does this type of thing happen in your marriage? One of you is talking, but "no one is there" on the other end of the conversation. Listening is not as easy as talking for most of us. But we all know from frequent experience that talking gets us in trouble, while attentive listening encourages the speaker.

The Scriptures urge us, "Let everyone be quick to hear, slow to speak and slow to anger" (James 1:19). Usually, however, we are slow to hear, quick to speak, and quick to anger.

If you can become a better listener, you will experience less tension in your marriage. How does that happen? Listen to what follows!

How Not to Listen

Did you take a communications or a speech course in high school or college? That course most likely taught you the basics of public speaking. The problem is, most of us have had little training in how to listen. We know how to argue and win our points, but we are neophytes at really hearing what someone else is saying. As a result, poor listening habits show up in several forms:

Pseudolistening. The husband is often guilty here. After a long day, he comes home with his mind still whirling from events at work. Over dinner, his wife comments, "Did you know Jill has a new job?"

"Uh-uh."

"She will be moving to Florida next week."

"Uh-huh."

"She's going there to rob banks."

"Uh-huh."

"You aren't listening, are you?"

"Uh-uh."

Pseudolistening isn't listening at all. It's a fake. You're not really there. You will soon be in trouble with your spouse.

Selective listening. A problem with learning to listen well is that all of us can listen at least five times faster than anyone can talk. While your spouse is trying to express something important, you may be thinking of things you want to do around the house and phone calls you have to make. Or you may drift off into that well-known territory called "a million miles away."

Another form of selective listening can happen when you're having an argument. You listen only for what you want to hear, thinking, *Aha! Weak reasoning there. I'll nail her to the wall on that one. What's her next point? Aha! Got her again.* With selective listening, you're not trying to hear what your mate is saying; you're building your case.

Protective listening. The protective listener doesn't want to hear much at all, especially something threatening. His mate may have been trying to tell him things for months, but he has insulated his heart from hearing. Every time the topic is raised he changes the subject, acts bored or annoyed, or may say, "I don't want to talk about that now."

This avoidance technique may so frustrate the spouse that she gives up. Ultimately, inadequate communication will cause great harm and bring the emotional death of the marriage—whether or not the couple actually divorces.

Surface listening. This form of selective listening concentrates on hearing just enough to keep the conversation going but not enough to connect emotionally with the mate. A husband may pour out his heart for a half hour about a dilemma at work, and then his wife says, "Sounds like you had a bad day! Oh, did you remember to take the clothes to the cleaner this morning?"

This response makes the husband think, *What's the use of sharing this stuff? She's not really listening.*

You must learn to put away your poor listening habits and give your mate your undivided attention.

The Listening Gold Standard: Focused Attention

Focused attention is the cure for bad-listener disease, as illustrated by the old story of some workmen who were storing huge blocks of ice in deep beds of sawdust in a dark icehouse. One of the workmen dropped his watch into the thick sawdust and searched for it in vain for several days. Finally, a boy offered to help him find it. Asking everyone else to remain outside, he went into the icehouse and came out in a few minutes holding the watch. "What happened?" asked the incredulous workman. "How'd you find it so fast?" "Simple," said the boy. "I went to the middle of the room, put my ear down next to the sawdust, and listened."

In your marriage, focused attention will detect what is ticking in your mate.

Another term to describe focused attention is *active listening*, which means that you are interested in understanding your spouse's feelings, not just in hearing the pertinent information. You listen to the meaning of what is being said rather than the words. Never tell your spouse, "That's dumb; you shouldn't feel that way."

Perhaps the way your spouse feels is not based on facts or reality. This is how your spouse feels; it is his or her reality. To tell your spouse that the feelings are dumb or invalid interferes with oneness and understanding.

To practice active listening, try sending back messages of empathy that let your spouse know that you are trying to put yourself in his or her shoes. Don't try to evaluate or offer advice; just reflect the feelings that you hear being communicated.

For example, I may come home and Barbara will greet me with, "I'm about ready to ground that child. She's impossible!" (I'm being purposely vague here to protect the guilty!)

My first inclination is to move in and play Mighty Leader and ask, "What did she do now? Where is she? I want to talk to that kid!"

But to listen actively to Barbara, I will face her eye-to-eye so that she knows she has my attention. Then my first comment might be, "It sounds as if you and 'that child' have had an 'interesting' time today."

Then Barbara will give me details of the problem or tell me about how tired she feels, which may be the issue on her mind.

Once you establish communication with your mate through focused attention and active listening, seek clarification by asking questions. Questions act like crowbars to dislodge thoughts and emotions from another person's heart. But you have to use the crowbars deftly and gently. Asking the right questions is particularly valuable if you're married to a person who is reserved and has a hard time opening up.

Gain all of the skills you can to become a better listener. Then genuinely listen to your mate. Saint Francis of Assisi was never married, but he gave all married couples golden advice when he prayed, "Lord, may I seek to understand more than to be understood." An attentive listener will bring answers to that prayer.

(For more information on this topic, see Chapters 6 on communication, 10 on conflict, 17 on intimacy and transparency, and 45 on blessing and encouraging your spouse.)

HomeBuilders Principle

Two good listeners create a marriage filled with understanding.

TO THINK ABOUT INDIVIDUALLY

1. Which of the following bad listening habits are a problem for you and your mate?

Me   My Mate

_____   _____   Pseudolistening that fakes interest.

Me   My Mate

_____ _____   Selective listening that tunes in only now and then.

_____ _____   Protective listening—"don't bother me."

_____ _____   Surface listening—emotionally unconnected.

2. What can you do to break bad listening habits?

3. What is one action point for you to give better focused attention to each other?

TO DISCUSS TOGETHER

Sit down together and share your answers to the questions in the previous exercise. Use the following ground rules: Listen carefully to what the other person is saying, and if you start to get irritated and find yourself headed for conflict, call time-out and review Chapter 10.

TO TAKE ACTION TOGETHER

Give each other a Listen Gift. On different occasions, take turns allowing each other to talk without interruption for up to one hour. It may seem awkward at first, but both of you will be amazed at what is said and learned.

33

Dad University

A QUICK COURSE ON BEING A GODLY FATHER

BY DENNIS RAINEY

A father has the privilege of imprinting young lives that will carry the torch to the next generation. Unfortunately, most men starting out in marriage haven't fully grasped their role as a husband before their wives inform them that they will be a father! As a newlywed, you know life is full of changes, but children may be something you hadn't bargained for so soon.

To be better prepared for this thrilling, frightening moment—however far in the future—you should ask yourself now, *What does it mean for a man to become a father?* The responsibilities and challenges comprising the job description of fatherhood are the three M's—manager, minister, and model.

Manager

Many men, who prepare themselves diligently and work hard to become efficient managers on the job, hardly give a thought to their role in managing a complicated and important organization like a family. When you think of it, much like a company, a family needs attention in the areas of personnel, capital reserves, facilities, cash flow, planning, inventory control, suppliers—even competition (for example, cultural influences seeking to undermine the family's well-being).

The mother shares some of these managerial duties, but ideally, the father should look at the big picture and provide the security that results from responsible and faithful leadership. Here are some components for your new job description as the family manager:

- Know the strengths and weaknesses of those you supervise: "Know well the condition of your flocks, and pay attention to your herds" (Prov. 27:23).
- Exercise self-control, and train those under your authority: "And, fathers, do not provoke your children to anger; but bring them up in the discipline and instruction of the Lord" (Eph. 6:4).
- Engage in ongoing enhancement of personal skills and exemplify high character: "He shepherded them according to the integrity of his heart, and guided them with his skillful hands" (Ps. 78:72).
- Abide by instructions and bylaws contained in the company policy manual (the Bible): "By wisdom a house is built, and by understanding it is established; and by knowledge the rooms are filled with all precious and pleasant riches" (Prov. 24:3–4).

Minister

To be a family minister, a dad does not need to prepare a five-point sermon he will deliver in the family room while wearing a floor-length robe. But he does have the responsibility to oversee the spiritual well-being of those under his care. Another word describing this role is *shepherd.*

That's right—a little flock of sheep share your living space, and a good dad will minister to his flock by voluntarily and eagerly caring for their needs. Just as you now should be caring for the needs of your wife, you will bear a new responsibility to care for those of your children.

The Shepherd's Psalm begins with the sentence, "The LORD is my shepherd, I shall not want" (Ps. 23:1). What will your children "want"? They'll want a lot of stuff—everything from the latest computer games to name-brand shoes. But God gives you the responsibility to provide for their most basic needs—physically, emotionally, and spiritually. By providing them with basic security (a big part of this is loving their mom), you will help them "lie down in green pastures."

Above all, the family minister-shepherd must bear the weight of transferring God's truth to his children:

> Hear, O sons, the instruction of a father,
> And give attention that you may gain understanding,
> For I give you sound teaching;
> Do not abandon my instruction. (Prov. 4:1–2)

You'll learn more specifically about what this means, but for now remember: Your children will need you to lead them spiritually.

You can take advantage of daily opportunities to equip your children. What you want to teach your children needs to be clear in your mind. Early in the lives of my children, I started carrying around a list that started out as "Twenty-five Things I Am Teaching My Kids." This list always faces my daily "to do" list. On this page, Barbara and I have listed things such as "being faithful in little things," "becoming a man of character," and "becoming a woman who has a gentle and quiet spirit." This list reminds me of what is important beyond my daily tasks. Now the list has grown to more than fifty items!

Transferring truth includes life-skill training about sex education, morality, and manners. For example, your kids should know what to do in an emergency, such as a fire in the house. Or train them to know how to handle being bullied.

What's your vision for your family? Determining your vision for your children and family doesn't have to wait for your wife to say, "Honey, we're going to have a baby." You can formulate your ideas right now as you prayerfully ask God to help you gain *His* vision for what He wants your family to become.

Model

If "all the world's a stage," as Shakespeare said, then every dad is always in the spotlight doing a one-man play for an audience that never leaves the theater—the tykes who always watch their daddy and don't miss a thing. Every dad is the family role model, whether or not he wants the job.

My father played that role well, modeling integrity and honesty for me every day of his life.

A weighty proverb states, "What a man is determines what a man does." I like a quote by playwright Eugene O'Neill even better: "You do not build a marble tower out of a mixture of mud and manure." You do well to begin the process of becoming the man your family will someday look up to.

I'm comforted by the fact that a man's character is shaped by his relationship with God. That's where my hope lies. God hasn't given up on me. He's still squeezing the mud and manure out of my life, building the strong, enduring marble tower instead.

Have you ever run on a relay track team or participated in a relay race at a picnic? Scripture speaks of running a different kind of relay that has God's eternal truth as its baton. The psalmist said about the Lord and His works and intentions for all generations:

> For He established a testimony in Jacob,
> And appointed a law in Israel,
> Which he commanded our fathers,
> That they should teach them to their children,
> That the generation to come might know,
>   even the children yet to be born,
> That they may arise and tell them to their children,
> That they should put their confidence in God,
> And not forget the works of God,
> But keep His commandments. (Ps. 78:5–7)

I want to run the father-son/daughter relay to the best of my ability. The dad finishing with his torch still burning brightly, though not necessarily first, will make an impact. And I want to run and give that torch of my love for Christ to my children, instructing them to carry it to the next generation.

An incredible way to model God's care is to lavish affection and encouragement on your children. We dads should never stop embracing our children, hugging them, and running our hands through their hair. And let's not forget to say "I love you" every day.

If I were to go to my grave today, one of the highest compliments to me would be to have it said that I was a father known for his love for his kids. Someday, I hope you will hear your wife tell you, "Sweetheart, you're going to be a father!"

(For additional understanding of this topic, see Chapters 27 and 30 on parenting, 34 on being a mom, and 51 on legacy.)

HomeBuilders Principle

> A good family shepherd doesn't lead
> any faster than his sheep can follow.

TO THINK ABOUT INDIVIDUALLY

Think about how you will fulfill the roles of family manager, minister, and role model when you have children. Write out specific objectives for each area:

As a family manager, I will _____

_____.

As a family minister, I will _____

_____.

As a family role model, I will _____

_____.

TO DISCUSS TOGETHER

Sit down with your wife and share your responses from the previous exercise. What additional ideas does she have on how you could increase your potential as family manager, minister, and role model?

TO TAKE ACTION TOGETHER

Make arrangements to visit with your dad or another mature father you respect. Ask him to answer these questions: "What do you wish a wise father had told you before you became a dad?" "What would you do differently?" "What are your happiest memories as a father?"

34

Mom University

BECOMING A MOTHER OF INFLUENCE

BY BARBARA RAINEY

*S*omeday, I hope you will experience the amazing joy that comes from being a mother. Motherhood can be the source of incredible fulfillment as well as an area of tremendous challenges, difficulty, and worry.

Jesus said about a mom, "Whenever a woman is in travail she has sorrow, because her hour has come; but when she gives birth to the child, she remembers the anguish no more, for joy that a child has been born into the world" (John 16:21). This verse well describes not only the emotions of childbirth, but also the entire roller-coaster experience of being a mother: sorrow-joy-sorrow-joy.

As a mother, I have days when everything is relatively easy, the children behave lovingly toward one another, and I wonder why I ever struggle. But on other days, I wonder whether mothering will ever be fun again. I ask myself, *Am I ruining my kids for life?* You will find someday (as I have) that being a mom is tough enough without the identity attacks that can come from your emotions, other people's perceptions and expectations, and your abilities and failures.

I'm especially prone to guilt and discouragement. I have high standards for my children and for myself. When I fail to respond to my kids with love and kindness, or when they disobey or act irresponsibly, I experience disappointment. In the middle of life's daily stress, I often find myself on a seesaw of emotion, one moment feeling down and discouraged, and the next rewarded as only a mother can be.

Though motherhood can be hard work, frustrating, and lonely, priceless moments come every day in the form of crayon-scrawled notes, a quick hug and a kiss, or something expressed as only a child can say it. I think God gives mothers those moments to spur us on, to help us hang in there and not give up hope. One of my favorite verses is, "Let us not lose heart in doing good, for in due time we shall reap if we do not grow weary" (Gal. 6:9).

I believe that if I persevere, God will give me a ministry of influence to the next generation. Mothers literally shape the future by making specific choices about how we raise our children.

A Mom Must Be a Critical Thinker

Another of my favorite verses is Paul's advice to "not be conformed to this world, but be transformed by the renewing of your mind" (Rom. 12:2). I yearn for God to transform me by continually renewing my mind so that I never unconsciously adopt the worldly wisdom of the culture in which I live.

Our society sends the wrong signals to mothers, telling them they are dispensable. Trained caretakers, nannies, and workers in daycare centers meet the physical needs of children. Mothers provide maid service and shuttle service, and they offer purchasing advice. This state of affairs implies that mothering is not important—that someone with special training can raise children as well as—or better than—their own moms.

Four Key Questions a Mom Should Ask

I often use four questions to challenge what our culture tells me about my role as a mother. As you think ahead to becoming a mom, keep these questions in mind as a way of determining what you want for yourself and your family.

1. Why am I doing what I'm doing? For example, ask yourself, *Why would I want to send my child to daycare?* or perhaps, *Why am I involved in the mid-week women's Bible study?* or, *Why am I working sixty hours a week at the office?* Will these activities and responsibilities contribute to your being a mother of influence? Will they distract you from your primary role? Mothers should ask *why* about everything they do.

2. What am I communicating to my child by what I do and by what I say? What will my children perceive, based on my actions? What will they learn? What values will I model?

One day at home I heard the sound of porcelain shattering, and I knew it was my Hummel figurine, *Little Apple Girl*. I had just reminded my two boys they couldn't play ball in the house, and I felt like wringing their necks. When I arrived at the scene of the crime, I found the guilty party, Samuel (then four years old), sheepishly awaiting his sentencing. I told him to sit on his bed because he was going to get a spanking. Then I picked up the pieces of my apple girl and discovered she was not beyond repair.

Holding them in my hand, I went to Samuel's room, took his precious blue-eyed, blond-haired face in my other hand, and showed the pieces to him. I said, "Samuel, do you see this?" His eyes became little blue saucers, and he nodded. When his eyes met mine, I made my point: "I want you to know, Samuel Rainey, that I love you more than this." Glancing down at the remnants I cradled in my hand, I added, "And I love you enough to spank you for disobeying me."

I haven't always responded with such grace, but on that occasion with the Holy Spirit's help, I gave Samuel a strong and true message about my ultimate values.

3. Am I willing to deny myself? Answering this question honestly now, while you don't have children, can reveal what and how much you're holding onto. Not until you actually become a mother do you learn how much of yourself must be given up to fulfill your role as God intended. Before my first child was born, if God had asked me, "Are you willing to deny yourself in order to be a mother?" I would have readily answered yes. But if God had said to me, "Barbara, are you willing to deny yourself your watercolor painting, your sewing, quilting, and handiwork, your time with your friends—in fact, nearly all of your personal interests and talents—in order to be a better mother?" my response would have been much more hesitant and deliberate.

I'm thankful God didn't ask me to give up all these things at once because they were very important to me. Over the years He has guided me gently in setting aside most of these talents and interests so I can be a more focused mom.

4. Am I willing to take risks to be a mother of influence? In an Old Testament story, Jochebed, the mother of Moses, hid him for the first three months of his life after Pharaoh decreed that all Hebrew baby boys were to die. When she could hide him no longer, she made a little boat out of a basket and sent baby Moses floating down the river.

Pharaoh's childless daughter found Moses and adopted him. In that way, God rescued Moses from certain death and honored his mother's faith. Jochebed willingly took a risk for her child's sake because she feared God more than she feared Pharaoh.

What would you be willing to risk for your child? Would you risk the ridicule of family and friends to stay home full-time when they don't think it's necessary? What if your children needed you to move to a smaller town with a safer environment? What if doing so meant taking a smaller family income?

When you become a mom, I urge you to hang on tightly to your kids, not allowing the world to drag them to destruction. I'm not advocating "smother love." I'm saying that being a mother today calls for courage, determination, and tenacity that will never quit, no matter how confused things get.

(For further reading related to this topic, see Chapters 27 and 30 on parenting, 33 on being a dad, and 51 on legacy.)

HomeBuilders Principle

The prescription for mothers: patience, prayer, perseverance.

TO THINK ABOUT INDIVIDUALLY

1. Find a quiet place to be alone and ask yourself these questions:

- *Why am I doing what I'm doing?* (What is necessary? What could I drop? What could I change?)
- *What might I need to deny myself in order to be a good mother?* (What would I rather be doing? Am I resentful?)

- *What messages will I send my children with my lifestyle?* (Will my actions match the values I say I believe in?)

2. Based on your answers to those questions, rate yourself between 1 (strongly disagree) and 5 (strongly agree) with the following statements:

____ My children will know I love my husband.

____ My children will know I love them.

____ My children will know I sacrifice myself for them.

____ My children will know they are a top priority.

____ My children will know my home is a priority.

Where did you score below a 4? Think about why and what you can change or improve.

TO DISCUSS TOGETHER

Sit down with your husband and discuss your answers to the questions in the previous exercise. Get his input to see where he believes you are being too hard on yourself and where he may have suggestions on how you can improve or change.

TO TAKE ACTION TOGETHER

Make arrangements to visit with your mom or another mature mom you respect. Ask her to answer these questions: "What do you wish a wise mother had told you before you became a mom?" "What would you do differently?" "What are your happiest memories as a mother?"

Part 4

35

Great Escapes

GETTING AWAY TO DREAM, PLAN, REFRESH, REFUEL

*D*o you remember the jingle from the fast-food restaurant with golden arches that went, "You deserve a break today"? By tweaking that jingle, I can give every couple a message worth remembering: "*Your marriage* deserves a break today!"

How long has it been since you spent extended, focused time with your mate? Not just an evening at a fantastic eatery, but a couple of days away from your usual environment to catch up? In too many marriages, the ordinary grind seems to overwhelm the possibility of extraordinary excitement.

Because of our fast-paced culture, we need to pause once or twice a year to rest, count our blessings, and dream some dreams. Barbara and I take what we call planning weekends, an opportunity to evaluate our marriage and parenting and, if necessary, redirect plans.

The getaway is effective in keeping our communication current, and it's just plain fun. Without any of the everyday distractions, we can concentrate on romancing each other. I can give Barbara flowers and speak tender words. She can give me undivided attention as I unwind and share from the heart. We can stay up munching snacks, listening to music, or talking and not have to get up in the morning to meet a demanding schedule.

In this chapter we offer basic guidelines for a great escape. Each couple needs to find the place and schedule to satisfy unique needs. However, we think every couple should avoid skimping on the time—even if it means going less often. We have found that the best scenario is to be gone at least two nights, which involves part of three days.

Purposes for a Getaway

We've settled on three general purposes for our getaways.

First and foremost, *it is time together with each other and with God.* We want to have plenty of unhurried, quiet time to listen to the Lord, to pray together, to just sit. If our lodging has a fireplace, we may plop for hours in front of the fire with our feet up, not going anywhere, not doing anything, not answering any phones, just sitting quietly talking—or not talking. Sometimes we read Scriptures or another good book to each other. To busy people like us, these hours satisfy almost beyond description.

A second getaway purpose is *planning.* This activity is especially important to our family planner—Barbara. Sometime during our escape we pull out our calendars and talk about where we are headed for the next week, the next month, the next six months, the next year. We also talk about upcoming vacations and how to make them meaningful for our children. The process of planning always helps you revisit your values.

A third purpose of these getaways is *romance and pure pleasure.* We reconnect soul to soul, heart to heart, and body to body. There should be no pressure to this aspect, and it certainly shouldn't feel like a performance situation—just a time of caring and sharing and meeting each other's spiritual, emotional, and physical needs.

If one or both of you are uncertain about how to act during a getaway time or need ideas, refer to the lists of a man's and woman's needs for romance (Chapters 25 and 26). If she likes to take walks and talk, then take an entire morning to walk and talk. If he likes to wake up and enjoy making love followed by a steak and eggs breakfast, go for it. The point is that you need to concentrate on satisfying the needs of the other person.

Getaway Preparation, Ideas, Activities

Cost is often the first objection raised to the getaway idea. You don't need to be wealthy—a little creativity goes a long way. An inexpensive place we've found is a cottage in a state park. We've also stayed in the off-season at no cost in a friend's apartment on a lake. Another excellent idea is to add a day or two at a suitable spot at the conclusion of a business trip.

Childcare arrangements and expenses are often barriers for younger couples. You may want to try to work out a deal with friends to take care of your kids for a weekend and then do the same for them later. (Husband: You will come out a big winner if you take responsibility for making get-away arrangements, including lining up the baby-sitter.)

One of the best tools we've found concerning a getaway was written by friends of ours, Bill and Carolyn Wellons. It's called *Getting Away to Get It Together*. This excellent guide will help you schedule the entire weekend. It's not available in bookstores, but you can order it from the FamilyLife resource center at 1-800-FLTODAY.

Here are more ideas:

- Don't drive too far. A maximum of two and a half hours in the car is plenty. If you drive much farther—perhaps on a Friday night—by the time you arrive, it will be late and you will be exhausted. And you still might have to buy groceries if you are staying in a cabin or condo.
- Go somewhere remote. If you are far off the beaten path, you will have to turn to each other for your entertainment and conversation. Get away by a stream, in the woods, a place that doesn't have the usual distractions—no TV, no newspapers, no Internet. The thought of such a media-deprived setting may send you into withdrawal. Just try it! Peace and quiet will grow on you, and you both may be pleasantly reminded of dating days that were more carefree and spontaneous.
- Don't stay by a mall. We've tried that, but it is tempting to while away too many hours shopping, eating, seeing movies. We avoid staying in tourist-trap-type locations too.

Getaway Activities

Here are additional suggestions for making the time romantic and memorable once you've arrived at your getaway location:

- Write a love letter, then read it to your spouse.
- Build in surprises over the weekend for your spouse. What would truly meet her needs for romance? What would spell delight for him? Be a student of your spouse, and do something special.

- Work on an area of your marriage or family that needs attention, such as planning, scheduling, or lovemaking.
- Do the fun things both of you enjoy but seldom take time for.

A Getaway Fight?

Sometimes your beautiful weekend may be marred by conflict. We know all about this too. By being together in a strange place with plenty of time on your hands, it's possible that unresolved matters will surface. If you ever find yourself in such conflict, be the first one to repent and initiate restoration of the relationship, even if you believe you are only 10 percent wrong. The truth is, you are probably more guilty than 10 percent! But back off, admit your fault, and realize that enjoying the relationship, not fighting, is what your getaway is all about.

And don't forget that new jingle, "Your marriage deserves a break today!"

(For more information related to this topic, see Chapters 25 and 26 on romance and 44 on rest.)

HomeBuilders Principle

> Every couple needs the refueling
> and refreshing that come only through
> focused, extended time alone.

TO THINK ABOUT INDIVIDUALLY

1. What about a getaway is most appealing to you (for example, the location, the mood, the activities, the peace and quiet)?

2. Which of your personal needs, ones that usually may not be met, would you like to have met during a getaway?

TO DISCUSS TOGETHER

Take turns sharing answers to the questions in the previous exercise.

TO TAKE ACTION TOGETHER

If you've never had a getaway, or it's been a long time since you've made an escape, how about planning a getaway now?

36

The Best Day of the Week

CHOOSING THE CHURCH WHERE YOU WORSHIP GOD

How important is a local church to the health of your marriage? The question may surprise you. With all of the current discussion on how to strengthen marriage, prevent divorce, and stabilize families, we don't hear much about the role of the church. Particularly in America, individual freedom and personal responsibility for spiritual growth are emphasized so much that it's tempting to forget we need outside assistance—particularly with our "private" relationships.

Let me answer the question by saying that perhaps no other choice you make, besides deciding to make Christ your daily Master, will have as significant an impact on your marriage as the church you join and commit to.

If you follow Jesus Christ, you are connected to the church: "God has placed the members, each one of them, in the body, just as He desired . . . Now you are Christ's body, and individually members of it" (1 Cor. 12:18, 27). And the church provides not only spiritual nourishment, but also strength and support that will help you honor your marriage covenant and build a godly family.

Although church attendance remains quite high in America, many younger people particularly have bought into the idea that regular involvement in a local church is an optional part of their Christian life: "Isn't God everywhere?" "Can't I meditate or catch a TV service or listen to a tape?" Of course, God can be worshiped anywhere and at any time, and meditating and using Christian resources are beneficial. But God has made us part of His living body, and others need us as much as we need them in dynamic relationships that typically occur in a local church.

The writer of Hebrews explained the importance of active engagement with other believers:

> Let us hold fast the confession of our hope without wavering, for He who promised is faithful; and let us consider how to stimulate one another to love and good deeds, not forsaking our own assembling together, as is the habit of some, but encouraging one another; and all the more, as you see the day drawing near. (Heb. 10:23–25)

The beloved pastor Chuck Swindoll spoke to this issue:

> When it's functioning correctly, *nothing* beats the church for effectiveness. Babies are cradled, children are loved, teenagers are challenged, parents are instructed, seniors find fellowship, singles are strengthened, and families are nurtured . . . Above all, the church is a family; in fact, it's a family of families.[1]

Trust me: You *need* a family of families. You need that family now, and you'll need that family later.

Choosing a Church

The issue of where to worship is usually decided before marriage, but perhaps because of new issues, unforeseen circumstances, or a move, you as a couple now face a choice about where to go to church. It's not a decision to be made lightly; you are choosing where you will worship God and where you will raise your family.

Barbara and I are aware of situations where the husband goes to one church, the wife to another, and the children to a third. They seem to have overlooked the best interest of family unity or the spirit of true family worship.

Choosing a church is another area where leaving and cleaving may be necessary to establish a new family identity. I have known couples married up to twenty years who felt compelled—even though they were drying up spiritually—to attend their parents' church. It wasn't good for them, their marriage, or their children.

CHURCH CHECKLIST

Spiritual value is the number one driving factor in choosing a church. You will need to consider other issues, too, and come up with your own tailored list. No church will be perfect, but this checklist of questions will help you consider areas that shouldn't be compromised.

_____ *Do you agree with the church theologically?* On the major matters of faith, can you align yourself with a particular local church's teaching and doctrine? As long as you have no significant reservations, if your spouse is less willing to try someplace different, you should be able to join that church to maintain family unity.

_____ *Is the church alive spiritually, and are both of you fed spiritually from the Scriptures?* You won't thrive spiritually in a dead church. You need a church that believes in the power of the Holy Spirit and the authority of Scripture—a body where the pastors and others preach and teach from the Word. Without these things you won't grow.

_____ *Does the worship engage you and draw your attention and heart to God?* Many different worship styles involve a wide variety of music. Assuming a church meets other important criteria, its services should help you enter God's presence in heartfelt worship.

_____ *Is it a church where you can experience true Christian community?* As I discussed in Chapter 23 on support and accountability, I believe all couples—especially younger ones—need to be part of a small group. Even in a relatively small congregation, you need a group of like-minded couples or a group led by an older mentor who will challenge you to grow spiritually during the early years of your marriage. Don't minimize this! You need Christian community.

_____ *Does the church hold its members accountable to obey Scripture?* A Bible-believing church will expect its people to seek to be like Christ in all of life. The church leaders will conduct scripturally appropriate and loving discipline with members when required.

_____ *Does the church eagerly welcome strangers and have an "outreach mentality"?* Nothing is worse than an ingrown church that is one large clique or a collection of smaller ones. How active is the church in evangelism? In helping the poor and needy? In supporting missions at home and abroad? Positive answers to these questions are good signs that a church is "outgrown," not ingrown.

What If You Can't Agree on a Church Choice?

This has never been much of an issue for Barbara and me, but I know it is for some couples. If it is a point of disagreement, pray about it individually and jointly for at least a week. If you still can't agree on a decision, I believe the husband should prayerfully make a choice, then encourage his wife to trust God and follow him in that decision without becoming embittered. It's amazing how our perceptions can change once we decide to accept rather than fight against a choice.

As newlyweds, Barbara and I moved five times in six years, and we made the mistake of not joining a church but instead visited many churches. We church-hopped! We didn't disagree; we just couldn't definitely decide where to go. I'm convinced our spiritual lives suffered because we didn't sink roots down into a body of believers and plug into a fellowship. Five years into our marriage, we finally committed ourselves. And when we did, we experienced what we had been missing.

A couple not part of a dynamic, growing, spiritually alive church puts their marriage at an enormous risk. If you move and have to find a new church, make it your objective to find a good church within four to six weeks.

Why the Local Church Needs You

The pollster George Barna, who has written extensively on the future of the church in America, observes,

The only way in which the Church will thrive in the future is if families lead the process of directing and furthering their own spiritual growth ... *The future of the Church in America depends largely upon the spiritual commitment of families* ... As the Church continues to decentralize, the spiritual development of our families will make or break the vitality of the Christian Church.[2]

I couldn't agree more. What an incredible challenge for all of us—to take greater responsibility for the spiritual growth of every person in our homes and then to join together with other maturing believers in building dynamic local churches that will be beacons of light in our darkening world.

Barna concludes, "For the sake of the future of the Church, we must ensure that spiritual development remains one of the key elements that our families integrate into the mix of activities and goals to which they are committed. However, we must go far beyond where our families are today in their spiritual commitment."[3]

A Special Message to Men

Too many men are missing in action when it comes to involvement in the local church. George Barna reports that of 94 million American males age eighteen and older, only about 26 million step through the door of a church.[4] And even those who go to church demonstrate a high level of lethargy.

For the good of the kingdom, your family, and yourself, I encourage you to involve yourself in your church. And as I've already suggested, one of the best ways to support that involvement is to take the lead in providing spiritual leadership at home.

Here are some ideas on how to do this:

1. Be faithful in your prayer life and study of the Bible.
2. Minister to your wife through daily, joint prayer.
3. Lead your family weekly in some type of family worship. It doesn't have to be complicated—perhaps a brief reading of Scripture, discussion, and prayer. Sticking with it is the key.
4. Help your wife with the children when it's time to get ready for church. Doing this may seem a small thing, but many families get off to a bad start on Sunday morning because Mom has too much to do.

(Other information on this topic can be found in Chapters 9 on building a spiritual foundation, 21 on growing faith, 23 on accountability and support, and 51 on legacy.)

HomeBuilders Principle

> Your family needs the church
> as much as the church needs your family.

TO THINK ABOUT INDIVIDUALLY

1. Do you agree or disagree that involvement in a local church is important to the health of your marriage? Why do you feel this way?

2. What attitudes did your parents have toward church attendance? How do they impact your attitude about church now?

3. What issues guided your choice of your local church? Are you satisfied that you are involved with the right local church? What about your spouse—do you think this local church is a good place for him or her to grow spiritually?

4. Do you feel you are actively supporting your church with your resources and time? Why or why not? Are there any changes you want to make?

TO DISCUSS TOGETHER

Discuss your answers to the questions in the previous exercise. Decide as a couple what decisions need to be made about church choice or church involvement.

TO TAKE ACTION TOGETHER

Determine together how you might give a special gift to your local church. Perhaps you can volunteer to weed the flower beds, paint the nursery, or take a meal to an older member. Or you may want to give money or a needed item. Remember, your church needs you.

37

Refresher Course

REVIEWING THE BASICS TO KEEP YOUR
MARRIAGE ON TARGET

*A*t some point while reading and applying the information in this book, you may ask yourself, *There's a lot of material in this book. Do the Raineys have a* Cliffs Notes *version of the critical ideas that I need to remember above all else?*

We are happy you asked! We think all of the topics covered in this book are important, but to make your marriage last, we will discuss seven core principles—the basics—in this chapter.

1. Intimacy and Passion

Marriage is more than romance, but without intimacy and genuine passion, a relationship will dry up like a stream in the desert.

I may have been a country boy from the hills of southwest Missouri, but I knew our honeymoon needed to have a romantic flair—on a budget! While Barbara engineered the wedding plans, I spent weeks meticulously detailing a fourteen-day trip in the Colorado Rockies.

We camped out (one night in the snow) and also stayed in a cabin by a roaring river. There was plenty of time to talk and share our thoughts and dreams—the perfect environment to know each other better.

Before a couple marries, attaining intimacy seems easy. You draw close as though you are compelled by the force of gravity. But after marriage, the forces feel reversed, and passion and closeness take persistence and hard work.

Throughout our marriage, Barbara has allowed me to know her fully, and I, too, have risked letting her learn what's inside me. But this didn't come naturally on our wedding night. It has taken years of sharing, adjusting—and yes, some arguing—to find the total communication of body, soul, and spirit.

2. Commitment

At its core, marriage is a lifelong commitment not merely to stay married but to love another person. During our wedding, Barbara and I pledged to stand by each other "in riches and in poverty, in joy and in sorrow, in sickness and in health." When I looked in Barbara's eyes and said the vows, I meant every word. But in our fourth year of marriage, a health crisis that nearly took Barbara's life tested the depth of my commitment.

Understandably, Barbara became preoccupied with her health. For weeks, which turned into months, there weren't many romantic feelings in our relationship. But I had promised to stand by her. Barbara couldn't give much to me, but she needed my love more than ever. That's what commitment comes down to—digging your fingers into a rock and hanging on when it feels as if your marriage might slide off a cliff.

3. Respect

I'll never forget the feelings of being trapped that hit me not long after the honeymoon. Barbara was so *different* from me. We would go to parties, and she would follow me around the room, hardly ever speaking, clinging to me like Velcro. I had more of an outgoing personality, but she was struggling with her self-confidence. What was going on? And Barbara had similar questions about me. Some of my endearing traits made her feel so confined that one day she locked herself in the bathroom, thinking, *What in the world am I going to do? I can't get away from this!*

A fork loomed in the road of our marriage. Was I going to love her or criticize her for her apparent "weaknesses"? Would she love me in spite of my grating qualities?

Fortunately, we made the right choices: Each of us decided to respect the other person's uniqueness and to work on letting our differences bind instead of divide us.

4. Self-denial

As a single man, I was used to going fishing on Saturday, watching the game of the week, or generally doing my own thing. I'll never forget one of our first weekends together after the honeymoon. All of a sudden it hit me like a blast of chilly arctic air: *I can't do what I want to do on Saturday anymore! I have someone else's needs to consider besides my own.* That was a startling realization—I couldn't live my life as I had in the past.

Since then we've made great strides, but at other times selfishness has shown its ugly face in our relationship. We have discovered that at the heart of a great marriage must be two people who know how to deny themselves. If both people are willing to sacrifice their own desires, it's amazing how individual needs are met over time.

5. Communication

Barbara and I became good friends before we got overly serious in our relationship. We spent hours going on picnics, exploring outdoors, shopping, and even fishing. And we talked and talked, sometimes forgetting the clock until 1:00 or 2:00 A.M.

When we married and were together all the time, the discussions past midnight no longer seemed necessary or productive. Since communication takes energy, we didn't talk as openly, frequently, and deeply. When communication is ignored, problems are likely to occur.

The same focus and time for communication we savored while dating are needed in marriage. For a relationship to grow and bloom, partners need time to communicate—time to listen and speak, time to be real, time to share disappointments, frustrations, and failures.

6. Negotiation

Once in just a few hours, because of a sickening run of insensitive words and actions, I hurt Barbara's feelings—big time.

A long day had exhausted me, and though I knew Barbara was upset about something, I was so tired that I eagerly crawled into bed. A few minutes later Barbara joined me, but instead of giving me a goodnight kiss, she grabbed a pillow and smacked me on the head! And it wasn't a playful whack either.

That made me mad. I rolled over to stare at the wall.

"Don't you want to talk?" Barbara asked.

I grunted a noncommittal answer. A long, long silence followed.

Finally, in a chilly monotone, I said, "Sweetheart, neither one of us is doing well in this relationship now. Let's reschedule our conflict for tomorrow."

"Okay," she said softly. We turned out the lights and tried to pretend we had not let the sun go down on our anger.

In the darkness I was wide awake, still red hot, facing the wall. But as the hours ticked away, my simmering sulk dissipated. I knew my attitude was wrong, and I asked God to take away my anger and desire to punish Barbara.

The mood was still tense the next day when I told Barbara I had blown it and was sorry. She said she was sorry, too, especially for blasting me with the pillow. Even though our feelings were still raw, we used a classic approach to negotiate an end to our conflict: We forgave each other *by an act of the will.* This is necessary because feelings are hardly ever good during a conflict.

7. Vision

Many marriages consist of two purposeful and successful people who are unable to arrive at a common vision as a couple. They are like two contractors building the same house from two sets of blueprints.

Although I had known about God and the Bible when I was growing up, I didn't take God seriously and give control of my life to Him until I was in college. I was excited to learn that Barbara shared this passion.

Because we both knew that our differences and our selfish inclinations had the potential to turn our romantic dream into a disaster, we agreed that God would need to be the center of our marriage. I am convinced that this joint vision to give God our very best not only cemented us together as a couple but has given us individual purpose, direction, and significance in all of life. I wouldn't want to put our relationship at risk by not seeking God's direction and help continually.

There you have them—the seven big ideas that can bring every marriage safely through life's storms to a safe harbor.

HomeBuilders Principle

> When you're not sure what to do in your marriage,
> stick to the basics.

TO THINK ABOUT INDIVIDUALLY

1. Rate yourself on each of the seven basics of marriage (1 = low–poor; 5 = high–outstanding).

_____Intimacy and passion

_____Commitment

_____Respect

_____Self-denial

_____Communication

_____Negotiation

_____Vision

2. If you rated yourself low on any item, which of these basics do you think should receive attention from you now in your marriage?

TO DISCUSS TOGETHER

Share anything you discovered in answering the questions in the previous exercise. How might you help each other make progress on areas that were rated low?

TO TAKE ACTION TOGETHER

Share prayer requests. Each person should identify one basic about which prayer is desired from the other spouse. Promise to pray faithfully for each other for at least a month. Offer each other encouragement as progress is made.

38

Taming Time Together

SCHEDULING BUSY LIVES

*H*ow are you doing at keeping all the plates spinning in your home? Let me explain.

When I was a boy, each week I watched the classic variety program *The Ed Sullivan Show*. I will never forget the guy who spun plates on sticks.

The performer strolled out on the stage with a stack of porcelain plates. He set the stack on a long table, then took a plate, and started it spinning on a stick. Then he started another plate spinning on another stick. In a few seconds he had six, seven, even eight plates spinning away.

But as he moved to the end of the table and got his last plate going, the first one lost steam and began to wobble. He dashed to that end of the table and gave that plate a spin. Then, of course, the next plate was wobbling, and he'd give that one a new spin. Back and forth he dashed, catching up to precariously wobbling plates at the last second and somehow keeping them all going.

Finally, when I was sure he couldn't keep it up any longer because of sheer exhaustion, he started at one end of the table and collected each teetering plate until he had the entire stack safely in his hands.

That spinning plate act is a good visual summary of how most marriages start. A starry-eyed bride and groom walk the aisle and say, "I do." They begin at the end of the table and spin that first big plate called marriage. They're madly in love. It's just fantastic, playing house, keeping that plate spinning.

But then the inevitable happens. They discover there is more than one plate. They have careers, and perhaps they move to a different community and make new friends. Maybe they join a new church. Those plates need spinning, too, and that first plate called marriage slows down, maybe even wobbles.

Then some little saucers come along, and things get more interesting. The average number of saucers is around two, but some of us wind up with as many as six. Husband and wife are pulled their separate ways—meeting deadlines, scratching off "to do" lists, putting in twelve- to sixteen-hour days, and falling into bed exhausted. Inevitably, that first big plate suffers neglect. Isolation takes its toll, and oneness begins to waver. The wonder of marriage is replaced by a wobble.

The apostle Paul urged us to make the most of our time (Eph. 5:16). Just how can we maximize our time wisely so that the important "plates" in our lives keep spinning?

Mastering Your Schedules

We all want our lives to be meaningful, to count as individuals and as a couple. To do this well, Barbara and I have had to acquire the equivalent of a Ph.D. in managing and merging schedules. We certainly don't pretend to have all the answers, but here are our best tips (so far):

Early in your marriage, decide together what's ultimately important. If you don't know where you are going in life and what your values are, deciding where to spend a spare Saturday, what activities to join at church, and how to integrate schedules can create significant conflict. Shared values will help you decide where to invest your time.

Work on schedules together. This point seems obvious, but too many couples overlook it. Almost every Sunday night we go out for dinner and discuss schedules. We pull out our calendars and plan for the next week or longer. (We've found it healthy to take a hard look at our calendars as far as twelve to eighteen months in advance.) Without this action plan our lives would quickly deteriorate to stressful chaos. Start the date night habit now, before you have children or while they are young.

Hold each other accountable. Staying focused and abiding by schedules take unwavering personal discipline, in fact, more self-control than most of us have. You need to give your mate the freedom to ask hard questions about your schedule and commitments to help you stay on target.

Discard optional responsibilities. Many good causes and activities are waiting for you with open arms. If you and your spouse can't stick to the main things in your lives, soon your list of commitments will bulge, and communication and intimacy in your marriage will be on standby.

Practice saying no. Many of us are so accustomed to saying yes that we almost need speech therapy to say no. You may think this is weird, but sometimes Barbara and I go outside in the woods near our home and use the trees to practice saying no: "No, I'm sorry; I can't do that." "No, I've got a commitment that weekend." "No, that won't work."

Know when to say yes. On the other hand, we need to know when to say yes to enjoyable activities and opportunities for service. The key is to feel confident that the activity or opportunity will help achieve your key goals and values as a couple and a family. In special situations God will lead a couple to sacrifice some of their personal or family goals to accomplish spiritual agendas in the community or around the world.

Post a master calendar listing all activities. It starts out as an aid to husband and wife, but after children arrive and get older, everyone benefits.

Plan times of rest. Even Almighty God knew when to take a break. During the seven days of creation, He set aside one whole day of rest. He wants us to follow His lead and catch our breath and get our bearings before plunging into each week's demanding schedule.

Humble yourself and regroup when schedules slip out of control. There are points where you've been too busy and going in different directions. You must pull back, say "time-out," and get life back into perspective. Things can quickly come unraveled, even in a family that's trying to do it right.

You Can't Do It All

People occasionally ask us, "How do you do it all?" That one is easy to answer: "We don't." We prayerfully, rigorously decide how many plates the Rainey family can keep spinning. We have to say no to many wonderful, exciting opportunities.

The reality is, no one does it all. No one can have a busy social life five nights a week and grow spiritually, work on the marriage, do home chores, have a family night, build a deepening relationship with each child, and so on. Something has to go. We decided years ago to pull back from certain social and even certain church meetings in order to concentrate on the *best things*.

To keep schedules in balance, we all need the guidance and control of the Holy Spirit. If God isn't in control of everything, we are prone to lose focus and become slaves, not masters, of our schedules.

(For additional insight, see Chapters 12 on family values, 22 on balancing work and family, 35 on planning getaways, 44 on rest, and 49 on stress.)

HomeBuilders Principle

> Every couple must learn how to master their time—making
> sure they are accomplishing the *best things*.

TO THINK ABOUT INDIVIDUALLY

1. Make a list of all the "plates" you are spinning—anything that regularly requires a significant investment of your time, energy, and other resources.

2. Do you think there are too many "plates" in your life? Why do you feel this way? If you need to cut back, how will you decide which activities to reduce or eliminate?

3. What about your spouse? From your perspective, do you think your wife or husband is overcommitted? If so, how might you help bring his or her life back into balance?

TO DISCUSS TOGETHER

Share your answers to the questions in the previous exercise. As you compare notes on the state of your schedules, what solutions or conclusions are emerging about how as a couple you need to make adjustments—if any? (If you are unsure or not united on your goals, take another look at Chapter 12 on family values.)

TO TAKE ACTION TOGETHER

If you are not doing so already, arrange your first weekly family schedule planning meeting. Do what works for you—share a meal, go to a park, meet in the kitchen. And plan a getaway for the two of you (see Chapter 35).

39

Facing Troubles

PULLING TOGETHER IN TOUGH CIRCUMSTANCES

In life the sky is not always clear and blue. Storms appear on the horizon.

Barbara and I have learned from life's storms that God is interested in our growth. He wants us to trust Him in the midst of the storms and to grow together as a couple. And yet couples pull apart and marriages die during tough times like these:

- A child drowns in a swimming pool. The wife blames herself, then abruptly turns on her husband.
- A husband's lost job and subsequent financial disorder cause a wife to stop believing in him. Their disappointment in each other causes them to retreat from meeting each other's needs.
- An unplanned pregnancy and increased pressures at work provoke a couple to question their commitment to each other.

Most couples don't realize that trials represent opportunities for them to sink their roots deeper and gain stability in their relationship. As followers of Christ, we are to recognize that difficulties benefit us: "Consider it all joy, my brethren, when you encounter various trials, knowing that the testing of your faith produces endurance. And let endurance have its perfect result, that you may be perfect and complete, lacking in nothing" (James 1:2–4).

We know well the stress—and benefits—that come with trials and troubles. Early in our marriage, Barbara and I endured a tough twelve-month period.

It started one summer. Barbara and I were not getting along very well—nibbling and picking at each other. Our sexual relationship was at an all-time low. And when we arrived in Little Rock, our new home was so filthy, it took days to clean. Later we discovered that in purchasing the home, we had been cheated out of several thousand dollars.

Our troubles were starting to pick up speed. We got a call one Sunday morning in August. My brother said, "Dennis, Dad died this morning." My dad had always been one of the stronger figures in my life. A sudden heart attack had taken him at the age of sixty-six.

In February I came home from work to learn that our son Benjamin needed major abdominal surgery. He came through fine, but the financial stress was heavy.

Fortunately, the spring months passed quietly. Then in June, Barbara was doing her morning exercises. I hadn't left for work at my usual time and was still there, admiring her energy as she did sit-ups. Suddenly, she stopped and put her head between her knees. I said, "Sweetheart, what's wrong?"

"I feel faint."

"Well, can I help?"

"I think my heart is beating fast."

"Well, maybe you should get up and try to walk it off. Let me help you to your feet."

We got exactly three feet, and she collapsed on the bed, nearly passing out. I checked her pulse, and her heart was racing so fast, I couldn't count the number of beats. I called an ambulance, which rushed Barbara to the hospital.

Throughout the morning, Barbara's heart raced at 280 to 300 beats a minute. Her blood pressure dropped alarmingly low.

Just before noon, I began to despair. I had just lost my dad. Was I going to lose my wife too? I called Kitty Longstreth, a widow who had become one of our good friends in Little Rock, and asked her to pray.

"Of course I will, Dennis. I'll start right now."

At 4:00 P.M. the doctors told me they were going to try to stop Barbara's heart with electric shock and retime it as they shocked it into starting up again. There was no choice. But at 4:05 a doctor came back out and said, "We didn't have to use the shock treatment. Your wife's heart suddenly returned to normal."

Because they wouldn't let me see Barbara, I decided to call Kitty and tell her the good news. When I told her what had happened at 4:05, she said, "That's when I stopped praying! Somehow I knew at that moment that everything was okay."

For the next thirty days, Barbara had extra heartbeats, I had extra heartbeats, and so did the kids. Then at the end of that month, we discovered that she was pregnant.

That ended our one-year adventure in trials, but we faced eight more months of suspense wondering whether Barbara would give birth to a healthy baby. Three weeks past her due date, she delivered a nine-pound, five-ounce boy whom we named Samuel.

I acknowledge that what we went through was not the worst possible series of traumas a couple can face. But our troubles taught us that without a plan and the inner resources to move through trials, marriage will suffer.

Grasp God's Perspective Together

Couples fail to respond properly to adversity in two major ways. First, and most typically, they fail to anticipate the inevitable trials and problems. Second, when the troubles do hit, many husbands and wives mistakenly turn against each other rather than turning together to God to pray through the trials.

Part of the strategy for facing troubles is realizing that God allows difficulties in our lives for many reasons. I'm not saying He *causes* difficulties. I believe He allows them for many reasons, but difficulties do not mean something is wrong with your marriage.

Trials do not bring neutral results: They drive two people together or apart. The natural tendency is to go through a difficulty alone and not share it as a couple. The following are some principles we've learned:

• *Give your mate time and the freedom to process trials differently from the way you do.* The problems Barbara and I faced that year brought us to a crossroads: Would we share our difficulties with each other and give the other person room to process the problems? I remember feeling tempted to think that Barbara was wrong for being so introspective during the months that followed her heart episode. I had to fight the urge to discount her emotions and give her the typical noncompassionate male response: "Snap out of it, Dear. Everything is going to be fine." But Barbara wanted to share her fears with me. She needed me to listen. Men and women process suffering differently, so don't try to make your spouse like you.

• *Realize the temptation is to become self-focused and to withdraw from each other.* The desire to pull away is greatest during these periods because it is very difficult for another person to carry your burden. As a result, you end up thinking the other person doesn't understand, and the pain associated with that conclusion makes you want to pull back to safety.

• *Respond to trials by embracing God's perspective of suffering together as a couple.* The spouses who learn the art of facing storms together by seeking God's perspective can develop a sweet and robust spiritual oneness. As we struggled with our trials, Barbara and I learned a principle for handling problems: "In everything give thanks" (1 Thess. 5:18). It isn't a simplistic excuse to put your head in the sand and ignore reality. On the contrary, I believe when we give thanks in all things, we express faith in a God who knows what He's doing and can be trusted. As Martin Lloyd-Jones said, "Faith is the refusal to panic."

• *Remember that your mate is never your enemy.* Realize that your struggle is not against your spouse; resist the urge to punish or think that he or she is the problem. Your spouse is your intimate ally, a fellow burden bearer who is there to encourage you as you go through a difficult time.

• *If the burden or suffering persists, seek outside help.* If you feel you are slipping off in a deep ditch as a couple, don't wait until you have all four wheels stuck before you seek help. Find godly counsel by calling your mentoring couple, your pastor, or a biblical counselor to gain outside perspective.

Suffering is common to all marriages. The way in which you respond to it will determine whether your marriage flourishes or flounders.

(For more on this topic, see Chapters 19 and 20 on teamwork, 23 on a support system for your marriage, 45 on blessing and encouraging your spouse, and 47 on knowing when your marriage needs outside help.)

HomeBuilders Principle

To handle the hard times,
learn God's perspective and face troubles together.

TO THINK ABOUT INDIVIDUALLY

1. Take inventory of your marriage. Have there been any major trials or troubles? Did they result in stronger oneness or in isolation of some kind? Why or why not?

2. How well do you follow Paul's exhortation to "give thanks in everything"?

___I do it all the time.

___I do it most of the time.

___I do it some of the time.

___I seldom, if ever, do it.

When is it easiest for you to give thanks? When is it hardest?

TO DISCUSS TOGETHER

1. Talk together about the trials and troubles you have had as a family. Which ones stand out, and why? Which ones brought you closer together? Which ones seemed to separate you?

2. What can you do now that will prepare you for the inevitable troubles to come?

TO TAKE ACTION TOGETHER

Schedule a Be Thankful Day in your family. Encourage every family member to think of one thing each hour for which to be thankful. Write the items down and put them in a bowl or jar. At dinner, read each one. Then pray and give thanks to God for His goodness.

40

Vacations

MAKING THEM DELIGHTS, NOT DISASTERS

"Daddy, how long is it going to be till we get there?"

"How much farther?"

"What do you mean it's another hour?"

Like me, do you have nightmares about comments like these?

Although we joke about these vacation conversations, I am astounded that a lot of families don't take a vacation. I'm not thinking of trips to exotic, expensive locales, but an extended time away together to take a break from responsibilities—to refresh and refuel your own lives as well as provide experiences and memories for your children.

Rest and recuperation are necessities. When Jesus sensed His disciples needed a break, He told them, "'Come away by yourselves to a lonely place and rest awhile.' . . . And they went away in the boat to a lonely place by themselves" (Mark 6:31–32).

Just what is the purpose of a vacation? Perhaps a better question is, What do you, your spouse, and your family need from vacations at this stage of life? As always, Barbara and I bring different perspectives to developing goals for our vacations. Barbara enjoys doing research on the history of our destination, while I bring the "let's party" perspective: Be sure to have too much fun rather than too little fun on vacation. Together, these attitudes have made our family vacations memorable.

Our favorite vacation as a (briefly) childless couple remains our honeymoon. We started our family during our second year of marriage, but that didn't stop us from taking off in a Rambler station wagon and driving through Michigan to Canada. We camped in our car, swatted mosquitoes, and went fishing.

Vacations Just for Couples

Your quiver may fill quickly with children, or you may spend the first five years (or longer) of the marriage without children. Although we didn't experience many vacations without children, we have some wisdom we've gained over the years.

Experience each other's ideal vacation. Just as Barbara and I differ in our tastes for vacation experiences, you will likely have contrasting values. Take turns exploring what the other really likes.

In our first years of marriage, we grabbed several minivacations. Barbara took me to museums and to the theater. I took her hiking, fishing, and exploring. I took Barbara on a one-day road trip around the Olympic Peninsula near Seattle, Washington. Neither of us has forgotten the clear January day when we saw pristine lakes, jagged cliffs overhanging the ocean, and a rain forest. As we shared these experiences with each other, our interests expanded, and we learned tons about each other.

Give yourselves plenty of time for each other. Many couples spend too much time being entertained and *not* focusing on each other. Our favorite times have almost always included an open schedule so that we were able to sleep in, hang out, and just be together. That's why we head for the woods for a vacation.

Don't use all your vacation to visit family. Now, this may sound selfish, but I would advise you to make sure you get time away just for yourselves.

Consider going on a short-term missions trip together. Early in our marriage, we went to South Africa and Kenya and held FamilyLife Marriage and Parenting Conferences together. Many organizations specialize in taking lay couples like you on these adventures. You don't have to travel to Africa or China to go; North America has many mission fields where you two could invest your lives.

Planning and Outfitting

With or without children, the husband and wife should plan and set vacation goals as far ahead of time as possible. Do this now when you don't have kids; the habit will be in place when you do.

Set summer vacation goals within the broader purposes for your family's summer. At times we have overscheduled activities and done too much before, during, and after vacation. A good vacation does not have to include all the amusement parks in the area. For some of our most enjoyable vacations, we stayed put in one spot for a solid week, such as at a family camp. And we went home far more relaxed.

As far as detailed preparation goes, for smaller children I (Barbara) always packed little travel games, books, coloring/activity books, and markers and crayons. I tried to get something new each trip so they wouldn't say, "The same old thing!" We had travel games I kept in a box and didn't allow the children to play with or see from summer to summer.

When our children were four or younger, we wouldn't tell them about the vacation until the day before we left. Children of this age have little understanding of time, so there's no point in saying, "We're going on vacation two weeks from now." Tell them the day before and save yourself grief.

The Car Trip

How do you survive the car ride?

With six children, we've had some interesting car trips. One time, we had eight family members to carry in a seven-passenger van. Since some of the current child safety laws weren't in place, behind the driver's seat we installed a porta-crib where two-year-old Laura rode. She stood behind the driver—usually Dennis—for the entire two-and-a-half-day trip, banging toys on top of his head, sometimes yelling in his ear.

I learned after several long trips that I needed to introduce new items each day into the children's activity packs. I used these things as incentives or rewards for good behavior. We also listened for hours to Bible story tapes, *Chronicles of Narnia* tapes, and music. Nowadays, keeping individual children occupied is even easier because each can have an inexpensive cassette player with headphones.

All of the preplanned activities and distractions helped, but inevitably, our bunch would start griping because they had been in the car too long. After a couple of trips, we came up with an idea that was a lifesaver for us—the Dime Jar.

Before heading out, we filled a glass jar with dimes—about ten dollars in all. We set the jar on the dashboard where everyone could see it and let the kids know that whenever they complained or bickered, we would take dimes out of the jar until they became quiet, talked in a reasonable tone of voice, or stopped complaining. Whatever money was left over at the end of the day or the trip was theirs. They could split the proceeds equally and buy ice cream, soft drinks, or whatever they wanted. It provided motivation for the whole trip because they knew every time we took a dime out, that left less money for goodies. As they got older, we substituted quarters for dimes.

We also insisted on a quiet period of sixty to ninety minutes a day during car trips, especially when the younger ones had to take naps. Dennis and I looked at our watches and said, "Until exactly 3:30, you can't talk; you can't say a word." (Of course, we made sure we had a potty stop beforehand!)

As I (Dennis) look back on the sanity we protected on those trips, I'm convinced the effort Barbara expended for the time in the car was the most valuable preparation for our entire vacation.

Reentry After a Vacation

When you pull up to your home, there's a reentry process. It can be grim. The weeds are growing, and the lawn needs cutting. There's almost no food in the house. You've accumulated piles of laundry. To lessen the pain of this moment and to have time to ease back into the routine, we try to come back a day early rather than on Sunday afternoon late, just hours before work starts on Monday morning.

On the trip home, talk about the memories you made and what you'd like to do again. Unpack the car together, and spend a quiet evening settling in so that you'll be ready to go—recharged and energized from your time away.

(For material related to this topic, see Chapters 35 on getaway escapes, 43 on holidays, 44 on rest, 50 on building memories, and 51 on legacy.)

HomeBuilders Principle

Every family needs
the anticipation, experience, and memories
of well-planned vacations.

TO THINK ABOUT INDIVIDUALLY

1. Reflect on your family vacation memories from childhood. What is your favorite memory? Why? Which trips were great, and which ones were disasters? Why?

2. How did your parents work together to prepare for the trip and then help the family to re-enter after coming back? What effect did this have on your family?

3. Make a list of five purposes or goals that you think would be profitable for your family's vacations.

TO DISCUSS TOGETHER

Review each other's answers to the questions in the previous exercise. Combine your lists of purposes and goals for a vacation. Be gracious to each other. It's likely, having come from different families with different ways of doing vacations, that you will need to compromise as you come up with a list agreeable to both of you.

TO TAKE ACTION TOGETHER

1. Take an hour or two and gather information for a future vacation. You could scan the Internet, stop at a travel agent, visit the library, and/or buy a tour book. A vacation provides pleasure in three phases—planning/anticipation, doing (the vacation), and remembering the memories.

2. For a couple with children, brainstorm together on ways you can entertain your children while maintaining discipline and positive attitudes (e.g., the Dime Jar) on your vacations. Be creative!

41

"Where's the Remote Control?"

MANAGING THE MEDIA MONSTERS

Would you be upset to learn that someone was competing for your mate's heart, subtly sending negative messages about you, and seeking to intrude on your marriage by robbing the two of you of time alone for talk and intimacy?

Upset? You probably would explode with anger and hurt. No marriage has room for another lover.

But each day assorted voices lure your spouse and you away from each other: TV, cable, Internet, E-mail, radio, magazines, newspapers, music, movies, and video games.

Have I gone over the edge on this topic? Hear me out.

Daily, we face a barrage of communication from various media sources. Nothing is wrong with the media per se. Through the media we receive information, inspiration, quality entertainment, and spiritual nourishment via Christian materials and programming. For every media pearl, however, there seems to be a bucketful of garbage.

Without careful evaluation and control, the media can consume our lives—through time invested as well as the value-assaulting messages delivered. More often than not, the media communicate worldly values, which the enemy uses to advantage in his ongoing war against godly families.

Media Threats to Marriage

The media present at least three significant threats to marriage:

First, the media will take time away from the relationship. Take TV, for example. Many people consider renting a movie or watching TV together to be a family evening. We've been guilty of doing this and have found that these extremely passive activities do not build relationships. Families must do something other than stare at the screen to acquire special identities.

Second, the media can twist your sense of reality, creating unreasonable expectations for your mate. The media usually present a distorted picture of real life. How often in a movie or on a television program do you see ordinary-looking people fall in love, get married, and remain committed through good times and bad for life? More often, the norm is two extremely attractive people—groomed beautifully and photographed in the best possible light—falling in love and into the sack without much thought about moral issues. If you constantly feed these images into your head, doesn't your spouse stand to lose in the long run? Competing with fantasy is difficult.

Third, through pornography and Internet liaisons, the media can facilitate emotional adultery. Pornography fosters a lust for images of other people, which can be as damaging to the mental and emotional health of a marriage as a physically realized affair. Anyone with a computer, modem, and Internet access can download pornographic materials anytime at home. Also, people can use Internet chat rooms to meet strangers of the opposite sex and engage in intimate, sexually oriented conversation. In some cases spouses have left a marriage to rendezvous with a chat-room "friend," and divorce resulted. Although the benefits of using the Internet are obvious, its costs and risks are not always so plain. We must carefully guard our eyes, hearts, and minds against the possible temptations that can come through it into our homes.

Taming the Media Monster

The words of Psalm 101:2–3 apply well to media use:

> I will give heed to the blameless way.
> When wilt thou come to me?
> I will walk within my house in the integrity of my heart.
> I will set no worthless thing before my eyes.

That last phrase grips me. How many times a day must I turn away if I am to avoid setting a "worthless thing before my eyes"? It's not just what we see that leads to trouble. Suggestive music lyrics and the increasingly sexually oriented topics of certain radio and television talk shows are two nonvisual temptations.

Here are some thoughts from both Barbara and me concerning mastering the media instead of being manipulated by the messages:

• *Know what you believe.* How will you be able to distinguish the truth from lies in media if you don't know the Scripture's values on a variety of issues?

• *Be aggressive—not passive—about the media.* A media monster will enter our eyes, ears, minds, hearts, and houses like a flooding river washing over a dike if we allow it. Set some standards! For example with TV, watch on purpose. Decide in advance what you will view; don't just turn it on and surf. And when something offensive catches you by surprise—*turn it off!* Hold one another accountable to your standards.

• *Control the flow.* Watch what comes into your house. We haven't subscribed to cable TV because it would encourage us to watch more television. We know great programming exists on cable, but we don't think spending more time in front of the tube is a good idea. Someone needs to stand sentry at the media entrance to the family, carefully and prayerfully deciding what will be allowed in.

• *Guard your mind and heart.* If you allow yourself to create fantasy lovers through media sources, you stand in the courtyard of the house of adultery. This includes advertising as much as programming. Even news programs—with the increasing emphasis on celebrities—feed this fantasy mentality.

• *Don't depend on the movie rating system and movie reviews.* The movie rating system can be highly inconsistent. Find out about movies from friends who share your values. Consult reviewers with a similar Christian worldview. (The excellent Web site <www.screenit.com> describes the quality, morality, and specific language of any film being released.) Additionally, when you read movie reviews, pay attention to what the reviewer says about how sex and violence are used in the movie.

• *Control Internet access.* If you must have Internet service in your home, construct safeguards. Subscribe to an Internet access provider that screens out offensive material (one possibility is FlashNet Communications, 1-888-FLASHNET). Consider placing any computer with Internet access in a very public, heavily traveled place in your home, such as the kitchen or family room. Men, in particular, will benefit from accountability to another man—someone who asks, "Are you clean in what you're viewing?"

• *Use technology to your advantage.* Use the media to strengthen your marriage and family. (For instance, <www.familylife.com> contains down-loadable resources for your marriage and family.) Make the media serve your needs.

• *Realize that popularity doesn't always mean something is good.* Much of popular media, which reflects popular culture, is extremely low-brow. Just because something is popular, even within the church, does not mean it has redeeming value. Frequently, the opposite is true.

• *Consider cutting back on or even fasting from media use.* Have you ever tried going a whole day or week without watching television? What might happen in your marriage if you did? Our society has become media-dependent; we think we need media stimulation for entertainment. We're missing numerous enjoyable activities because we're lazy about unhooking our media umbilical cord.

• *Be accountable to one another for your use of different types of media.* During our first year of marriage, I wanted to go to a scary flick, but Barbara did not want to go. She told me she had trouble emotionally pro-cessing frightening films. Understanding her fully took me several years, but I came to realize she was a source of accountability for me. I have learned to honor her by not taking her to these kinds of movies and by not going alone. She has sharpened me when it comes to media consumption.

The Ultimate Media Filter

The apostle Paul gave us perhaps the best screening tool regarding the media: "Whatever is true, whatever is honorable, whatever is right, what-ever is pure, whatever is lovely, whatever is of good repute, if there is any excellence and if anything worthy of praise, let your mind dwell on these things" (Phil. 4:8).

(*For additional information on related topics, see Chapters 12 on family values, 23 on accountability, 42 on affair-proofing your marriage, and 44 on sabbath rest.*)

HomeBuilders Principle

For the good of your marriage,
guard what you allow to enter your eyes and ears.

TO THINK ABOUT INDIVIDUALLY

1. In what areas—if any—do you think the media threaten your marriage: time lost, distorted reality and expectations of your spouse, pornography, or Internet liaisons?

2. Do you need to make any changes in media use in your home? List ideas.

TO DISCUSS TOGETHER

Share your responses to the questions in the previous exercise. If you agree that changes in media use need to be made, write down new guidelines now.

TO TAKE ACTION TOGETHER

Together, keep a log for several days of all the different ways the media enter your home and daily activities. For example: "6:00 A.M.—woke up to morning radio talk show; 7:00 A.M.—briefly watched local forecast on the Weather Channel and checked Wall Street opening on the Internet; 8:00 A.M.—drove to work listening to radio talk program." What does your log indicate about the daily media consumption in your home?

42

"I Only Have Eyes for You"

AFFAIR-PROOFING YOUR MARRIAGE

I want to talk straight with you about one of the most dangerous issues you'll ever face in your marriage: an extramarital affair. An illicit relationship probably seems unimaginable right now, and that's good. But someday you or your spouse may be tempted. Read carefully.

Affairs are not always what we think they are. An extramarital affair is an escape from reality that begins with loneliness and isolation at home and ends with a search for need fulfillment outside marriage.

Although extramarital affairs are often sexual, other types of affairs occur. Career, hobbies, church work, sports, and entertainment can become escapes from the pain of a real relationship and hunts for fulfillment without your spouse.

The desire to escape is driven by our selfish, sinful nature and the pressures of the secular culture in which we live. From one end of the country (Madison Avenue) to the other (Hollywood) comes a barrage of advertising, TV programming, movies, and other schemes—all urging us to seek self-satisfaction. "You can have it all," they assert. "You deserve complete happiness."

Because of this pressure, you may embrace an improper perception of reality. As you compare your expectations and fantasies with your real life, you may wonder, *Why doesn't my love life match up with the one led by my favorite movie star? Why can't my mate be that cool/sexy/romantic?*

From there you may take a short, slippery step to questioning reality.

Instead of challenging your fantasies, you may look at life and think, *Wait a minute. Why don't we have all that passion and chemistry?* Instead of being wise, you may become a fool and trade God's plan for the world's (Rom. 1:22–23).

It's no wonder, then, that too many people take the next step into an extramarital affair. Instead of finding happiness and satisfaction in the real world with a real spouse, real children, and a real God, they chase their fantasies.

The Chemistry of Emotional Adultery

As I have mentioned, affairs occur in more than one way, but for the purpose of this chapter, I'm going to focus on emotional adultery.

High school chemistry taught me a valuable lesson: When certain substances come into close contact, they create a chemical reaction. One day during my senior year of high school, I decided to conduct an experiment. I dropped a jar full of pure sodium into a river and nearly blew up the bridge I was standing on. In my naïveté, I didn't realize how powerful the chemical reaction would be.

Husbands and wives don't always respect the laws of emotional chemistry. They mix volatile ingredients without giving much thought to the chemical reaction that can happen with someone other than one's mate. I'm not talking about sexual attraction per se. Before sexual indiscretion starts, a reaction of two hearts, the chemistry of two souls, takes place. In other words, people commit emotional adultery before they commit physical adultery. It starts when two people of the opposite sex talk with each other about intimate struggles, doubts, or feelings. They share their souls in a way that God intended exclusively for the marriage relationship. Emotional adultery is friendship with the opposite sex that goes too far.

Let's look at the typical scenario. The busy young computer programmer arrives at work, still simmering over the argument about finances with his wife the night before. He finds it increasingly difficult to talk to her about *anything* without fighting. When he walks into the office, he sees a coworker who is *always* easy to talk to, and she *always* treats him with respect.

One night they end up working late on a project together. It's innocent enough, but as they relax their guard during the late hours, they talk in ways they never did before about their lives, their struggles.

They stay and work late again, and he takes her home afterward. Nothing happens. Just a friendly, "Thanks for the ride," and he drives away. But then they have lunch together, and soon they decide that they need to discuss business over lunch at least once a week. Before long an attraction develops. The young programmer knows his coworker is really interested in him—and vice versa.

Back home, perhaps his wife is nagging him to fix the deck and change her car's oil. She reminds him of family decisions he must make, and soon he feels he doesn't need all the hassles. The responsibility of home feels heavy and restrictive; he'd rather have lunch with his new friend at work.

This man may not know it, but he is already having an emotional affair. And almost inevitably, the emotional affair turns into a physical one. Meanwhile, his wife senses she's losing her husband. She becomes hurt and lonely, but she doesn't blow up. Instead, she plays it cool and throws herself into her job, trying to find an identity of her own. A nice guy at her office begins paying attention to her, compliments her, and unlike her husband, actually talks to her. Next, he asks her to have lunch, and then . . .

With the easy availability of the Internet, a new form of emotional adultery has surfaced as men and women meet in chat rooms and share intimate conversations. Their electronic liaisons have resulted in countless heartaches and even divorce, as spouses leave their mates and families emotionally for a love found on a computer screen.

Even our churches are full of people deceived by fantasies. They don't realize that something better than a fantasy is under their own roofs in the reality of their marriage relationship.

The Danger Signs of Emotional Adultery

Whenever you develop an in-depth relationship with someone of the opposite sex, an attraction to that person can take place. Consider signs that this reaction is beginning to occur:

• You feel that your mate isn't meeting a need—for attention, approval, affection—and that other person meets your need.

- You talk about problems you are having with your spouse.
- You rationalize the relationship by saying that it must be God's will to talk openly and honestly with a fellow Christian. You become defensive about and protective of the relationship.
- You look forward to being with this person more than with your mate.
- You hide the relationship from your mate.

When you find yourself connecting with another person who becomes—in even the smallest way—a substitute for your marital partner, you're traveling down a dangerous road. How do you protect yourself and your marriage?

1. Know your boundaries. Put fences around your heart, and protect the sacred ground reserved only for your spouse.

2. Be aware of isolation and concealment. One strategy of the enemy is to isolate you from your spouse by tempting you to keep secrets from your mate.

3. Extinguish chemical reactions that may have begun. A friendship with the opposite sex that meets any needs your mate should meet must terminate quickly. Heed this simple rule of chemistry: To stop a chemical reaction, remove one of the elements. This means you! Run! Get out! Both of you know where it's headed.

4. Ask God to remind you to fear Him. The fear of God has turned me from many a temptation. It would be one thing for another person to learn I had compromised morally, but quite another thing to realize that God would have knowledge of my infidelity faster than the speed of light.

It has been said, "A secret on earth is open scandal in heaven." My heavenly Father and my earthly father are there right now. Thinking of hurting them keeps me pure. (A superb resource on this subject is *Torn Asunder: Recovering from Extramarital Affairs* by Dave Carder [Chicago: Moody Press, 1995].)

(For more on this topic, see Chapters 6 on communication, 17 on intimacy and transparency, 23 on accountability to spouse and others, 25 and 26 on romance, 31 on isolation, 35 on romantic getaways, 41 on managing the media, 46 on work-related travel, 47 on knowing when your marriage needs outside help, and 52 on the seasons of marriage.)

HomeBuilders Principle

To maintain purity, know your boundaries,
avoid isolation and concealment,
extinguish chemical reactions, and fear God.

TO THINK ABOUT INDIVIDUALLY

1. Analyze your relationships with members of the opposite sex other than your spouse. Have you ever been (or are you being) tempted to commit emotional adultery? Are you facing any temptations to commit emotional adultery via the Internet?

2. What are some other ways you can have an affair besides straying away to another person? Have you ever considered your career as an adulterous relationship? Is this a problem for your spouse?

TO DISCUSS TOGETHER

1. In what areas might both of you face the greatest temptation to commit emotional adultery? How can you help each other with these temptations?

2. If one or both of you work, rate how serious a threat your careers pose to your marriage. (1 = low threat; 5 = high threat)

His career   1   2   3   4   5

Her career   1   2   3   4   5

Why did you assign these ratings?

TO TAKE ACTION TOGETHER

A marriage is significantly "affair-proofed" when partners communicate freely, openly, and profusely and make romance and passion a high priority on the schedule. Remember to spend time together every day, have weekly dates, and go on getaways as often as possible.

43

Holidays

HONORING PARENTS WHILE BUILDING
YOUR FAMILY'S TRADITIONS

The thought expressed by the song "I'll Be Home for Christmas" is as likely to give someone a knot in the stomach as a longing in the heart. The issue of how to handle family expectations for holiday gatherings probably came up early in your marriage, if not before. *Where* and *how* you celebrate may cause culture shock.

Barbara and I had to deal with this because both families have wonderful holiday traditions. We adopted a common solution; one year we celebrated Christmas with Barbara's family, then went later to my folks. Next year, the schedule reversed.

But during my first Christmas visit to Barbara's family, I was shocked that they did not open presents in the "correct" way! To me, the orthodox approach was for one person at a time to open a gift. Everyone focused on the person receiving the present and smiled when the gift was opened; the recipient dutifully looked surprised and pleased, and then came the next person's turn. At Barbara's house, they distributed all the presents, and then chaos erupted. The race was on to see who could open presents first. I thought, *This isn't right!*

We've all experienced the discomfort of being used to one custom and then having to adapt to another. However, the challenge of the Christmas holidays is mild until the first child comes along. Now your parents are *grandparents*, and the stakes jump dramatically. When our children arrived, we realized that we needed to establish our own holiday traditions.

Making the Holidays Happy

Every family is truly unique. What we do will not apply in every situation, but we've learned some principles that can help you negotiate the challenge of managing holidays.

Honor Your Parents

How can you possibly honor your parents' wishes but establish your own family traditions?

Jesus reminds us of the command found in Genesis 2: "For this cause a man shall leave his father and mother, and shall cleave to his wife; and the two shall become one flesh" (Matt. 19:5). Scripture also commands us to: "Honor your father and your mother, that your days may be prolonged in the land which the LORD your God gives you" (Ex. 20:12). These two commands are not in competition with one another.

I can't offer an ironclad set of rules on what honors or dishonors parents concerning holiday visits. Frankly, the Holy Spirit is much better qualified to help you because He knows your specific circumstances and relationships. Yet what could honor your parents more than building an enduring, love-filled, God-honoring marriage that creates a safe nest for the *grand-children?* Establishing holiday traditions in your family cements your marriage and family identity. What parent could oppose that?

Your response might be, *Oh, yeah? You don't know my mom, dad, in-laws, and stepparents.* Like anyone else, parents are sinful; they may want you at home for selfish reasons. Some parents are manipulative. Ultimately, honoring your parents doesn't mean giving in to immature attitudes. You need to do what is right, long-term, for your marriage and family. And there is a way to do that and still honor your parents.

Cleave-Leave Tensions Often Surface in December

Letting a child go is one of the most difficult challenges of parenting. Don't be surprised that something as innocent as a holiday visit may reopen the "separation wound." If a mom or dad struggles with letting go, irritation over holiday plans may indicate that this is the case. This issue may help you appropriately sever the ties and better establish both your marriage and your family's holiday traditions.

Establish Your Own Traditions

You and your spouse need to establish your own holiday traditions. They include what you do in your own home, with your spouse and children, before and through Christmas Day. Of course, part of your traditions may involve activities with your parents. However, the focus needs to shift to *your home*.

Consider These Going-Home Guidelines

As part of honoring your parents, you will likely visit their home. Here are some ideas on how to do this without violating your emerging traditions:

• *Be flexible.* Perhaps occasionally, you will celebrate your family's Christmas a day or more early, then head to Grandma and Grandpa's.

• *Be proactive.* Address possible hurt feelings early. For example, call your parents and say, "We won't be coming home for Christmas this year because we want to establish our own family traditions. But we want to come home the weekend of Mom's birthday and have a tremendous celebration!" If parents know you aren't abandoning them, they will more easily accept potentially disappointing decisions.

• *Be brief.* We've found this rule to be helpful for any home visit (and we have a great relationship with all our parents): Never plan on staying more than three days on a family visit. A short visit that ends on a positive note is better than a long stay that rubs someone the wrong way.

• *Be firm.* Don't let nostalgia, the holiday spirit, or guilt-inducing comments sway you from doing what's right for your family.

• *Be kind.* Afterward, don't overanalyze or criticize your parents for mistakes. Parents need children to be compassionate to them too.

What About a Dysfunctional Family?

You may be asking, "But, Dennis, what if our family of origin is an ugly mess? What do we do if parents mistreat my spouse? Me? Or overindulge or hurt our children?"

You as a couple must establish guidelines and limits that protect you, your spouse, your relationship, and your family. In other words, if you go back home to an abusive parent or an alcoholic parent who ruins the time for everyone, you must decide in advance on your limits. Gently but firmly communicate those limits to your parents. Let them know what will happen if they behave in a certain way; then do exactly what you said.

Watch out for resentment. While visiting under difficult circumstances, you inevitably will see the unkind way your spouse is treated, or you will feel it. Practice forgiving and giving grace.

Holiday Tradition Tips for Your Family

As you establish your own family traditions, try these ideas:

• *Keep Christ central.* Make Christ the focus of your holidays. Continually ask yourself, What does it mean to be a follower of Jesus during the Christmas season? For starters, consider giving to those in need, inviting people without families to share your holiday joy, or especially emphasizing spiritual things in your home.

• *Deal proactively with holiday stress.* The season of peace and goodwill is the most stressful time of the entire year for many people. If you get uptight during the holidays, plan accordingly. Do you have too many holiday traditions? Has your focus shifted too much toward gift giving?

• *Confront your memories.* Holiday memories generally come in two varieties—good and bad. Both types can wreak havoc with your appreciation for Christmas's real meaning. If you have good memories, your expectations may rise so high that you end up disappointed with the state of your current experience. If your memories are bad, almost everything that happens around Christmas will renew your pain. Either way, it's better to deal honestly, openly, and prayerfully with your expectations about Christmas ahead of time.

• *Set and keep a budget.* Too many people get carried away with spending around Christmas. It often starts with a sincere desire to make children happy and then gets out of hand. Exchange gifts on a preplanned budget. Don't run up a large credit card bill to finance Christmas gifts.

- *Keep it simple.* Christmas traditions don't have to be elaborate, and you don't have to spend a lot of money to enjoy the season sincerely. Ultimately, love is all that is necessary.
- *Make it special.* Although the holiday season may bring problems, it is a fantastic time. With God's help, make Christmas memorable. Take your cues from Scripture, and use your common sense and creativity.

These are just a few ideas. The ones you come up with for your family will be better—the raw material of your own traditions and memories.

(*Additional information relevant to this topic is found in Chapters 4 on parents, 40 on vacations, and 50 on memory making.*)

HomeBuilders Principle

Your family needs its own holiday traditions.

TO THINK ABOUT INDIVIDUALLY

1. What are your childhood Christmas memories? Do you want holiday traditions in your family to be different? Why or why not?

2. What one tradition from your family of origin do you want to keep in your new family? Why?

3. What challenges to establishing your own family's traditions exist from your parents or your spouse's parents? What are some solutions that honor parents but also protect your family's need to build traditions?

TO DISCUSS TOGETHER

Share answers to the questions in the previous exercise. Agree on how to build proactively your own family traditions for next Christmas.

TO TAKE ACTION TOGETHER

Several months before Christmas, schedule an in-home date. Play some Christmas music and work together on specific ideas for the upcoming holidays. Discuss possible visits to parents, budget, special events to make Jesus central, and so forth.

44

"I Need a Break"

THE IMPORTANCE OF SABBATH REST

This woman's story expresses well how Barbara and I feel too often:

> My husband works a night shift, while I work days. Thus our cars always pass going in opposite directions on a street just a few miles from our house. When we pass, we both yell "I love you!" One day, after our rush-hour rendezvous, a man who had obviously witnessed this scene several times pulled up beside me at a stoplight. "Hey, lady," he said, "you two seem to like the looks of each other pretty well. Why don't you stop and introduce yourselves sometime?"

Like that couple, many others live lives that flirt with exhaustion. Wayne Muller writes that the standard greeting everywhere is "I am so busy." He goes on to say, "The busier we are, the more important we seem to ourselves and, we imagine, to others. To be unavailable to our friends and family . . . to whiz through our obligations without time for a single mindful breath—this has become the model of a successful life."[1]

He's right: We're a culture of weary people. And a significant part of our weariness is not because modern life is "so busy," but because we have forgotten or never learned how to rest.

Early in our marriage Barbara challenged how I spent the Sabbath. She questioned me when I worked. But mostly, she modeled a quiet Sunday, retreating to our bedroom to read a good book, study the Scriptures, and take a nap.

The decision to go on a Sunday night date also became part of our sabbath rest. We'd go out to eat, look over our schedules, and discuss issues in our marriage. Those dates became times of emotional and spiritual reconnection, islands of clarity for us as a couple (and later as parents).

How can you and your spouse break the day-in, day-out cycle of non-stop work and weariness?

Bring Back the Sabbath

Rest was important to God from the very beginning. He created for six days, then rested on the seventh.

But contrary to this pattern God established, the idea of sabbath rest is now foreign to our culture, and a rather novel thought for most Christians too. Gordon MacDonald states bluntly, "A rest-less work style produces a restless person . . . We do not rest because our work is done; we rest because God commanded it and created us to have a need for it."[2]

God knew we would need to get our bearings before plunging back into the daily grind. But adjusting to a sabbath pace isn't easy. Just try it! You'll probably experience how unnatural this day of rest is to us twenty-first-century Christians. We are definitely out of practice.

As I mentioned earlier, our family owes its sabbath practices almost solely to Barbara. She has fought for them in our home, and I have not always been cooperative. She wanted Sunday to be as God intended it— a day set apart to reflect and rest, to allow the soul to catch up with the body. I'll let her explain more of why the Sabbath is so important.

I (Barbara) find both parts of Exodus 34:21 intriguing. The first part is familiar: "You shall work six days, but on the seventh day you shall rest." However, we often overlook the second part: "Even during plowing time and harvest you shall rest." In other words, no matter how busy we are or how long the "to do" list is, we need a regular break. We're tempted to say, "I've got these few hours on Sunday afternoon. I could get a jump-start on the laundry, or I could run a couple of errands and catch up a bit." But if we compromise, we will miss what we desperately need the most—rest.

Dorothy Bass notes:

[In] *The Overworked American*, economist Juliet Schor reported that work hours and stress are up, and sleep and family time are down for all classes of employed Americans. Wives working outside the home return to find a "second shift" of housework awaiting them. Husbands add overtime or second jobs to their schedules. Single parents stretch in so many directions that they sometimes feel they can't manage. Simultaneously, all are bombarded by messages that urge them to spend more (and so, ultimately, work more), to keep their homes cleaner (standards keep rising), and to improve themselves as lovers, investors, parents, or athletes. Supposedly to make all this possible, grocery stores stay open all night long, and entertainment options are available around the clock. We live, says Schor, in "an economy and society that are demanding too much from people."[3]

That accurately describes our culture today. We don't know how to slow down, take a day off, or rest. And I admit it's not easy for us as a large family, either. But I wanted our children to learn that something needs to be different about Sunday. I wanted them to learn the importance of rest, to have time to think, to be still. I didn't want our children to grow up and be so busy, they couldn't hear God speak to them.

Suggestions for Successful Sabbath Making

One author said about the Sabbath, "We would do well to heed three millennia of Jewish reflection on the Sabbath commandment. Not good are *work* and *commerce* and *worry*."[4] That's a succinct summary of how "to do" Sabbath. Here are some other thoughts:

• *Recognize that work is not life.* Margie Haack comments on the proper attitude about work, which often inappropriately consumes us: "Work is never done. A lot of it doesn't need to be done today. If, while you are resting, someone else wants to run the country, let them do it . . . While I am obeying God's command to rest, he will kindly run the universe."[5]

• *Make Sunday (or your Sabbath) special.* Start preparing at least the day before the Sabbath. For example, if any of our children have homework due on Monday, we ask them to complete it by Saturday night. On

Sunday, we worship as a family. For the remainder of the day, we limit out-going phone calls to family members only. The house stays quieter—time for naps, reading, recreation, relationship building. We avoid the usual activities that drain energy and time and can bring worry, such as shopping or bill paying.

What if you have to work on Sunday? Many millions do—including all of those pastors who deliver sermons on Sunday morning. If necessary, observe your Sabbath on another day or part of a day. The *idea*, not strict observance, counts.

• *Work together as a couple to learn what brings true rest for you as individuals, as a couple, and later as a family.* For some, rest means recreation, such as a hike or jogging. For others, rest may include taking a nap or hanging out with the family.

• *Remember that worship is an integral part of a day of rest.* Without question, worshiping in a local church is necessary on the Sabbath and can continue at home after the church service. Fill your home with the soothing sounds of hymns or praise music that exalts the Lord God Almighty and turns your heart toward Him.

• *Without becoming legalistic, continue to discuss and refine together the ways you experience sabbath rest.* Some of the most stimulating discussions Barbara and I have had concern the activities that encourage sabbath rest. Should we rake leaves, fix meals, watch football, wax the car? To what extent will we try to protect our lives, marriage, and family from the world on this special day? Be purposeful about your day of rest together. Make it a spiritual discipline.

Honoring the Sabbath is like having a family wheel alignment once a week. If you're not able on a regular basis to reflect on where the family is headed, in two or three months you can slowly drift off track and end up in a ditch. For the spiritual, emotional, and physical health of everyone in your family, take a sabbath break every week.

(For further study of this topic, see Chapters 12 on family values, 22 on balancing work and family, 35 on getaway escapes, 38 on scheduling, 40 on vacations, 50 on building memories, and 51 on legacy).

HomeBuilders Principle

Rest restores relationships.

TO THINK ABOUT INDIVIDUALLY

1. What has been your experience with the idea of sabbath rest—from childhood until now? What would you like to change in your life and the life of your family concerning sabbath observance?

2. Dream awhile: What activities—or lack thereof—would be included in your perfect Sabbath?

TO DISCUSS TOGETHER

Discuss your answers to the questions in the previous exercise. What similarities emerged in your ideas of the perfect Sabbath?

TO TAKE ACTION TOGETHER

If you've never done this as a couple/family, plan a sabbath rest. Don't expect this to go without a hitch the first time—we compulsively busy people usually have a difficult time slowing down. But if you stick with it, you won't want to go back to living week after week without your sabbath break.

Part 5

45

Say Something Nice

BLESSING AND ENCOURAGING YOUR SPOUSE

I clearly recall the day my high school typing teacher leaned over her desk after I had disrupted class again and said, "Dennis Rainey, you'll never amount to anything!"

Those words really hurt. I've never forgotten them. Fortunately, I had many other teachers and parents who believed in me.

You, too, have likely been wounded by words hurled at you like sharp arrows. And some of the most hurtful verbal missiles come from those closest to you, including your mate. Thoughtless words can chip away self-esteem and erode intimacy in your marriage.

The opposite is also true. You can build your mate's self-esteem with the words you speak. Your tongue can be a paintbrush that adds splashes of vibrant color through words that affirm and encourage.

When you're first married and entranced with the other person and with what he or she does right, you're oblivious to what your spouse does wrong. But by the end of the first year, your thinking reverses; having become oblivious to what your spouse does right, you focus on what he or she does wrong, harping and nagging on the negative things.

Robert Louis Stevenson said some wise words that apply: "Make the most of the best and the least of the worst."

The Power in Blessing Your Spouse

The apostle Peter offered this advice: "Let him who means to love life and see good days refrain his tongue from evil and his lips from speaking guile. And let him turn away from evil and do good; let him seek peace and pursue it" (1 Peter 3:10–11). When Peter talked about refraining your tongue from evil, he meant you should change your natural tendency to lash out, fight back, or tell your mate off. But you can't do this without God's help, without yielding to the Holy Spirit's power.

Peter went on to say that being a blessing means turning away from evil. To apply this to marriage, picture stepping aside or refusing to retaliate when your partner gets angry. Perhaps circumstances—the end of a tough day or too much hassle—have aroused hostilities in your spouse. Instead of digging in to fight for your rights, step aside and give a blessing.

And how do you do that? Peter said, "Do good." Doing good depends on the situation. Sometimes doing good means a few words spoken gently and kindly, or perhaps a touch, a hug, or a pat on the shoulder. Being a blessing also means seeking and pursuing peace.

I see many newly married couples getting assaulted by the same problems that lie in wait for them, much as a mugger lies in wait in a darkened doorway. You don't have to do this! When conflicts and problems come up, you can say together, "No, we're not going to respond with hurtful words. Instead, we can seek peace and oneness by giving a blessing."

Encourage Her with Affirming Words
A MESSAGE TO HUSBANDS FROM DENNIS RAINEY

To encourage and bless your wife, consistently affirm her with pleasant, loving words. Let her know verbally that you value, respect, and love her. I've discovered that I can't express too much affirmation.

Some evenings I come home, and I'm absolutely amazed at how busy Barbara has been for me and the children. Running errands, settling squabbles, fixing meals—the list is endless. Occasionally, I'll miss my cue to encourage her, and she'll say, "You know what I would like you to do? Just tell me you appreciate what I'm doing for you!"

When Barbara says something like that, I realize I've failed to notice that her emotional tank is running low. I can try to refill it by saying, "Sweetheart, you're terrific!" or "You're the greatest!" And it's even better when I'm more specific:

- "I appreciate your efforts to keep my clothes clean and pressed. You're incredible!"
- "Thanks for looking so nice today."
- "Thanks for being there—for always putting the children and me ahead of yourself."
- "I appreciate always being able to count on you to follow through, no matter what."
- "Thank you for being faithful to me."

Solomon had such words in mind when he wrote, "How delightful is a timely word" (Prov. 15:23).

Show Him Respect Through Appreciation
A MESSAGE TO WIVES FROM BARBARA RAINEY

Today society often emphasizes a woman's personal needs, wants, and desires—in short, her fulfillment. I don't believe a woman is supposed to have no interests nor activities outside her husband and family, but the biblical approach for every person, regardless of gender, is not to focus on self. We're called to give attention to our husbands and what they need.

And our husbands have many needs. The macho man who is self-contained, independent, and invulnerable is a myth. To bolster Dennis's confidence, I encourage him by being his fan, by believing in him.

I demonstrate my confidence in Dennis by offering him abundant respect, which includes reverencing him, noticing him, regarding him, preferring him, esteeming him, and appreciating him.

The word *appreciate* means to "raise in value." When I tell Dennis that I appreciate him, I raise his value in his own eyes as well as mine. That gives him more self-esteem and a better self-image as a man. Here are some statements I often make to Dennis:

- "I appreciate how hard you work to provide so many things for me and the family."
- "I love the way you interact with and nurture our children."
- "I admire your commitment to become a more godly man."

- "You are really good at _____."
- "I know you're facing a big challenge at work now, but I know you can do it. You're so talented."

For both husband and wife, learning the art of encouraging and affirming each other is a prerequisite for a healthy and godly marriage.

(For more on the topic, see Chapters 6 on communication and 32 on listening.)

HomeBuilders Principle

Encourage each other with words
that build up instead of tear down.

TO THINK ABOUT INDIVIDUALLY

1. In the past seven days, how many specific instances can you recall where you blessed your spouse with encouraging words? Do you want to make any changes?

2. In what ways does your spouse bless you with his or her words? Think of some specific examples. Write down how you feel when your spouse speaks to you in this way.

TO DISCUSS TOGETHER

Take turns sharing your answers to question 2 in the previous exercise. If either or both of you are having difficulty blessing the other with encouraging words, pray about this as a couple. This is not the time for accusations; rather, encourage each other with the help of the Holy Spirit to improve as time goes on.

TO TAKE ACTION TOGETHER

Take paper and pens, and go out for coffee. Spend fifteen to twenty minutes writing a "blessing note" to your spouse, listing all of the qualities and deeds for which you are thankful. Read your list to each other.

46

Road Warrior

KEEPING YOUR MARRIAGE TOGETHER
WHEN TRAVEL HAS YOU APART

*H*ave you heard the old saying that "absence makes the heart grow fonder"? I think that saying misses the mark. If anything, especially for newly married couples, absence can make the heart *wander*. In reality, the problems you experience when you are together are exacerbated when you are separated by travel. And our adversary uses your being divided by distance as a means to diminish your oneness.

To disarm travel-related issues, the two of you must agree that the work necessitating the travel is important and God's plan for the road warrior. If after prayer and discussion you both agree that the job is God's will, then dealing with the stress and inconvenience will be easier.

While both men and women take business-related trips in significant numbers, men make more than women do. Consequently, our discussion will center on the scenario of the husband on the road while the wife stays near the home front.

A Map for the Road Warriors

We hope that these ideas reduce the damaging effects of business travel on your marriage:

Planning and Preparation

As much as possible, don't leave packing and preparation until the last few hours at home. If you're rushed and feeling stressed, the chances of upsetting your spouse and provoking conflict rise steeply. If conflict or an argument occurs, do your best to resolve tensions before you leave. The next best thing is to call from the airport or to stop immediately along the highway at your first opportunity. Say those powerful words: "I'm sorry, Honey." Don't let a negative situation fester.

When you say good-bye, always kiss, hug, and say tender words from your heart. Leave a memory that speaks loudly of your love and commitment.

Communication

Separation is the worst part of the road warrior scene. Probably the best communication tool for the road warrior remains the telephone. E-mail is another option, but then your wife can't hear your voice. When I'm gone, I try to call home once a day—sometimes more often if there is a lot happening in our family. And if I'm in my hotel room when I call Barbara, I turn the TV off—no ESPN with the sound muted!

Don't forget the ultimate communication method—prayer, which is a superb end to each phone conversation. As much as prayer binds you together when you are at home, it's needed more when you are separated.

Loneliness

Every person on the road has come back after dinner to a sterile hotel room and thought, *Oh, man, I wish I could be home. I feel so lonely.* It can be a time of real vulnerability. The tempter will attack. Cling to God's truth as you confront any desire to sin. Remember this promise found in 1 Corinthians 10:13: "No temptation has overtaken you but such as is common to man; and God is faithful, who will not allow you to be tempted beyond what you are able, but with the temptation will provide the way of escape also, that you may be able to endure it."

One of the solutions to loneliness is to spend time with people, but beware of the company you keep. The verse "Bad company corrupts good morals" (1 Cor. 15:33) is not just for teenagers battling peer pressure. It's far better for you to spend an evening feeling alone in your room, seeking the comfort and companionship of Jesus, than to find fellowship with the wrong crowd.

A friend shared with me what he does: Take a bit of "home" with you by packing a framed picture of your wife and setting it beside your bed in the hotel room. It will remind you of your love and commitment to her.

Spiritual Life

Avoiding temptation and walking with God while on the road demand deliberate choices:

• Be accountable. Find a sincere Christian brother who will keep you honest by asking what television shows or movies you're watching, what kinds of business entertainment you're pursuing, and what other choices you're making that are a potential problem. Tip: When you check in, ask that all movie channels in your room be turned off.

• Do not neglect your devotional life. I know how hectic it gets, but schedule an "appointment" for at least fifteen minutes of prayer and Scripture meditation each day.

• Seek outside spiritual support. Jim Cote, coauthor of the book *On the Road Again*, advised on our radio program, "Give yourself some structure out of town that helps you to grow and mature in Christ. Go to a Wednesday night church service . . . If you go to the same cities, develop an accountability group of people in those cities that you can meet with when you are there."[1]

Decisions and Emergencies

An immutable law of life is that the washing machine will spring a leak or the car will die when the road warrior is away. Be prepared. Keep your cars well maintained. If your washing machine sounds as if it's about to hemorrhage, call the repairman when you are home. But when the inevitable decision concerning a family member or an emergency occurs and you're a thousand miles away, don't wimp out on your responsibility. Do what you can. Focus on the most critical, pressing items first. And if your wife has a long list of decisions and problems, listen respectfully to all of them. She may just need to talk and know that you are listening.

Before you leave, check with a friend or two at home who can be available to help out in emergencies.

Special Touches

It's always nice to bring home a surprise. Be creative—you don't have to buy an overpriced coffee mug at the airport gift shop. Maybe your surprise will be a love letter you wrote that night when you were lonely in the hotel room. Maybe it's a single rose you bought from the corner vendor. Do something! It always says, "I care about you and I thought about you while I was gone."

Reentry

The road warrior's arrival at home can be a letdown. The anticipated welcome-home-honey embrace may instead be a half-hearted hug from a weary mate. Lower your expectations. Go home anticipating reality. Check out the situation and the mood. Do what you can to serve your mate instead of expecting royal treatment. And don't initiate lovemaking within the first thirty minutes of your arrival. Waiting a night may say to your wife, "I love you more than I love me!" After crises are resolved, bruises bandaged, and the tire changed on the car, some of your expectations can be met.

If business travel regularly separates you and your wife, the two of you must have candid conversations about expectations regarding sex. God's plan is that both husband and wife share their bodies for the purpose of sexual pleasure. If you are both at home most of the time, how this happens can be more spontaneous. But if one person is gone frequently, you need to communicate honestly your needs and work together to make sure they are met. Neither wife nor husband should feel slighted, or the enemy will exploit this healthy desire for sexual intimacy. It is neither less romantic nor exciting to schedule a sexual encounter with your spouse.

Your wife has high expectations too. She looks forward to seeing you and being with you, but she also longs for affirmation and acknowledgment of the responsibility she has carried.

Travel is a necessary part of life for many of us. God knows that, and He will protect your marriage and family in the process. But if you ever sense that a demanding travel schedule threatens your marriage, ask God to help you find another job. This choice is excruciating, but there will always be another road warrior to take your spot. No one else can fill your unique role as a husband and father.

(For additional information on related topics, see Chapters 6 on communication, 17 on intimacy, 19 and 20 on teamwork, 22 on blending career and family, 25 and 26 on romance, 41 on managing the media, and 42 on affair-proofing your marriage.)

HomeBuilders Principle

Partners separated by travel
must work harder on their marriage.

TO THINK ABOUT INDIVIDUALLY

1. If you must travel often on business, are you convinced that this job is God's will for you? Why do you feel the way you do?

2. What issues of business travel and separation from your spouse cause the most difficulty for you? For your spouse? What might you do to make adjustments?

TO DISCUSS TOGETHER

Review answers to the questions in the previous exercise. If you both agree that the job and travel are necessary, thank God for His provision and discuss how to make your separations easier. If you're concerned that the job may not be God's will, pray together, seek godly counsel, and begin the process of finding new employment.

TO TAKE ACTION TOGETHER

If it's at all possible, make arrangements to travel together for all or some of a business trip. Doing this will heighten the wife's understanding of the road warrior's challenges as well as provide a fun getaway.

47

Help!

KNOWING WHEN YOUR MARRIAGE
NEEDS OUTSIDE ASSISTANCE

*E*very marriage needs help. Perhaps yours, after a few months or years of marriage, needs help now. Or maybe any real difficulty in your relationship is far down the road. But at some time during a crisis or trial, every marriage will benefit from the counsel and care of someone on the "outside."

In America, where we worship self-sufficiency, seeking help may seem shameful or weak. But those who are teachable and follow Jesus know better. We understand our limitations—the frailty of our flesh and our inclination to sin. We understand that we need others, just as they need us. This is the wonder of being part of the body of Christ: We don't have to be totally self-sufficient and independent. When necessary, we can lean on the gifts and strength of our brothers and sisters. We need one another.

Tune-up Help for Your Marriage

Before concluding that your marriage is falling apart, commit to praying about the problem. Ask God for insight and help on the issue you're struggling with.

Involvement with a local church and its members will only strengthen your marriage. Call a couple in your church and ask them to join you for lunch after Sunday worship. When couples get into trouble, especially early in marriage, they think they are the only ones in the world who have ever had this problem, whether it is finances, sex, communication, or in-laws. Meeting regularly with an older couple over a period of six to twelve months may be all you need to work through an issue.

It is also good for newly marrieds to spend time as individuals with another newly married person of the same sex. A kindred-spirit friendship will take some of the pressure off the marriage relationship. Women, who often have a higher need to talk about their feelings, may reap particular benefits from this idea. Marriage is a huge adjustment. Having the opportunity to share some of the built-up relational "heat" with someone on the outside will bring relief. It can be as simple as an occasional Saturday morning breakfast or lunch. But keep the discussion honoring to your mate, not a tear-down session.

Spending time with an older mentor of the same sex may also be very beneficial. During our third year of marriage, we moved to Dallas, our third move in as many years. Barbara hadn't really found a close friend in the previous two locations, and she *really* needed a female friend to talk to. Eventually, she started meeting every other week with a woman who'd been married fifteen years.

I will never forget the look on Barbara's face after one of her first meetings. It was the look of "I'm really not weird for feeling the way I feel." She found out that some of the challenges and adjustments she was facing in our marriage were normal. Meetings with this older mentor lifted a huge burden off Barbara's back. She no longer condemned herself or felt guilty for feeling what she was feeling. Even though I was telling her she was okay, it took a person of the same sex who could identify with what Barbara was feeling to reassure her fully.

Always focus on the positive as a couple. Review your marriage covenant or vows, which will remind you of your promises to each other. Our promises are the anchor that holds us steady when the marital storms blow.

Above all, don't wait until you are knee-deep in alligators in your marriage. Stay on the offensive in keeping your relationship out of trouble.

Crisis Help for Your Marriage

When is it time to get outside help for a marriage? That's not an easy question to answer because every marriage has pain. And part of growing toward deeper intimacy is resolving conflict and differences in a loving manner. But just as a broken arm requires a trip to the emergency room, certain events in marriage require outside assistance. This list is not exhaustive, and even some of the things I've mentioned are somewhat subjective, but every couple needs to pay attention to these danger signs:

• Unceasing conflict, vicious arguing, and/or yelling, that never seems to get any better.
• No sex, unusual demands for particular sexual behavior by one partner, persistent unhappiness of one partner with the sexual relationship.
• Abuse—physical or verbal, either spouse to spouse or parent to child. Verbal abuse is often subtle. If one person consistently uses his or her words to demean, control, and shame the other, especially with high doses of anger, this is verbal abuse.
• Regular, complete shutdowns of communication that persist for more than a day or two, with core issues never getting resolved. By this, I mean a husband and wife barely talking to each other or merely exchanging brief sentences without emotional warmth.
• An extramarital affair—either physical or emotional.
• Pornography use.
• Drug or alcohol abuse by one or both spouses.
• Other obsessive, destructive behavior, such as uncontrolled spending with credit cards.

In prayer ask the Lord to reveal to you where you should seek help and godly advice: "Blessed is he who walks in the counsel of the godly" (Ps. 1:1). Call on your church to rescue your marriage. If that does not seem satisfactory, call a counselor; share with a trusted friend; call a hot line—local or national; call your family. Help is available, and the Lord will provide. But you must be willing to go and seek help.

I recommend not seeking help in a lawyer's office. Many fine attorneys would work to keep a couple from divorcing, but many more make large sums of money from the divorce industry. Don't play into the enemy's hands and go to a lawyer who will create an adversarial relationship between you and your spouse. Remember, don't ever use the *D* word.

When you are in crisis, you can do the following:

• *Be patient.* Your situation probably took time to develop; it will take time to resolve. Men especially should heed this advice. We often want to fix a relational problem as we would repair a car: a two-hour tune-up at the service center. A guy may hover over his wife and not give her enough time and space. She needs to see and feel his love, not be bombarded with verbal promises.

When couples are stuck in a rut, they hope a magic wand can be waved over their relationship that will bring instant healing and love forever. That's not real life as God intended it to be. We grow through our struggles.

• *Show your true heart.* Too often when a husband and a wife are at odds, they allow the anger of the moment to cover up their true feelings. Don't do that. Tell the truth: "I'm mad at you, but I still love you. I want our marriage to be all that God intended. I want you to know that I'm going to pray. I'm going to be teachable. I want to hear from God about my responsibility for this."

• *Remind your spouse of your commitment.* I've repeated this several times, but a marriage covenant gives you the trust commitment that enables you to be real and solve problems. Without this covenant, your marriage is reduced to a contract that can be canceled at any time. Marriage is not a contract; it is a sacred and holy lifetime pledge to another.

• *Pray.* Pray for yourself, your spouse, and your relationship. Ask God for wisdom to handle your trials (James 1:2–8). Even when things are intense, do not stop praying with each other.

Marriage problems are not all bad. God can use such trouble in your marriage to drive you back to Him—the red light on the dashboard of your car letting you know that something is wrong.

Pain can cause you to go deeper in your relationship with each other. Early on, Barbara and I faced tough issues that challenged our commitment to one another. Not once, however, did we ever talk about quitting or getting a divorce. Our commitment to Jesus Christ and to each other saw us through. God will give you courage. He said, "Call upon Me in the day of trouble; I shall rescue you, and you will honor Me" (Ps. 50:15).

(For other information related to this topic, see Chapters 10 on conflict, 23 on accountability, 36 on choosing a church, 39 on facing tough circumstances, and 42 on affair-proofing your marriage.)

HomeBuilders Principle

Every marriage needs help.
When it's your turn, ask for it.

TO THINK ABOUT INDIVIDUALLY

1. What areas, if any, in your marriage might benefit from outside help—maybe just time spent with another couple?

2. If you ever experienced a crisis in your marriage, where and from whom would you seek help? List specific resources and names.

TO DISCUSS TOGETHER

Lovingly share your answers to question 1 in the previous exercise. If both agree that outside help is needed on a particular issue, discuss next steps. Where will you seek help? When?

TO TAKE ACTION TOGETHER

This was a heavy chapter. Express your joy and thanksgiving for the beautiful marriage God made when He put you two together. Go celebrate!

48

Don't Forget to Laugh

LIGHTENING UP YOUR MARRIAGE AND YOUR LIFE

I've always placed a high premium on fun and laughter in our marriage. In fact, a slight scar on the left side of my face reminds me of how much I like to make Barbara laugh.

One night in bed we were talking, and I started teasing her (something that comes naturally to me), and she teased me back. I looked over at her, sitting there feeling smug, pleased with herself for her clever jab back at me. All of a sudden, I reached for her rib cage because she is ticklish. As she instinctively grabbed for my hands, her diamond ring scratched my cheek, taking with it a microscopic layer of skin and pigment. For days, I milked that for all I could. Now when I get a little sun on my face, that scar becomes slightly evident—reminding me that I shouldn't have tickled my wife!

God gave us the gift of laughter to ease the difficulty of life on this troubled planet. Solomon wrote that there was "a time to laugh," and I agree with Martin Luther, who once said, "Heaven is the birthplace of laughter." I like to think of laughter as one of God's lubricants for life. Maybe that's another way of saying, "A joyful heart is good medicine, but a broken spirit dries up the bones" (Prov. 17:22).

I learned many wonderful things from my parents, but one of the best lessons was to enjoy laughter. A treasured memory from childhood is being made to laugh so hard that tears streamed from my eyes. My mom and dad knew how to have fun and laugh. Practical jokes, teasing, and spontaneous fun filled our home. My dad, Ward, had a rumbling laugh, and my mom has a finely tuned sense of humor, which she still uses with consummate skill at age eighty-seven. She has always been a real character. One Christmas, she gave herself a new vacuum cleaner. Under the tree was a huge wrapped package with a tag that read, "To my dear wife, from Ward."

Early in our marriage Barbara accused me of going to great lengths to get her to smile. She said more than once, "Your goal in life is to make me laugh, isn't it?" I replied, "Sounds pretty good to me!" (Nearly twenty-eight years later, she's still saying that!)

We should never take life so seriously that we think God's entire kingdom work depends upon us. We should never be so busy that we have no time for fun. And we should not become so weighed down by the cares of this life that our spouses seem to hinder us from achieving our "important objectives."

Laughter is the medicine intended to cure the disease of self-importance. It's hard to puff yourself up to weather-balloon size if you can deflate yourself with a good prick of self-directed humor. How many laughs are you having—some at your own expense? Have you as a couple claimed the promise, "He will yet fill your mouth with laughter, and your lips with shouting" (Job 8:21)? Before the wedding ceremony, many couples need to have a bold objective for their first year of marriage: *Over the next year, we will be found guilty of having too much fun rather than too little fun.* That's not a bad objective for *any* year of marriage.

The joy of courtship, coupled with romance and laughter, usually characterizes dating, but this joy can quickly dry up after marriage. Courtship, romance, and laughter go hand in hand because they demand focus. After we get married, our focus splinters in many different directions, especially after we have children. That's why we need to make it a priority in marriage to find ways to participate in the fun, laugh-generating antics we did when we first dated. That means we must flee from the television, telephone, and computer and *focus* on each other.

When couples stop laughing together, they stop sharing intimately. You'll find plenty of moments in your marriage—even in the early days—when you mourn over a loss or over what marriage may have cost you. That's why it's so important to find time to laugh and seek to please each other.

Pleasing Each Other with Laughter

The apostle Paul knew that it would be natural in marriage for each person to want to please the other (1 Cor. 7:33). At the heart of pleasing another person is the desire to create a smile on your spouse's face. Here are some ideas on how to please each other with smiles and laughter:

• *Become a student of what pleases your mate.* What brings a smile to the face, to the soul? Keep a list in your computer or calendar filled with all sorts of ideas of what makes your partner happy.

• *Consider what made your spouse laugh early in your relationship.* Don't think that you always need new material! This "audience of one" who loves you will appreciate the old gags, expressions, and words that first sparked laughter in your relationship.

• *Do something absolutely unplanned and positively spontaneous.* Marriage has robbed many a relationship of its fun. We forget what it's like to drop everything and do something for the sheer fun of it.

• *Relive the times you have enjoyed the most pleasure and fun together.* You will find that some of the great laughs came about spontaneously because you were together doing fun stuff.

• *Learn the art of not taking each other or life too seriously.* Life has a way of becoming heavy and weighing you down. If you're not careful, you will lose the joy and sheer pleasure of being together.

• *Spend focused, regularly scheduled time together.* Barbara and I have our Sunday night date. Often we do the same things we did while dating. These weekly times together don't always bring nonstop laughter. But because we are together, away from the usual distractions and pressures, there's a good chance we will have some fun.

• *Read your spouse a funny story.* Call from work to share a humorous situation. Don't be guilty of dumping heavy emotional loads on your spouse.

• *Do something absolutely frivolous with your spouse.* When was the last time you did something really silly with your wife or husband—something that couldn't help provoking laughter? You took those risks when you dated. Why not try them now? Having a few laughs a week is not excessive.

We all know that life is definitely not a barrel of laughs. But laughter is a gift given to help us keep life in balance, to put the "frosting" on the joy that God has promised us even in the middle of difficult times.

> There is an appointed time for everything. And there is a time for every event under heaven . . .
> A time to weep, and a time to laugh;
> A time to mourn, and a time to dance. (Eccles. 3: 1, 4)

In your lives together there will be plenty of times when you will mourn. Why not work on laughing and dancing in your marriage?

(For more on related topics, see Chapters 25 and 26 on romance, 35 on get-away escapes, 40 on vacations, 44 on sabbath rest, and 50 on building memories.)

HomeBuilders Principle

Laughter is the daily medicine that helps keep every marriage healthy.

TO THINK ABOUT INDIVIDUALLY

1. How was laughter a part of your home when you were a child?

2. Does laughter spill from your heart into the lives of others? Why or why not?

3. What about your mate's sense of humor attracted you when you were dating? What's your favorite fun moment together?

4. What ideas do you want to implement that will insure your marriage is "guilty" of having too much instead of too little fun?

TO DISCUSS TOGETHER

Share and reflect on your answers to the questions in the previous exercise. Together take the laughter pulse of your marriage: How are you doing in taking daily doses of this merry medicine?

TO TAKE ACTION TOGETHER

Do something that will make you giggle, laugh, roll on the floor with glee—just completely lose it in fun. Maybe you need to rent the funny movie that always cracks you up. You know what to do—laugh it up, live it up!

49

Stress

TAMING LIFE'S PRESSURES

*I*f you want your marriage to go the distance, you will have to manage stress effectively. I frequently tell our children, "You have the least amount of responsibility you will have for the rest of your lives!" This, too, is true of you as a newly married couple. Life will never again be as simple as it is right now. Growing complexities of life (and stress) will come with job promotions, moves, house mortgages, yard work, children, and even church.

The young couples I've known and counseled over the past two decades of ministry have underestimated the unending demands of life that cause them to be overcommitted, overextended, and overloaded. The hustle and bustle of life turn into a blur of hurried activity.

Pressures come from two directions: what other people expect of you and what you expect of yourself. You can easily let yourself be driven by the agendas of other people. Externally, their voices form a deafening chorus, incessantly telling you what you ought to do.

When we were in our first years of marriage, I made a list of a few things expected of me by outside forces:

• My CPA wants to know why I'm not keeping better records and whether I'm staying within my budget.

• My employers and colleagues want me to meet deadlines and do each task quicker, better, cheaper, always with a Christian attitude.

• Barbara wants me to help with redecorating and remodeling, moving furniture, and keeping things repaired.

• I need to consider personal exercise for my health, community involvement, church involvement, and parental expectations for how often we should visit.

• I need to be an understanding father and spiritual guide for my family.

• I'm expected to spend time and play with the kids, impart values to them, know their friends and what their parents stand for, be involved at their school, build a savings nest egg for their college education, and prepare them for adulthood.

Now here's the *real danger*: Pressure from a list like that could easily isolate Barbara and me from each other. I could be pulled one way and she another, our lives touching only at points. Many married couples who look as if they have it all together are nothing more than two highly productive and successful people doing their own thing. There is little time or energy for in-depth relating. While an illusion is created of the successful family, privately, the pressure can pry us apart.

Pressure and Stress Can Be Good or Bad

Hans Selye, a pioneer and expert in the study and treatment of stress, pointed out that stress itself is neither good nor bad. It depends on what it's doing to your system (e.g. your body, your company's organization, or your family).[1] All of us need some stress to conduct daily activities. The only people who lack stress are dead. The secret is to manage stress, not let it manage you. (One of the best stress managers is observing sabbath rest—a topic discussed in detail in Chapter 44.)

J. Hudson Taylor, a missionary who served in China for many years, said this about pressure: "It matters not how great the pressure is, only where the pressure lies. As long as the pressure does not come between me and my Savior, but presses me to Him, then the greater the pressure, the greater my dependence upon Him."

These words give me a tool to measure the pressures of life. As long as our schedules draw us closer to Christ, the stress is good. There is no such thing as a pressure-free, stress-free life. Perhaps in heaven we'll feel no pressure or be stress-free—knowing only total peace and contentment.

But here and now we have responsibilities, and responsibilities bring pressure and stress.

Barbara and I repeatedly find that we need to deal with stress in a way that builds oneness rather than creates isolation. This process is ongoing because every year the incline steepens and the pace accelerates.

A Stress Detector

Every marriage needs an early alarm system that can help the partners identify the tension level before a crisis. An excellent alarm system is accountability to each other, the scriptural principle that tells us to "be subject to one another in the fear of Christ" (Eph. 5:21). I choose to submit my life to the scrutiny of another person in order to gain spiritual strength, growth, and balance. Marriage is a perfect arena for this to happen as husbands become accountable to wives and wives to husbands.

What do I mean by being accountable to each other in marriage? Accountability gives each marriage partner freedom and access to the other. Accountability means asking the other person for advice, giving him or her the freedom to make honest observations and evaluations about you. It means you're teachable and approachable. It means you're willing to seek your spouse's opinion on a matter, and you're willing to hear what he or she has to say.

Early in our marriage, I began a habit of not saying yes to speaking engagements without first talking with Barbara. It was *not* the road of least resistance. On most occasions it would have been easier to have said yes. But this discipline has enabled us to be one in our schedules. She has been my anchor on more than one occasion—an anchor that brings me out of our stress-filled culture and back to a family that needs a husband and father.

Who Is in Control?

When dealing with stress or chaotic situations, I often ask myself, *Who is controlling you, Dennis? Is it your job, your neighbors, your friends, your children? Or is the Holy Spirit controlling you with your full permission?*

Solomon was right: "Like a city that is broken into and without walls is a man who has no control over his spirit" (Prov. 25:28). I know that if God isn't in control, my lines of defense will be down. People, schedules, and other forces will break in and control me and my family.

I want to challenge you now, early in your marriage, to establish the spiritual discipline of being dependent upon God and accountable first to Him, next to your mate, and then perhaps to a close same-sex friend. Otherwise, life will continually jerk you around, leaving you defeated—instead of a conqueror—over stress.

A Special Message to Husbands

While visiting with men, I often ask, "Are you accountable to anyone? Are you accountable to your wife? Does she have access to your life?"

Over the years, I have seen a number of men in the ministry bomb out due to sexual sin, materialism, bitterness, or carnality. I noticed a recurring pattern: Their lives were increasingly busy. They became isolated from the people who cared the most about them. They created for themselves invulnerable emotional walls, refusing to submit their lives to the scrutiny and advice of others. And they fell.

As a result, I have sought to lead a life full of accountability. I certainly have much to learn on the subject, but I have resolved to be teachable, approachable, and willing to hear what Barbara wants to say to me.

True accountability involves letting another person (in addition to your wife, a good same-sex friend) into the interior of your life. You have the choice to submit to another human being for perspective or advice, or even to be taken to task on something. Solomon declared that a wise man welcomes a helpful rebuke (Prov. 9:8).

I know of two men who hold each other accountable each month, asking each other tough questions about how they've spent their time in the past thirty days. And the last question is always, "Did you just lie to me?" In many cases, they have to admit to each other that they did fudge a little on the truth, then they discuss what they can do about it.

Finding a friend to hold you accountable can make a real difference. But you already have one friend to whom you should automatically be accountable—your wife.

(For more on this topic, see Chapters 2 on expectations in marriage, 19 and 20 on teamwork, 22 on blending career and family, 23 on accountability, 35 on getaway retreats, 38 on scheduling, and 44 on sabbath rest.)

HomeBuilders Principle

> Life's pressures will pull you away from God
> and your mate or press you closer to them.

TO THINK ABOUT INDIVIDUALLY

1. Take a serious look at your schedule. Where are the pressures coming from? At what points do you choose to put pressure on yourself because of your expectations or the expectations of others? At what points are the pressures caused by forces out of your control?

2. Pray about how accountable you are—first to God and then to your mate. How accountable are you willing to be?

TO DISCUSS TOGETHER

Talk about what is causing stress and pressure in your lives. Discuss what can be eliminated and what must be kept. Categorize the things that you can change and control and the things that you can't.

TO TAKE ACTION TOGETHER

Here's our gift to you to reduce some of your pressure—no "Take Action" assignment this time!

50

Celebrate!

MEMORIES HELP BIND A MARRIAGE
AND FAMILY TOGETHER

*T*he shared memories of a husband and wife beginning their married life, and later on with the addition of children, are like thick ropes binding a family into one tight unit. But you should know at the outset of your marriage and family that family identity and solidarity do not just happen. As you begin your family's journey together, you need to become skilled at producing memory makers and being memory collectors.

I'll never forget stopping at an overlook on Highway 36 just outside Boulder, Colorado. Barbara and I had been married only four days, and we were driving to our little apartment in Boulder. I pulled over to show her a view of our new home's setting. At that point all we had were wedding gifts, the same last name, and four days' worth of experiences together. Our family was brand new.

Nearly twenty-eight years later, our walls and bookshelves hold pictures and the memorabilia of experiences we've shared together. Thanks to these memory makers, and to Barbara for being a memory collector, our family has a clear fingerprint—a family identity uniquely ours among the six billion people in the world.

Memories are powerful family possessions profoundly linking hearts together. Both partners need to be diligent in planning memories (as well as enjoying those that come as surprises) and take necessary steps to save or catch memories.

Memory Making

Nearly any event has the potential to become a treasured memory. Let me illustrate. One weekend during our first few weeks of marriage, Barbara and I decided to drive four hours north to Wyoming to go fishing. When we arrived, we discovered the lake had been drained, so we impulsively decided to go to Yellowstone National Park and watch Old Faithful erupt. Eight hours later, we arrived just in time to see the eruption. We looked at our watches and realized we'd better head home! Obviously, that is *not* the way to see Yellowstone. But we had an absolute blast driving, talking, and laughing together. To this day, that adventure remains a fun memory of our early days together when we had no children.

Someone once said, "God gave us memories so that we could enjoy roses in January." Let me share with you what we've learned about creating a vase full of long-stemmed roses in the winter:

• *Memories are best made with those you love being with.* That's why a marriage and family is a ready-made unit for rich memories. Memories give us a common language of shared experience.

• *Memories take time.* Our best memories have been born out of extended time together. If we could have driven to Old Faithful in thirty minutes, I doubt that we'd even recall going.

• *Memories are made of varied adventures.* Too many of us get in a rut and don't realize the many wonderful ways to share our lives together. Barbara and I camped out on our honeymoon, got snowed on, and nearly froze to death, but I saved the day by zipping our sleeping bags together. We've traveled to forty-eight of the states and to faraway places (South Africa, Kenya, Egypt, Austria, France, Estonia, to name a few).

• *Memories are both planned and unplanned.* It's good to plan a great vacation. Memories are made as we create family traditions, such as our annual family Christmas tree cutting. But watch for the serendipitous memory. One midwinter night, the power went off, and we cooked supper over the fireplace. Don't lose your ability to be spontaneous and impulsive.

• *Memories are celebrated.* A memory isn't a memory if you don't talk about it, look at pictures of it, laugh or cry about it. "Do you remember the time . . ." can be a joyful introduction to a family conversation. One of our favorite questions to revisit as a couple or as a family is, If you could keep only one memory of all our years together, what would it be? Why?

Barbara and I have worked hard at creating a storehouse full of memories. Here's how we made many of the best of them:

Vacations

For me, vacations are times to strengthen relationships, have fun, and make memories. (See Chapter 40 for more on building vacation memories.)

Car Trips

In our first year of marriage, Barbara and I drove to Crater Lake, Oregon. The picture of Barbara in overalls climbing that mile-long trail still hangs in my office. It's my favorite shot of her.

Later when the children came along, we found that car trips are great for games. We often played a game called Beetle, Beetle, which involved spotting Volkswagen Bugs on the highway. Points were awarded depending on the color or position of the Beetle. We would yell, "Multicolor Beetle moving; that's four points!"

On one vacation I knew we were approaching a roadside junkyard that contained at least twenty Volkswagens. When we rounded a corner, I was ready! Before they knew what hit them, I rattled off about thirty points. The children groaned, one of them yelling, "Dad, you cheater." *Great fun!*

Holidays

Holidays are obvious memory makers, although holidays don't automatically guarantee they will be all good. (See Chapter 43 for more ideas.)

Family Celebrations

Anniversaries and birthdays should be observed with the same intensity we give to holidays such as Thanksgiving and the Fourth of July. By making a big deal of your anniversary, you not only honor your mate but also send a strong message to your family and others about the importance of your marriage covenant. And a birthday—this is the one day of the year when each person should feel totally unique, honored, and loved.

Achievements

When dad gets a promotion, when mom completes her master's degree, when a child hits a home run or takes first place at the music festival, celebrate and create a family memory.

Service to Others

At various times, Barbara and I—as individuals and as a couple—have taken our children on mission projects in America and overseas. Talk about great memory builders! We've shared exciting experiences while spreading the gospel and helping others.

Memory Collecting

I'm grateful for Barbara on this one. She has become the family curator and historian. You or your spouse needs to assume this role, or you'll forget a thousand memories.

A certain amount of record keeping and documentation helps a memory last. Taking still photos or having your video camera handy is a good way to do this, but also collect concert programs, tape recordings, newspaper articles—any object that records and preserves the memory. Creativity opens many possibilities.

In our house two entire sections of bookshelves are dedicated to family scrapbooks. They begin when we were single, and then every year from 1972 on has a scrapbook. Each singular, irreplaceable page logs the "official, authorized" history of our early married years and our family's memories.

Some years ago Barbara had the inspired idea of putting together a vacation book for each of the children. She'll tell the story.

When I (Barbara) was home-schooling our children, I had them keep a daily journal as a way of teaching them writing skills. This idea extended naturally to our vacations. I brought my camera and took pictures throughout the vacation.

Many times the children didn't want to journal, but I made them do it anyway. With the younger ones, I acted as scribe. I said, "Tell me what you did today," and wrote as fast as I could what they told me. Then they scrib-bled pictures.

They didn't appreciate the discipline then, but they appreciate having the books now. Many times they pull the journals off the shelf and enjoy looking at their drawings and pictures and reading about events.

These vacation books are humorous, but they record serious memories too. Here's an entry from Benjamin's journal written on a trip to Colorado in 1984. Beside a drawing of what must be an oil pump, he wrote, "We saw 200 oil pumps." Next he wrote, "Samuel invited Jesus into his heart, age 6." That important moment wouldn't be chronicled in any other formal manner if Barbara had not taken the time to encourage the children to do their memory books.

(For more on this topic, see Chapters 4 on the relationships with parents, 25 and 26 on romance, 35 on great escapes, 40 on vacations, 43 on holidays, 44 on sabbath rest, 51 on legacy, and 52 on the seasons of a marriage.)

HomeBuilders Principle

Memories are the unique language and history of every family.

TO THINK ABOUT INDIVIDUALLY

1. What are your best childhood memories? Why are they special to you?

2. What will you do personally to make sure your marriage and family have a large collection of good memories?

TO DISCUSS TOGETHER

Take turns sharing answers to the questions in the previous exercise. Having shared your individual thoughts on memories, how might you work together to be good memory makers and catchers?

TO TAKE ACTION TOGETHER

Take a memory break. If you haven't done well at collecting memories thus far, begin compiling a short history of your great family memories over a cup of coffee or a soft drink. Then start your family scrapbook ded-icated to a specific year of your marriage or a trip you took together.

51

A Legacy of Light

BUILDING A VISION FOR YOUR FAMILY'S FUTURE

Your marriage is not just for you. God intends for you as a couple to positively affect your family, your neighbors, and the world. This is called leaving a legacy.

The concept of leaving a legacy may be unfamiliar to many people. Leaving a legacy means that together spouses use their talents, treasure, and time to impact their world for Jesus Christ. Some understand leaving an inheritance but are not thinking much about leaving their kids with a legacy that reminds them of who they are, what is important in life, and what is their purpose.

Considering your legacy cuts against the grain in our selfish age. It requires pursuing personal spiritual growth, developing a godly family, and reaching out to others in the name of Jesus to change the world.

How to Leave a Legacy

There are two ways for you as a Christian couple to leave a legacy that is uniquely your own. The most obvious way is through physical descendants if God blesses you with children. You nurture them in Christ, seeking to develop their character so they become independently dependent on God. Then they carry their own Christian torch and hand it on to their children.

Maybe you don't have children yet. As you think about the legacy you would like to leave to your children, may I challenge you to evaluate your commitment to Jesus Christ? I've mentioned this earlier (see Chapter 9), but the most important thing we did in our first year of marriage was to give God the gift of our lives at Christmas.

Nearly twenty years later, when we reread what we had given God, we were amazed to realize that what we had given God was nothing (although it was everything at the time and felt like a huge sacrifice) compared to what He had done in our lives. He had given us a family beyond our expectations, a ministry that encircles the globe, and a marriage that has become more valuable with each passing day. He took a "smaller than a mustard seed" act of faith and blessed us profoundly.

Please don't miss this point as you begin this adventure with God: If you settle the issue of who has the ownership of your lives, you have no way of knowing how the Creator of the universe can use your surrender to Him to make your legacy mighty.

Maybe you already have children. When you look around the dinner table, what do you see? Runny noses? Cheeks streaked with spaghetti or the remains of an M & M overdose? Or do you see the next generation—the next mothers and fathers who will carry the torch of the gospel to a needy world?

I heard of one father who discovered the importance of his legacy and took steps to preserve and cherish it. He was addicted to television. He came home from work, turned on the tube, and watched it all evening until he fell in bed. He spent little or no time with his two children or his wife. The kids hardly knew they had a dad.

Needless to say, his marriage was hurting. His wife finally pulled this potato off his couch, and the two attended a FamilyLife Conference. That weekend God changed his life. He realized that his priorities were totally wrong and that he was setting a bad example for his children.

When the man got home the evening following the conference, he took the television set from the family room and hauled it to the garage. Then he took a family portrait he had stuffed away in a closet and hung it on the wall behind where the television set used to sit.

Next he called his wife and two children into the family room for a family council meeting. As he shared with them his new set of priorities and asked for their forgiveness, his twelve-year-old son interrupted him and said, "Daddy, now that there is a picture of our family where the television used to be, does this mean we are going to be a family?"

This husband and father made a giant step, from spending night after night doing nothing of value to deciding to be a dad who cared about his family. That's what a legacy is all about.

A second and equally important way to leave a legacy is through the investments you make while on planet earth to change people's lives for Christ. Your spiritual descendants—people you influence through the use of your talents, gifts, abilities, finances, and prayers—are the second component of your legacy.

You need to see beyond the problems in your family and look to a world that lacks the peace offered only by Jesus Christ. One of God's primary purposes for your family is to be a part of fulfilling the Great Commission, which Jesus gave His disciples: "Go therefore and make disciples of all the nations, baptizing them in the name of the Father and the Son and the Holy Spirit, teaching them to observe all I have commanded you; and lo, I am with you always, even to the end of the age" (Matt. 28:19–20).

When Jesus said, "Go therefore and make disciples of all the nations," He was talking to His disciples, common men like you and me. God never depends on paid professionals or highly trained technicians to do His work. Of course, He uses well-trained professionals, but He usually works through the average, available person.

Every day, over a quarter million people die around the world. How many of these precious souls go to their final destination without hearing about Jesus? What are we going to do to rescue the perishing? Reaching the world must begin where we live with a reality of Christ in our lives that gives credibility to a bold witness for Him.

Helen Keller was once asked if there was anything worse than being blind. She replied, "Yes, the most pathetic in all the world is someone who has sight but has no vision." We must open our eyes! We work alongside people whose marriages are hell. We live next to neighbors whose kids are one step short of going to jail. And you and I have the solution. We know the Maker and Designer of marriage, and we are armed with principles from His Word that will help us explain to people how they can make marriage and family work. You can help make that happen.

We may tend to believe that we can do nothing for our culture, that we are caught in a vast tidal wave of pagan unbelief and immorality and all we can hope for is to barely stay afloat. We become used to seeing friends end their marriages with "no-fault" divorces. But isolation and divorce do not have to be the norm. Yes, there are tough situations in many marriages. For many there is anguish involved in staying in the relationship—pain and hard work to try to make the marriage go. But which legacy do we want to leave behind? A legacy of selfishness caused by our personal pursuits, or a legacy of love, caring, and commitment to the family for the glory of God?

Everyone in your family should realize he is part of something that will outlive him. What greater investment could there be than to make your marriage and family work and then to reach out to help others do the same? That's how you can build a godly legacy.

As you conclude these pages, may I challenge you as a couple to set goals for your marriage by considering several questions? If you died right now, what would your legacy be? What do you want your legacy to look like in two years? Specifically, what goals would you like to set together that would stretch your faith and cause you to sacrifice for God? Then look ahead ten years and ask the same question: What do you want your legacy to look like after ten years together as a couple?

The choice is yours: What kind of legacy will you leave? The world is full of people erecting monuments to themselves but leaving nothing of real value behind. Why not determine with God's help that you will leave behind a legacy that will last forever?

(For additional information related to this topic, see Chapters 12 on family values, 21 on growing faith, 27 on deciding to have children, and 52 on coming seasons in your marriage.)

HomeBuilders Principle

The legacy you leave is determined by the life you live.

TO THINK ABOUT INDIVIDUALLY

1. What legacy did you receive from your parents? What was good and not so good about this legacy?

2. What legacy do you want to pass to the future? Write down the key points.

TO DISCUSS TOGETHER

Share answers to the questions in the previous exercise. What common themes emerged in the legacy both of you want to pass to the future? What do you want your legacy to look like in two years? Ten years?

TO TAKE ACTION TOGETHER

In addition to influencing your children, your role in reaching the world for Christ can begin with a neighbor. Invite a neighbor(s) who does not know Jesus to your home for a meal. Begin the process of becoming a friend and reconciling him or her to God "who reconciled us to Himself through Christ, and gave us the ministry of reconciliation" (2 Cor. 5:18).

52

"What's Next?"

UNDERSTANDING COMING SEASONS IN YOUR MARRIAGE

Do you think your marriage is great now? Well, just wait! As you allow God to shape you and your relationship in the years ahead, your love will mature and sweeten into your most precious earthly possession.

With broken relationships all around us, and the bad press that marriage receives these days, embracing this idea requires significant faith. But God desires true, growing lifelong marital joy for every couple. His model for the marriage merger was unveiled in the Garden of Eden—two people designed to complete and satisfy each other perfectly in an unending relationship. Yes, we live "east of Eden" in a world where people are scarred and broken by sin, yet God has given us the resources to overcome all this and experience oneness and happiness.

Just what can you expect in the years ahead, and what can you do to make sure your marriage reaches its full, vibrant maturity?

I've said many times to parents, "Your marriage must be built to outlast your children." Even if you do not have children yet, the principle remains the same for any marriage regardless of the season of life—your marriage must be built to grow through every life stage and still be on its feet at the finish line.

Solomon wrote, "There is an appointed time for everything. And there is a time for every event under heaven" (Eccl. 3:1). In this closing chapter, I want to explain what I believe are the six appointed "times" of marriage. Like the seasons we experience in nature, they often overlap and change gradually. I'll conclude by offering three ideas for ways to see your marriage grow and bear fruit, no matter what the season.

The Seasons of Marriage

There are other ways to describe the path of a marriage, but after years of reflection and input from others, I've found the following helpful to explain the stages of a family's life, especially in America.

Season 1: Newly Married. Generally, this includes the first five years of marriage. Everything is new, and challenges are numerous. The marriage's mood swings tend to be frequent and dramatic—in a single day you can experience deep disillusionment and awesome pleasure. But the habits and disciplines formed in this season will significantly determine what your marriage becomes later on.

Season 2: Full Nest I. This occurs when children arrive and lasts until they are about age five. Little tykes toddle and romp through the house, absorbing enormous amounts of attention from both mom and dad. This season often takes a young couple totally by surprise. Get ready for changes in your lives like nothing you've ever encountered before! You will experience the unspeakable joy and awe of ushering a human being into life on this earth. But beware: During this season, much marital drift toward isolation can begin because children are so demanding that they can leave adults emptied of time, energy, and emotion.

Season 3: Full Nest II. This may be the most placid period of the entire family experience. For us, this time was golden. The children are between the ages of six and twelve. They don't yet have wheels or jobs, and you can easily schedule family events. Basically, you're able to exert significant control. Although there are challenges, life seems predictable and manageable. Don't be deceived and think this will last forever. The golden years will give way to the challenging years of raising teens. As a couple, review and make sure that you agree on your basic family values.

Season 4: Full Nest III. Now your children are teenagers in junior high or high school. You are on the road a lot. You must not resent having to be mobile during this season, transporting your nondriving teenagers to a multitude of activities, such as athletic, church, music, and drama events.

Gone for good is the predictable daily schedule that allowed everyone to gather for a pleasant evening meal at the appointed time. Now you need to plan carefully those family times, and be ready, available, and flexible to grab moments of intimacy with your children on their terms and at their timing. You spend as much time as possible being a subtle spectator as they "do their thing." A warning: If you as a couple don't protect your intimacy and privacy, you will find it withering as your teenagers roam the house until all hours of the night talking on the phone, snacking, listening to music, and working on the computer. Set boundaries. There will be times when the door to your bedroom is shut and you are not to be disturbed—even if your children are still awake and needing you. Remember, your marriage must be built to survive the teenager season.

Season 5: Empty Nest I. The children have moved out of the house, and it's quiet. You now have only each other to talk to over the dinner table or in the family room. One or both spouses are still employed, but preparation is under way for reduction of commitment to work or retirement. You're still involved in your children's lives because they may need financial and emotional support during college or in transitioning to adulthood.

This season should be reminiscent of those newlywed days when there was much more time to enjoy each other, to make last-minute plans to do something fun. This season that should be a reward for a job well done as parents for too many couples becomes a nightmare of broken dreams and cold isolation. Because they may have accepted the idea that their marriage existed primarily to raise the children, too many couples crash and burn in this stage. Don't wait until this season to nurture the relationship that drew you together in the first place. This is a time of celebration! Your marriage is seasoned, and you can enjoy marital intimacy and give fully to each other without so many distractions.

Season 6: Empty Nest II. With grandchildren arriving, you have the joy of helping shape another generation to love and follow Christ. A man enters the patriarchal phase of leading and loving his family and continuing to set the spiritual direction he initiated decades before. A woman can be the matriarch, guiding her daughters in how to truly love their husbands and nurture their children. These are the golden harvest years for a couple to savor before their sacred marriage covenant is broken by death.

Three Things Necessary in Every Marriage Season

I grow excited and motivated when I think about each season of marriage. If you want your life to follow this pattern, here are some thoughts on how to get from here to there, regardless of your marriage season:

1. Grow today as individuals and as a couple. Pray together; share spiritual truths; share your experience with God together. Don't wait until tomorrow when you think you will be "more spiritual." Respond to life's circumstances today in faith and obedience. Your marriage will become the sum total of every choice made along the way. That's why it's so important for you to be content and grow spiritually now.

2. Seek to understand what your spouse is facing in this season of your marriage. I regret that I was not more sensitive to Barbara during some of the early seasons of our marriage. As a new bride, she needed my understanding, love, compassion, and a listening ear. I'm not saying I never did this, but I wish someone had challenged me to set that as a goal.

3. Prayerfully anticipate the next season of your life as a couple. Some couples don't fully prepare for the seasons of their marriage. It doesn't take a lot of preparation, but it takes prayerful, thoughtful application of Scripture, for example, to prepare for a child. Work on your values as a couple and what you want to build into children *before* you welcome your first one.

If you do these things, you'll grow strong in the seasons of life, and you'll grow deep.

(For additional material on this topic, see Chapters 3 on God's blueprint, 12 on family values, 21 on growing faith, 28 on the marriage covenant, 37 on a refresher course for marriage, and 51 on family legacy.)

HomeBuilders Principle

Every season of marriage
brings unique challenges and joys—
and prepares you for the season that follows.

TO THINK ABOUT INDIVIDUALLY

1. As you look ahead in your marriage, what season(s) do you think will be the most enjoyable for you? What season(s) might present more of a challenge? Why do you feel this way?

2. What about your spouse—which season(s) do you think will be most enjoyable or challenging for him or her? Why do you feel this way?

TO DISCUSS TOGETHER

Take turns sharing your answers to the questions in the previous exercise. What can you learn and do *now* that will help you prepare as individuals and as a couple for the next season, as well as other future seasons, in your marriage?

TO TAKE ACTION TOGETHER

Congratulations on completing this book! You may return now and then to review particular chapters when you need assistance and encouragement on a specific topic. Best wishes to you as you apply the principles we have shared—all a part of God's blueprints for starting—living—and ending your marriage *right*.

Appendix A: The Four Spiritual Laws*

Just as there are physical laws that govern the physical universe, so are there spiritual laws that govern your relationship with God.

Law One: God loves you and offers a wonderful plan for your life.

God's Love

"For God so loved the world, that He gave His only begotten Son, that whoever believes in Him should not perish, but have eternal life" (John 3:16).

God's Plan

[Jesus said] "I came that they might have life, and might have it abundantly" [that it might be full and meaningful] (John 10:10).

Why is it that most people are not experiencing the abundant life? Because . . .

Law Two: Man is sinful and separated from God. Therefore, he cannot know and experience God's love and plan for his life.

Man Is Sinful

"For all have sinned and fall short of the glory of God" (Romans 3:23).

Man was created to have fellowship with God; but, because of his stubborn self-will, chose to go his own independent way, and fellowship with God was broken. This self-will, characterized by an attitude of active rebellion or passive indifference, is evidence of what the Bible calls sin.

Man Is Separated

"For the wages of sin is death" [spiritual separation from God] (Romans 6:23).

This diagram illustrates that God is holy and man is sinful. A great gulf separates the two. The arrows illustrate that man is continually trying to reach God and the abundant life through his own efforts, such as a good life, philosophy, or religion.

The third law explains the only way to bridge this gulf . . .

Law Three: Jesus Christ is God's only provision for man's sin. Through Him you can know and experience God's love and plan for your life.

He Died in Our Place

"But God demonstrates His own love toward us, in that while we were yet sinners, Christ died for us" (Romans 5:8).

He Rose from the Dead

"Christ died for our sins . . . He was buried . . . He was raised on the third day according to the Scriptures . . . He appeared to [Peter], then to the twelve. After that He appeared to more than five hundred . . ." (1 Corinthians 15:3–6).

He Is the Only Way to God

"Jesus said to him, 'I am the way, and the truth, and the life; no one comes to the Father, but through Me'" (John 14:6).

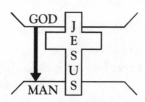

This diagram illustrates that God has bridged the gulf that separates us from Him by sending His Son, Jesus Christ, to die on the cross in our place to pay the penalty for our sins. It is not enough, however, just to know these three laws . . .

Law Four: We must individually receive Jesus Christ as Savior and Lord; then we can know and experience God's love and plan for our lives.

We Must Receive Christ

"But as many as received Him, to them He gave the right to become children of God, even to those who believe in His name" (John 1:12).

We Receive Christ Through Faith

"For by grace you have been saved through faith; and that not of yourselves, it is the gift of God; not as a result of works, that no one should boast" (Ephesians 2:8–9).

When We Receive Christ, We Experience a New Birth

(Read John 3:1–8.)

We Receive Christ By Personal Invitation

[Christ is speaking] "Behold, I stand at the door and knock; if anyone hears My voice and opens the door, I will come in to him" (Revelation 3:20).

Receiving Christ involves turning to God from self (repentance) and trusting Christ to come into our lives to forgive our sins and to make us the kind of people He wants us to be. Just to agree intellectually that Jesus Christ is the Son of God and that He died on the cross for our sins is not enough. Nor is it enough to have an emotional experience. We receive Jesus Christ by faith, as an act of the will.

These two circles represent two kinds of lives:

SELF-DIRECTED LIFE
S—Self on the throne
†—Christ is outside the life
*—Interests are directed by self, often
   resulting in discord and frustration

CHRIST-DIRECTED LIFE
†—Christ is in the life
S—Self is yielding to Christ
•—Interests are directed by Christ,
   resulting in harmony with God's plan

Which circle best
represents your life?
Which circle would you
like to have
represent your life?

The following explains how you can receive Christ:

You Can Receive Christ Right Now By Faith Through Prayer

(Prayer is talking with God.)

God knows your heart and is not so concerned with your words as He is with the attitude of your heart. The following is a suggested prayer:

"Lord Jesus, I need You. Thank You for dying on the cross for my sins. I open the door of my life and receive You as my Savior and Lord. Thank You for forgiving my sins and giving me eternal life. Make me the kind of person You want me to be."

Does this prayer express the desire of your heart?

If it does, pray this prayer right now, and Christ will come into your life, as He promised.

Fellowship in a Good Church

God's Word admonishes us not to forsake "the assembling of ourselves together" (Hebrew 10:25). Several logs burn brightly together; but put one aside on the cold hearth, and the fire goes out. So it is with your relationship with other Christians. If you do not belong to a church, do not wait to be invited. Take the initiative; call the pastor of a nearby church where Christ is honored and His Word is preached. Start this week, and make plans to attend regularly.

If you have come to know Christ personally through this presentation of the gospel, write or call FamilyLife for a free packet of materials especially prepared to assist you in your Christian growth. A special Bible study series and an abundance of other helpful materials for Christian growth are also available.

FamilyLife
3900 North Rodney Parham
Little Rock, AR 72212
1-800-FLTODAY

*Written by Bill Bright. Copyright © 1965 Campus Crusade for Christ, Inc., all rights reserved.

Appendix B: Family Budget Worksheet

I. INCOME

	Monthly	One Time	Annual Total
Husband			
Wife			
Dividends/interest			
Gifts			
Bonuses			
Tax refunds			
Other			
Total			

II. SET EXPENSES & OBLIGATIONS

	Monthly	One Time	Annual Total
Tithe			
Rent or mortgage			
Second mortgage			
Electricity			
Heat/cooling			
Telephone (not cell)			
Water & sewer			
Garbage			
Child care			
Education loans			
Income tax			
Property tax			
Home insurance			
Life insurance			
Med./dental insurance			
Disability insurance			
Auto loan or lease			
Other installment loans			
Savings			
Other			
Total			

III. RECAP AND SUMMARY

	Monthly	One Time	Annual Total
1. Total income (from I. above)	_____	_____	_____
2. Total set expenses (from II. above)	_____	_____	_____
Available funds (**Deduct** line 2 from line 1)	_____	_____	_____

IV. VARIABLE EXPENSES

	Monthly	One Time	Annual Total
Food	_____	_____	_____
Clothing	_____	_____	_____
House supplies	_____	_____	_____
House furnishings	_____	_____	_____
House maintenance	_____	_____	_____
Animal care	_____	_____	_____
Car gas/maintenance	_____	_____	_____
Car license/fees	_____	_____	_____
Car tolls/parking	_____	_____	_____
Other transportation	_____	_____	_____
Cell phones	_____	_____	_____
Gifts	_____	_____	_____
Medical/dental	_____	_____	_____
Prescriptions	_____	_____	_____
Cleaners	_____	_____	_____
Toiletries	_____	_____	_____
Husband personal care	_____	_____	_____
Wife personal care	_____	_____	_____
Cable TV	_____	_____	_____
Internet	_____	_____	_____
Magazine/newspaper	_____	_____	_____
Eating out	_____	_____	_____
Dates/entertainment	_____	_____	_____
Baby-sitters	_____	_____	_____
Clubs/activities	_____	_____	_____
Vacation	_____	_____	_____

	Monthly	One Time	Annual Total
Other	_____	_____	_____
Total	_____	_____	_____
Available funds	_____	_____	_____
(from III. Recap)			
Plus/minus*	_____	_____	_____

*If your plus/minus is zero in the Annual Total column, this is your family budget. If you have a plus balance, apply this amount to reducing debts or savings. If you have a minus balance, more work needs to be done on cutting variable expenses. If you still cannot reach a balanced budget, you will have to examine your set expenses to see how you might adjust your style of living to "live within your means."

Appendix C:
The HomeBuilders Couples Series®

IDEAL FOR NEW GROUPS

Building Teamwork in Your Marriage
Building Your Marriage
Growing Together in Christ
Keeping Your Covenant

GREAT FOR OUTREACH OR SPECIFIC NEEDS

Improving Communication in Your Marriage
Managing Pressure in Your Marriage
Mastering Money in Your Marriage
Resolving Conflict in Your Marriage

FOR EXPERIENCED GROUPS

Building Your Mate's Self-Esteem
Expressing Love in Your Marriage
Life Choices for a Lasting Marriage

ADDITIONAL HOMEBUILDERS RESOURCES

Leader's Guide: Preparing for Marriage
Orientation Manual: An Introduction to HomeBuilders
Preparing for Marriage

To obtain any of these materials, visit your local Christian bookstore, call 1-800-FLTODAY, or visit the FamilyLife Web site at <www.familylife.com>.

Notes

Chapter 3

1. We were first taught these purposes for marriage by a mentoring couple, Don and Sally Meredith. We remain indebted to Don and Sally for their investment in our lives and marriage.

Chapter 4

1. Dan Allender and Tremper Longman III, *Intimate Allies* (Wheaton, IL: Tyndale House Publishers, 1995), 218.

Chapter 5

1. *The Inspirational Writings of C. S. Lewis* (New York: Inspiration Press, 1994), 278.

Chapter 6

1. Eugene "Red" McDaniel and James L. Johnson, *Scars and Stripes*, American Defense Institute, 1050 North Fairfax Street, Suite 200, Alexandria, VA 22314. To order, call 703-519-7000.

Chapter 8

1. "A Weekend to Remember," FamilyLife Marriage Conference Manual, FamilyLife, P.O. Box 23840, Little Rock, AR 72221-3840, 87.

Chapter 14

1. Radio interview with Larry Burkett, "FamilyLife Today." To order, call 1-800-FLTO-DAY. Larry Burkett is the founder of Christian Financial Concepts, an organization dedicated to teaching biblical principles of money management. For more information, visit the Web site <www.cfcministry.org>.

2. Ron Blue, *Master Your Money* (Nashville: Thomas Nelson, 1986), 33.

3. Radio interview with Larry Burkett, "FamilyLife Today."

4. Ron Blue's *Mastering Money in Your Marriage* HomeBuilders study is available through your local Christian bookstore, by calling 1-800-FLTODAY, or the FamilyLife Web site <www.familylife.com>.

Chapter 16

1. *Webster's New World College Dictionary*, Third Edition (New York: Macmillan, 1996), 529.

Chapter 19

1. Will Durant, *Caesar and Christ: The Story of Civilization III* (New York: Simon and Schuster, 1972), 57.

2. Scott Stanley, *The Heart of Commitment* (Nashville: Thomas Nelson, 1998), 175.

Chapter 20

1. Robert Lewis, *Building Teamwork in Your Marriage*, The HomeBuilders Couples Series, (Ventura, CA: Gospel Light, 1993), 113.

Chapter 22

1. "Home Is Where the Parent Should Be," *Christianity Today*, 15 June 1998, 22.

2. James Dobson, *What Wives Wished Their Husbands Knew About Women* (Wheaton, IL: Tyndale House Publishers, 1975), 55–56.

3. Burton White, "Should You Stay Home with Your Baby?", *Young Children*, November 1981, 3–5.

4. Marc Peyser, "Time Bind? What Time Bind?" *Newsweek*, 12 May 1997, 69.

Chapter 24

1. Cris Evatt, *He & She: 60 Significant Differences Between Men and Women* (Berkeley, CA: Conari Press, 1992), 150.

Chapter 25

1. Many of the ideas listed are from *Simply Romantic* (Little Rock, AR: FamilyLife, 1995).

Chapter 26

1. Most of the ideas listed are from *Simply Romantic* (Little Rock, AR: FamilyLife, 1995).

Chapter 28

1. Portions of this chapter originally appeared as an article by Dennis Rainey, "Marriage Covenant," in *Living Way* magazine, February 2000. Used by permission.

Chapter 30

1. Stephen R. Covey, *The Seven Habits of Highly Effective People* (New York: Simon & Schuster, 1989), 148.

2. Charlie Shedd, *You Can Be a Great Parent* (Waco, TX: Word Publishing, 1970), 63.

Chapter 31

1. *Statistical Abstract of the United States*, 119th Edition, 114.

2. Philip Zimbardo, *Psychology Today*, August 1980, 71–76.

Chapter 36

1. Ed Hayes, *The Church* (Nashville: Word Publishing, 1998), x.

2. George Barna, *The Second Coming of the Church* (Nashville: Word Publishing, 1998), 191, 196.

3. Ibid., 190.

4. George Barna, "The Battle for the Hearts of Men," *New Man*, January–February 1997, 40.

Chapter 44

1. Wayne Muller, "Remember the Sabbath?" *USA Weekend*, 2–4 April 1999, 4.

2. Gordon MacDonald, *Ordering Your Private World* (Nashville: Thomas Nelson, 1984), 166, 174.

3. Dorothy C. Bass, "The Gift of the Sabbath," *Christianity Today*, 1 September 1997, 39.

4. Ibid., 43.

5. Margie Haack, "Sabbath Master," *World*, 23 May 1998, 29.

Chapter 46

1. Radio interview with Jim Cote, "FamilyLife Today." Order at 1-800-FLTODAY.

Chapter 49

1. Hans Selye, *The Stress of Life* (New York: McGraw-Hill, 1956), 62–63.

Since attending a FamilyLife Marriage Conference,
romance won't become old news in the Banks home ...

It's now a daily feature.

—— FAMILYLIFE MARRIAGE CONFERENCE ——

Get Away for a "Weekend to Remember"

Experience a fun, romantic weekend together and discover how to make
your marriage both strong and lasting. At the conference you'll learn how to:

- Avoid the five threats to oneness
- Receive your mate as a gift
- Experience a vital sexual relationship
- Resolve conflict in your marriage
- And much more!

To register or receive more information, call 1-800-FL-TODAY or visit www.familylife.com.